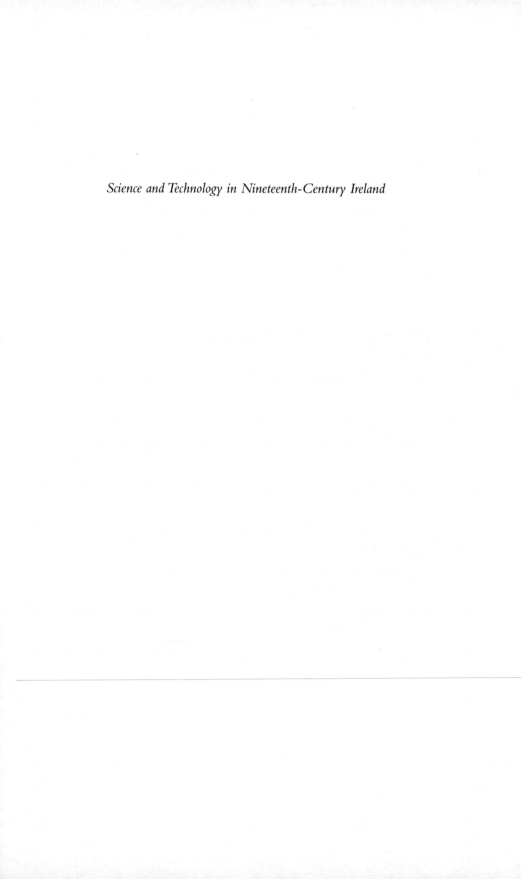

Science and Technology in Nineteenth-Century Ireland

Science and Technology in Nineteenth-Century Ireland

Juliana Adelman & Éadaoin Agnew

EDITORS

FOUR COURTS PRESS

Set in 10 on 12.5 point Bembo for
FOUR COURTS PRESS LTD
7 Malpas Street, Dublin 8, Ireland
www.fourcourtspress.ie
and in North America for
FOUR COURTS PRESS
c/o ISBS, 920 N.E. 58th Avenue, Suite 300, Portland, OR 97213.

A catalogue record for this title
is available from the British Library.

ISBN 978–1–84682–291–9

Printed in England
by Antony Rowe Ltd, Chippenham, Wilts.

Contents

Acknowledgments

The editors would like to thank each of the contributors not only for their articles, but for their willingness to engage with the review and editorial process. We would also like to thank the reviewers who reported on each of the articles in this volume and contributed valuable suggestions for their improvement. We would like to thank the Society for the Study of Nineteenth-Century Ireland and its council for entrusting us with the editing of this volume and the Royal Irish Academy, particularly Vanessa Carswell, for hosting the conference from which the papers were derived. Finally, we thank Four Courts Press for their support for this series.

Juliana Adelman would also like to thank the members of the RIA's National Committee for the History of Irish Science for keeping the history of science in Ireland an active area of research. Funding for a postdoctoral fellowship (2008–10) by the Irish Research Council for the Humanities and Social Sciences provided her with the opportunity to participate in both conference and volume.

Éadaoin Agnew would like to thank the Society for the Study of Nineteenth-Century Ireland for supporting the conference at which these papers were originally presented, and for continuing to cultivate the study of Ireland in the nineteenth century.

Illustrations

Abbreviations

BJHS	*British Journal for the History of Science*
CE	*Cork Examiner*
DMP	*Dublin Medical Press*
FDR	*Field Day Review*
FJ	*Freeman's Journal*
HC	House of Commons
IER	*Irish Ecclesiastical Record*
IT	*The Irish Times*
JRDS	*Journal of the Royal Dublin Society*
MNRAS	*Monthly Notices of the Royal Astronomical Society*
NLI	National Library of Ireland
ODNB	Oxford Dictionary of National Biography
OED	Oxford English Dictionary
OSI	Ordnance Survey Ireland
PIME	*Proceedings of the Institute of Mechanical Engineers*
PRI	*Proceedings of the Royal Institution*
PRIA	*Proceedings of the Royal Irish Academy*
PRO	Public Records Office
PTRS	*Philosophical Transactions of the Royal Society*
QUB	Queen's University Belfast
RCScI	Royal College of Science for Ireland
RDS	Royal Dublin Society
TNA	The National Archives, UK
UCC	University College Cork
UCD	University College Dublin

Contributors

JULIANA ADELMAN is an Irish Research Council for the Humanities and Social Sciences post-doctoral fellow in the Department of History, Trinity College Dublin.

ÉADAOIN AGNEW is a lecturer in English literature at Kingston University, London.

VANDRA COSTELLO is a landscape historian and historic gardens consultant.

CLARA CULLEN is a former academic librarian whose doctoral research was on the history and teaching of science in nineteenth-century Ireland.

THOMAS DUDDY is a senior lecturer in philosophy at the National University of Ireland, Galway.

IAN ELLIOTT is retired, but was formerly an astronomer with the Dunsink Observatory of the Dublin Institute for Advanced Studies.

PATRICK MAUME is a researcher for the Dictionary of Irish Biography.

JAMES H. MURPHY is professor of English at De Paul University in Chicago.

SHERRA MURPHY teaches Visual Culture and Cultural Studies at the Dun Laoghaire Institute of Art, Design and Technology and is currently pursuing a PhD in the School of History and Archives at University College Dublin.

ELIZABETH NESWALD is an associate professor for the History of Science and Technology at Brock University in Ontario.

SEÁN Ó DUINNSHLÉIBHE is a lecturer in the Department of Modern Irish, University College Cork.

TADHG O'KEEFFE is professor of archaeology at University College Dublin.

PATRICK RYAN is an independent scholar specializing in the history and archaeology of Dublin.

Introduction

JULIANA ADELMAN & ÉADAOIN AGNEW

> The world will be a dull world some hundreds of years hence, when Fancy shall be dead, and ruthless Science (that has no more bowels than a steam-engine) has killed her.
>
> William Makepeace Thackeray, 1843[1]

Driving rain prevented William Thackeray from leaving his Galway hotel room, so he whiled away the hours by reading romantic tales and 'Hedge-School Literature'. Although he enjoyed this respite from the practical and improving fare of English penny magazines, he predicted a day when *all* literature would be practical and improving: imagination would fall away as science became the only occupation of mankind. That Galway bore few of the marks of scientific progress seems not to have affected Thackeray's certainty in the eventual triumph of 'ruthless science'. In his travels through Ireland he found other towns similarly lacking evidence of scientific development. Cork's scientific institution, for example, was one of many 'swaggering beginnings that could not be carried through; grand enterprises begun dashingly, and ending in shabby compromises or downright ruin'.[2] To Thackeray, the appeal of Ireland in 1842 lay in its romantic landscapes and its quaint towns. Underdevelopment brought inconveniences to the traveller but was also further evidence that the country had not yet entirely succumbed to the empiricist and utilitarian spirit of the age.

Thackeray was neither the first nor the last to suggest that science and the arts, practicality and creativity, were in opposition. Likewise the notion of science as non-Irish has a long history and has prevailed until rather recently. Ireland's tourism industry reinforces the historical focus on creative and literary achievements rather than scientific ones. However, as the essays in this volume attest, science was an important element of nineteenth-century Irish life. Science never killed fancy in Ireland but should itself be seen as another form of creativity; it is a cultural phenomenon that can give us insights into the past.

The nineteenth century has dominated histories of science in Ireland and it may be fair to ask what another volume on the subject can add to our knowledge. Although the biographical details of Ireland's most famous scientific men (and some women) are now relatively well known, this book offers new insights into the participation of those beyond the intellectual elite. This book also serves to place Irish

---

1 W.M. Thackeray, *The Irish sketch book* (Belfast, 1985, [1843]), p. 163.   2 Thackeray, *The Irish sketch book*, p. 83.

perspectives on science into the historical study of Irish literature and culture, as well as the context of the well-developed historiography of Victorian science. Finally, this book continues the rich interdisciplinary tradition that has characterized the history of science in Ireland, offering perspectives from science, literature, history and archaeology.[3]

The essays in this book represent a diversity of topics and approaches, yet they cluster around three themes: innovations, individuals and institutions. These themes are significant strands in the current literature on the history of science in Ireland. Although the themes overlap, and many of the essays might have been included in more than one section, these divisions promote useful comparisons between the papers in each section. Innovations are at the heart of the history of science and this section examines the propagation and reception of particular scientific ideas. This process is dependent on the activities of the individuals who form the focus of the second section: not only scientific men but women, clergymen, writers, readers and the general public. Essays on individuals look at how specific people have engaged with science or scientific ideas. The final section on institutions encompasses broader scientific engagement on the scale of communities and the state. These essays deal with the ways in which individuals have banded together in order to promote scientific ideas, particularly in an educational context. Essays highlight how science was used to further political and social agendas in nineteenth-century Ireland.

INNOVATIONS

The modern-day significance of many innovations from the nineteenth century may be the reason why the period has attracted so much historical study. Nineteenth-century precursors of a sort can be found for many of the technologies we rely on and the scientific ideas we hold, although historians now eschew this approach to the history of science. The history of Victorian science is no longer dominated by the intellectual history of important discoveries.[4] Cultural and social context now form an important part of any examination of a scientific innovation. The definition of a scientific innovation, for the purposes of historical investigation, has expanded to include unorthodox and even folk knowledge about the natural world.

Histories of nineteenth-century science now include knowledge systems formerly considered marginal or unscientific, such as phrenology and mesmerism.[5] This change in subject matter has also signalled a change in approach to orthodox science. For example, the process by which Charles Darwin's theory of evolution by natural selection came to be accepted is now examined rather than assumed.

3 J.A. Bennett, 'Why the history of science matters in Ireland' in D. Attis and C. Mollan (eds), *Science and Irish Culture* (Dublin, 2005), pp 1–14. 4 B. Lightman, 'Introduction' in B. Lightman (ed.), *Victorian science in context* (Chicago, 1997), pp 1–14. 5 A. Winter, *Mesmerized: powers of mind in Victorian Britain* (Chicago, 1998); J. van Whye, *Phrenology and the origins of Victorian scientific naturalism* (Aldershot, 2004).

Competing ideas are given an equal share in the story. The instruments that men of science rely upon are now themselves interrogated alongside the knowledge they purport to produce. A broader definition of science and an emphasis on processes and artefacts means that studies of countries like Ireland, peripheral to the centre of the scientific world, need not be peripheral to the literature on the history of science. However, Irish scholars have been somewhat slower to embrace these subjects. For example, there is a single study of phrenology in Ireland.[6] Essays in this volume begin to redress this balance while suggesting avenues of future research.

No single innovation in the scientific thought of the nineteenth century has been so widely researched as Darwinian evolution. Nevertheless, the literature on Darwinism in Ireland is relatively small.[7] Thomas Duddy's essay contextualizes the cultural factors that affected acceptance, rejection and modification of Darwin's theory of evolution. By demonstrating that Ireland, like elsewhere, encompassed a variety of responses, Duddy dispels the notion that Irish people were simply divided between horrified creationists and hardened evolutionists. Duddy identifies four strands of thought, exemplified by individual writers, which display a spectrum of responses to Darwin's ideas. In this way, Duddy's essay reflects the aims of the volume as a whole and offers a more diverse reading of how science and technology were pursued, interpreted, disseminated and received in nineteenth-century Ireland.

Astronomy, like evolution and natural history, interested a broad section of Irish society beyond men of science. Nineteenth-century Ireland boasted a substantial scholarly community of astronomers as well as several significant female popularizers of astronomy.[8] Ian Elliott's essay supplements existing literature by providing a history of telescope manufacture in a Dublin-based family business. Grubb's manufacturing firm in Ireland was a unique high-technology enterprise that constructed many of the world's largest and best telescopes as well as producing a wide range of precision optical and mechanical instruments. Elliott's history of the Grubbs pays particular attention to specific telescopes, such as the Great Vienna and Great Melbourne Telescopes. At the same time, Elliott demonstrates how technological development and science were affected by political and social changes towards the end of the nineteenth and start of the twentieth century. For example, the Grubbs gradually turned their attention to military and surveying instruments in response to the demands of imperialism and war.

Just as the Grubbs' instruments were used to survey sky and land, empirical

---

6 E. Leaney, 'Phrenology in nineteenth-century Ireland', *New Hibernia Review*, 10:3 (2006), 24–42. **7** A good example is D. Livingstone, 'Darwin in Belfast: the evolution debate' in J.W. Foster (ed.), *Nature in Ireland* (Dublin, 1997), pp 387–408; a more general introduction is provided in G. Jones, 'Darwinism in Ireland' in D. Attis and C. Mollan (eds), *Science and Irish culture* (Dublin, 2005), pp 115–38. **8** See, for example, N. Whyte, '"Lords of ether and of light": the Irish astronomical tradition of the nineteenth century', *Irish Review*, 17/18 (1995), 127–41. On the female popularizer Mary Agnes Clerke, see B. Lightman, 'The visual theology of Victorian popularizers of science: from reverent eye to chemical retina', *Isis*, 19:4 (2000), 651–80.

observation can itself become a form of surveillance. The technologically innovative surveys of the nineteenth century, including the geological and ordnance surveys, were tools of governance as much as they were scientific enterprises. They were aimed at harnessing science to the realization of Ireland's economic potential. Tadhg O'Keeffe and Patrick Ryan's essay makes use of the Ordnance Survey maps to reveal representations of the 'Monto', Dublin's notorious red-light district. As O'Keeffe and Ryan argue, maps are less conveyors of information about places than media through which places are created and recreated. Thus, their essay questions the degree to which scientific observation can be said to represent factual reality.

Elizabeth Neswald's essay on the cold water cure grapples with the line between accepted and discredited science. Neswald uses hydropathy in Cork as a case study to examine the networks of cultural, social and political ideas that impact upon the dissemination and reception of science. Rejected by the metropolitan medical elite, hydropathy's resistance to suppression in Cork demonstrates the value of local Irish case studies. Such studies demonstrate local variety, but also enrich our overall understanding of the power politics of science during the period.

INDIVIDUALS

The engagement of an individual with science has continued to prove a fruitful means of examining the history of science. Among the most recent and valuable examples is a two-volume biographical dictionary of Irish physical and chemical scientists.[9] The *Dictionary of Irish Biography* also contains a generous complement of scientists. Yet there are still significant gaps in the literature. In particular, those chosen as biographical subjects in Ireland have often been valued by the significance of their contributions within the paradigm of modern science. This has tended to exclude women as well as non-scientific men from study.[10]

English literature, rather than history, has provided the impetus for examining individual engagement with science outside biographies of scientific figures. As Thackeray's words demonstrate, it would be difficult to study nineteenth-century literature and ignore the influence of science. The prevalence of popular science writing during the period has spurred an interest in the history of reading, writing and publishing scientific material.[11] The interaction between literary and scientific interests has been demonstrated many times over. In Ireland, the Wilde family is a good example.[12] Furthermore, literary historians have not neglected the study of

9 C.D. Mollan, *It's part of what we are* (Dublin, 2007). **10** For two exceptions, see M. Mulvihill (ed.), *Stars, shells and bluebells: women scientists and pioneers* (Dublin, 1997); M. Mulvihill (ed.), *Lab coats and lace: the lives and legacies of inspiring Irish women scientists and pioneers* (Dublin, 2009). **11** See, for example, J.A. Secord, *Victorian sensation: the extraordinary publication, reception and secret authorship of* Vestiges of the natural history of creation (Chicago, 2000) and G. Cantor et al., *Science in the nineteenth-century periodical: reading the magazine of nature* (Cambridge, 2004). **12** J. McGeache, 'Wilde, Sir William Robert

men of science in their own right: Seán Lysaght's biography of Robert Lloyd Praeger is an exemplary study of an Irish life in science which considers the fullness of Praeger's social, professional and domestic circles and presents a rounded picture of a Victorian/Edwardian intellectual.[13] Lysaght was aided by Praeger's desire to chronicle his own life in almost as much detail as the plants he studied, highlighting the merging of different forms of writing within a single author. This section offers new perspectives by examining a woman, an evangelical minister and a Gaelic-speaking poet.

As in other intellectual domains, women interested in science were placed in an auxiliary position. Thus, it is significant that the fascinating figure of Mary Ward is here brought to the fore. Although she has received some recognition of late, Éadaoin Agnew provides a new and interesting interpretation of her scientific writing, being interested in how science could proffer a literary mode of expression for those who found it difficult to engage in authorial authority. Agnew situates historically Ward's discursive negotiations while illustrating how science permeated various forms of literature, such as children's literature; this offers an interesting perspective on how nineteenth-century ideologies affected the ways in which science was presented to the public and asks why Ward writes about science in the way that she does.

Agnew's essay on Mary Ward sets her work in context considering closely the gender constraints of the time. Ward's family connections are relatively well known and her work on microscopy and telescopy has long been pulled out of obscurity.[14] Agnew's essay provides instead a reading of the formal properties of writing science, and asks why Ward writes about science in the way that she does.

Agnew demonstrates the value of recovering Irish women's interactions with science. Equally overlooked are nineteenth-century religious apologists, such as the figure examined in Patrick Maume's essay. While this area has been the subject of intense scrutiny in British and American historiography, few comparable studies exist in histories of science in Ireland.[15] In the Irish context, the struggle between Catholics, Protestants and the state over control of education affected each group's view of modern science.[16] Maume's study of the evangelical Dominick McCausland shows how McCausland's denunciations of evolutionary theory selectively imposed material from contemporary popular science over a framework supplied by the premillennialist school of biblical interpretation. McCausland blended a surprising array

Wills', *ODNB* online ed. (Oxford, 2004), [www.oxforddnb.com/view/article/29403, accessed 13 Sept. 2010]. **13** S. Lysaght, *Robert Lloyd Praeger: the life of a naturalist* (Dublin, 1998). **14** O. Harry, 'The Hon. Mrs Ward (1827–1869); a wife, mother, microscopist and astronomer in Ireland, 1854–1869' in John Nudds, Norman McMillan, Denis Weaire, Susan McKenna-Lawlor (eds), *Science in Ireland, 1800–1930: tradition and reform* (Dublin, 1988). **15** For example, D. Livingstone, *Darwin's forgotten defenders: the encounter between evangelical theory and evolutionary thought* (Grand Rapids, MI, 1987). **16** G. Jones, 'Scientists against home rule' in D.G. Boyce and A. O'Day (eds), *Defenders of the Union: a survey of British and Irish unionism since 1801* (London, 2001), pp 188–208.

of scientific ideas with anti-Catholic prejudice and ancient history to develop his own history of creation that would exclude evolution.

Finally, Seán Ó Duinnshléibhe's essay offers a completely new perspective on the impact of industrialization and technological change by examining a nineteenth-century Gaelic poem that parodies a group of Cork weavers. Dáibhí de Barra's *Parliament of Weavers* presented the weavers as greedy, crooked and scheming. De Barra's work provides not only humour, but also a technivocabulary of the weaving trade in Irish. At the time when the poem was written, traditional hand weavers were beginning to be challenged by the introduction of mechanized looms, but the *Parliament of Weavers* indicates that the decline of their trade was unanticipated. Ó Duinnshléibhe demonstrates that an examination of Gaelic writers such as de Barra can illuminate the interaction between traditional culture and technological change.

INSTITUTIONS

One of the chief aims of Irish scientific institutions was to modernize Ireland, thereby overthrowing a traditional culture that scientific men often saw as hampering progress. From the eighteenth century, the Royal Dublin Society supported scientific research with the specific purpose of improving agriculture and manufacturing. The RDS's programme included exhibitions, prize essay competitions, laboratory research and public lectures and its significance as a public institution was demonstrated by its substantial annual grant from parliament. The Cork Institution, which Thackeray saw as a shabby failure, had once boasted salaried lecturers in chemistry, natural history, botany, natural philosophy and agriculture. Universities, too, gradually increased their science provision, with the foundation of the Queen's colleges in 1845 proving particularly important.[17] Although ostensibly for the good of the public, each of the above institutions was occasionally embroiled in religious and political controversy and each demonstrated a decided lack of scientific neutrality. The essays in this section highlight the symbolic functions of science and scientific institutions as evidence of modernity and in battles between religious and political factions.

James Murphy's essay, through an examination of science in Castleknock College, contributes to the debate on Irish Catholic attitudes towards science. Murphy's study is one of few examinations of science in an Irish secondary school setting and shows the degree to which science was an important part of the school's education philosophy and public image. Murphy also argues that Catholic views on science are more complex than many authors have suggested. For example, Catholic students could replicate John Tyndall's experiments in physics for an approving audience of the hierarchy, even though the same audience most likely reviled Tyndall's views on religion and evolution.

The relationship between religion and science in nineteenth-century Ireland is

---

17 See J. Adelman, *Communities of science in nineteenth-century Ireland* (London, 2009), ch. 2.

further elucidated in Vandra Costello's essay on the Sunday opening of the Glasnevin botanic gardens. Costello's work adds to our understanding of the political and religious divisions at work within the Royal Dublin Society and its conflicts with successive liberal administrations during the mid-nineteenth century. Far from maintaining a separation between politics, religion and intellectual pursuits, the controversy over Sunday opening demonstrates the degree to which cultural and social values were enmeshed with scientific ones.

The Royal College of Science was in some ways a victim of political and cultural conflict within Ireland. As Clara Cullen demonstrates, the college's promise as an innovative institution offering a new type of practical scientific education was never fulfilled. Poor funding, internecine struggles and changing national priorities ensured that the Royal College of Science remained a peripheral organization. Nevertheless, it provided a haven for Irish scientific talent and opportunities for female students not available elsewhere.

If the Royal College of Science's limited success was the result of ambivalent Irish attitudes towards scientific education, such ambivalence was not evident in Dublin in 1857. Sherra Murphy demonstrates that in the year that the British Association for the Advancement of Science visited the city, the Dublin newspapers were united in their desire to impress its members and to prove Ireland's scientific credentials. The reception of the society in the popular press was almost universally positive, though the different political and cultural viewpoints of their writers ensured that Ireland's scientific presence was depicted as variously subject to or equal to that of Britain.

What each of the essays in this volume shows is the diversity of approaches to science in nineteenth-century Ireland. No homogenous approach to science was taken, no monolithic idea disseminated. By examining innovations, individuals and institutions from new angles and including a more diverse array of ideas and actors, this volume contributes both to expanding the existing literature on the history of science in Ireland and to sowing the seeds of future research projects.

The Irish response to Darwinism

THOMAS DUDDY

The response to Darwinism in Ireland, as elsewhere, was quite a varied one. It would certainly be a mistake to think that on one side there was a vocal majority of horrified, Bible-waving (or catechism-waving) creationists and on the other side a hard-pressed minority of scientifically minded, proselytizing Darwinists. In Ireland in the nineteenth century there existed, as elsewhere, a spectrum of responses, ranging from passionate endorsement to passionate rejection, and in between a number of different attempts at striking some kind of conciliatory balance, some kind of accommodation – or even some kind of positive standoff – between the claims of traditional belief and the claims of the new science. I have concluded that there were four fairly distinct classes of responders to Darwinism in Ireland – the pro-Darwinists, the outright objectors, the accommodators and the compartmentalists.

THE PRO-DARWINISTS

We can predict that most of the early defenders of Darwin will come from the educated elite, especially those who have been educated, or have educated themselves, in the sciences. What is clear from the scholarly work of David Livingstone, Greta Jones, John Wilson Foster, Peter Bowler and Miguel De Arce is that a small but influential number of Irish scientists, both professional and amateur, were receptive to Darwinism from the beginning.[1] The fact that Darwin was elected an honorary member of the Royal Irish Academy in 1866 is itself an indication that he had some influential supporters in Ireland. These early sympathizers included Robert Ball, for example, and William Ramsay McNab, both of whom were members of the Royal College of Science in Dublin. Ball, who held the chair of astronomy at the Royal College of Science, was among the first Irish converts to Darwinism. In a still very readable, even charming, essay on Darwinism, he reports that he can still remember the intense delight he felt when, as a student, he first read *Origin of species*. 'I was', he says, 'an instantaneous convert to the new doctrines, and have felt their influence during all my subsequent life'.[2]

1 See D. Livingstone, 'Darwin in Belfast: the evolution debate' in J.W. Foster (ed.), *Nature in Ireland* (Dublin, 1997), pp 387–408; J.W. Foster, *Recoveries: neglected episodes in Irish cultural history, 1860–1912* (Dublin, 2002); G. Jones, 'Darwinism in Ireland' in D. Attis (ed.), *Science and Irish Culture* (Dublin, 2004), pp 115–38; M. DeArce, 'Darwin's Irish correspondence', *PRIA*, 108B (2008), 43–56; P.J. Bowler, 'Charles Darwin and his Dublin critics: Samuel Haughton and William Henry Harvey', *PRIA*, 109C (2009), 409–20. 2 R.S. Ball, *In starry realms*

Of course, the outstanding pro-Darwinist of the nineteenth century has to be John Tyndall, best known to historians of Darwinism for the famous address that he delivered to the Belfast meeting of the British Association for the Advancement of Science in 1874. Tyndall was born in 1820 in the village of Leighlinbridge in Co. Carlow. In 1848, after spending some years with the Irish Ordnance Survey, he went to study science at the University of Marburg in Germany, graduating with a doctorate in 1851. In 1853, he was appointed professor of natural philosophy at the Royal Institution in London. He soon earned himself a reputation not only as a scientist but also as a campaigner in the cause of science, becoming the nineteenth-century equivalent of Richard Dawkins. What in fact makes his 1874 Belfast address so provocative is the missionary zeal with which he defends the scientific enterprise, especially against interference from not only religious authorities but also from the religious mind-set. In the address, he defends Darwin as part of a more general promotion of scientific practice and scientific method. More than that, he also declares a state of war between the scientific and the religious views of the world.

The most controversial feature of Tyndall's paper is its materialistic tenor. He begins by rewriting the history of Western thought from a naturalistic and material-istic perspective. He shifts the emphasis away from the traditionally time-honoured philosophers, including Plato and Aristotle, and brings into the limelight what we might call the more worldly thinkers, those who focus their attention on the earthly, physical world, and who do so without conjuring up too much in the way of super-natural entities or forces. The first beneficiary of his revisionary overview of Western intellectual history is the Greek philosopher, Democritus, whom he considers to have been, as Francis Bacon put it, a man of 'weightier metal' than either Plato or Aristotle.[3] He recounts with approval the story that when Democritus visited Athens when Socrates and Plato were active there, he did so without making himself known to them. He also recounts with equal approval the harsh judgment that Democritus later passed on Socrates: 'the man who readily contradicts and uses many words is unfit to learn anything truly right'.[4] When Tyndall summarizes the natural philos-ophy of Democritus, it is clear that he endorses the materialistic tenor of it. The principles enunciated by Democritus reveal his uncompromising antagonism 'to those who deduced the phenomena of nature from the caprices of the gods'.[5] Among the other early thinkers praised by Tyndall are Epicurus and Lucretius. Epicurus had the aim of freeing the mind of man from superstition and the fear of death, while Lucretius is admirable for his courageous denial that the existence of structure in nature must be attributed to an intelligent supernatural designer. According to Tyndall, the Lucretian philosophy of nature is summed up best by Lucretius himself when he says that 'nature, free at once, and rid of her haughty lords, is seen to do all things spontaneously of herself, without the meddling of the gods'.[6]

It is when Tyndall moves on to talk about the medieval period that he comes

(London, 1920), p. 344. **3** J. Tyndall, *Address delivered before the British Association at Belfast* (London, 1874), p. 3. **4** Ibid., p. 4. **5** Ibid. **6** Ibid., p. 9.

across most forcibly as a nineteenth-century version of Richard Dawkins. He sees the spirit of the middle ages, dominated by the church, as a menial spirit:

> It was a time when thought had become abject, and when the acceptance of mere authority led, as it always does in science, to intellectual death. Natural events, instead of being traced to physical [causes], were traced to moral causes; while an exercise of the phantasy ... took the place of scientific spec-ulation. Then came the mysticism of the Middle Ages, magic, alchemy, the neo-platonic philosophy ... which caused men to look with shame upon their own bodies as hindrances to the absorption of the creature in the blessedness of the Creator. Finally came the scholastic philosophy, a fusion of the least-mature notions of Aristotle with the Christianity of the West. Intellectual immobility was the result.[7]

Not until the sixteenth century does there occur (in Tyndall's view) the beginnings of a timely reaction against scholastic philosophy and its verbal wastes and intellec-tual haziness. The first of the new intellectual heroes is, of course, Copernicus, from whom Tyndall quotes the following defiant assertion: 'Not unto Aristotle, not unto subtle hypothesis, not unto church, Bible, or blind tradition, must we turn for a knowledge of the universe, but to the direct investigation of Nature by observation and experiment'.[8] The pivotal year is 1543, when Copernicus published his epoch-making work on the movement of the heavenly bodies, at the same time bringing about the crash of Aristotle's closed geocentric universe. Copernicus is the first great stepping stone into modernity, towards a new, more intellectually honest and coura-geous understanding of the world. Other stepping stones along the way are Giordano Bruno, Descartes, Locke and Newton, all of whom attribute great causal powers to matter and motion, and who see the universe as the outcome of material and atomic forces, despite sometimes granting God a position as originator. And then at last, Tyndall arrives at the most eminent of the new thinkers, namely, Darwin. Predictably, he is full of admiration for Darwin, for his method, his persistence, his gifts of obser-vation and comparison, and especially for the intellectual courage that led him to his revolutionary insight – namely, that small variations, where they benefit a living thing, will be selected for preservation and eventually lead to the emergence of new species. As far as Tyndall is concerned, the theory of natural selection removes once and for all the need to invoke acts of supernatural intervention, and this represents for him an important culmination in scientific, rational thinking about matter, nature and life.

Given his preparedness to set the principle of natural selection against the tradi-tional creationist account of the origin of species, there can be no doubt that Tyndall was not only a pro-Darwinist but also some kind of Darwinist. This may seem like an odd thing to say, but it is in fact necessary to say it in the context of some work that has been carried on in recent years by Peter Bowler and other Darwin scholars

---

7 Ibid., pp 12–13.   8 Ibid., p. 18.

who have suggested that most nineteenth-century supporters of Darwin were not in fact genuine or true Darwinists.[9] It is Bowler's contention that, despite assumptions to the contrary, Darwin's theory of natural selection did not begin to be widely accepted, even in the scientific community, until the twentieth century, after the rediscovery in 1900 of Mendel's work on genetics. All too often, according to Bowler, the early supporters of Darwin turn out to have been little more than pseudo-Darwinists, people who combined Darwinian rhetoric with attitudes that were really continuations of a pre-Darwinian understanding of evolution. These pseudo-Darwinists still thought in terms of a pre-Darwinian analogy between individual growth and the evolution of species. For them, evolution is developmental and progressive; it progresses not only from lower to higher forms of life, from simple to more complex forms of life, but also progresses towards a certain end or goal. Even as they were reading *Origin of species*, these early interpreters still believed that the history of life passes through a fixed sequence of stages towards a certain ultimate end. It is as if these early interpreters of Darwin are not getting the full Darwinian message, such is their commitment to an older conception or picture of evolution. Despite their pro-Darwinist rhetoric, these progressive evolutionists fail to appreciate the logic of Darwin's theory of natural selection – they fail to appreciate how haphazard, how open-ended, how undirected, how unpredictable natural selection actually is. Only in the twentieth century, after the synthesis of Darwinism with Mendelian genetics, did it become more and more apparent that the notion of preordained development and progress is more ideological than scientific. Contrary to the received assumptions of the early interpreters, natural selection does not follow some preordained pattern of development, and is certainly not goal-directed. There is no preordained pattern working itself out implicitly by means of natural selection. Natural selection doesn't do preordained plans. Indeed, natural selection, strictly understood, doesn't do progress at all, let alone progress in accordance with a preordained plan. As Richard Dawkins puts it, 'Evolution has no long-term goal. There is no long-distance target, no final perfection to serve as a criterion for selection, although human vanity cherishes the absurd notion that our species is the final goal of evolution'.[10]

The question we have to ask about Tyndall is this: is he a true Darwinist, according to Bowler's strict criteria, and not just a pro-Darwinist? Is he part of what Bowler calls the non-Darwinian revolution of the nineteenth-century? Or does he look ahead to the true, full-fledged, full-dress Darwinian revolution of the next century, when scientists and others begin to take on board all the implications of a theory of natural selection, and begin to question the whole notion of predetermined biological progress? It seems to me that Tyndall has a foot in both centuries, as far as the evolving interpretation of Darwin is concerned. One of the things that deterred the early interpreters from a whole-hearted endorsement of Darwin was

9 See P.J. Bowler, *The Non-Darwinian revolution: reinterpreting a historical myth* (Baltimore & London, 1988). **10** R. Dawkins, *The blind watchmaker* (London, 1988), p. 50.

their unhappiness with materialism, with the materialistic, non-theistic implications of Darwin's theory. But this is not a source of difficulty for Tyndall. From the very beginning of the address, it is clear that he is some sort of materialist. Secondly, Tyndall is not compromised by a desire to defend a scripture-friendly version of evolution. His enriched conception of matter and nature is intended as a kind of substitute for any form of theism or creationism. It should be said here that Tyndall is unlike Dawkins in one important respect – that is to say, he is sympathetic towards the religious sentiment or impulse. He makes the case for the 'naturalness' of the religious impulse, maintaining that religion is rooted in the emotional life, and therefore cannot be denied a role in human culture. At one point in his essay, he speaks of the 'mystery' that lies beyond the reach of science and to which the human mind returns 'with the yearning of a pilgrim for his distant home'.[11] He is not sympathetic towards the orthodox religions and their theologies, especially where these interfere with the practice of science. Science must be free to go its own way without hindrance from the dominant religions and their unscientific views of the world. We can see, then, that Tyndall is free of the kind of ideological pressures that caused some early supporters of Darwin to ignore the harsher implications of his theory of evolution by natural selection.

Was Tyndall a full-fledged Darwinist for all that? Did he succumb, after all, to some preconceived Victorian ideas? I believe he did. He was unable to resist the progressionist streak that was present in Victorian social ideology. The Victorians believed that they were at the cutting edge of new improving developments in the social and political world. They were therefore receptive to the idea of progress in nature as well as in society and were disposed to interpret Darwin in uncomplicatedly progressionist terms. One disconcertingly progressionist idea that crops up in Tyndall's address is the idea that everything that now exists somehow existed in a potential form before it evolved into its actual present state. He insists that there is a real continuity between inorganic and organic matter, as if the makings of life were already present in matter and were at the same time determined to emerge as they did: 'I discern in that Matter ... that we have hitherto covered with opprobrium, the promise and potency of all terrestrial Life'.[12] Tyndall's Darwinism, then, is somewhat compromised by his commitment to a metaphysical, almost animistic, view of matter. At the same time, it would be wrong to call him a pseudo-Darwinist. He is a pro-Darwinist who is perhaps not as much of a Darwinist as he assumed himself to be; but he has resisted more of the ideological pressures of the Victorian period than most of his fellow scientists, and is entitled to be called a Darwinist, at least in the nineteenth-century sense of the term. If Darwin himself is some kind of Darwinist, then so is Tyndall.

11 Tyndall, *Address*, p. 64. 12 Ibid., p. 55.

THE OUTRIGHT OBJECTORS

There was, of course, a highly critical response to Tyndall's Belfast address, mainly from those who felt that their time-honoured religious beliefs were under attack. Negative responses came from all the religious denominations in Ireland, from representatives of Roman Catholicism, from members of the Church of Ireland, from Presbyterians. A couple of months after Tyndall delivered his address, the Irish Catholic bishops issued a pastoral letter in which they condemned, in highly emotive terms, the emergence of a materialistic approach to life among scientists and other intellectuals. They accuse the 'professors of materialism' of obtruding blasphemy 'upon this Catholic nation'.[13] They use Tyndall's classical references against him, arguing that his supposedly scientific materialism is nothing more than a reiteration of the doctrines of a petty school of pagan philosophy that was long ago rejected not only by the early Christians but also by 'the very flower of human intelligence'. What most concerns the bishops is Tydnall's positioning of science within a materialistic framework. They accept that science is a worthy enterprise but insist that it is limited in its scope, that it is confined to matters of empirical cause and effect and should not range into areas where it has no competence, such as those areas of metaphysical concern that are the provenance of faith and theology. It is not possible for a scientific discovery to overturn revealed doctrine or dogma, for

> it will be found that the bloated discovery which creates [an apparent contradiction] is but an ephemeral theory, and not the truth: or, if its truth be beyond gainsay ... then the doctrine with which it is in conflict, will be found to be but a theological opinion, and not a dogma.

They cite the authority of the Vatican document *De Fide Catholica*, in which it is stated that there can be no real conflict between faith and reason, 'since the God who reveals mysteries and infuses faith is He who gives to the soul of man the light of reason; and God cannot deny Himself, nor can truth ever contradict truth'. The bishops also attack the new scientific materialism on the grounds that it offers a reductive, deterministic, mechanical view of the human personality, that it eliminates the soul, free will, and conscience from the scheme of things, and that it reduces the human being to the status of an instinctive automaton: 'In such a system, all moral dignity absolutely disappears from humanity, for neither truth remains, nor duty, nor charity, nor self-sacrifice'.[14] Interestingly, the pastoral letter makes only a passing dismissive reference to the theory of natural selection; it does not dwell on Darwinism specifically, despite the fact that Tyndall spends a good part of his address defending it.

For a more extensive critique of Darwinism, I am going to look at the work of

---

13 Cardinal P. Cullen et al., 'Pastoral address of the archbishops and bishops of Ireland', *IER*, 11 (Nov. 1874), 49–62 at 49. **14** Ibid., pp 52, 62, 61, 55.

Fr Jeremiah Murphy, who published a series of anti-Darwinist articles in the *Irish Ecclesiastical Record*. Born in 1840 in Inniscarra, Co Cork, Murphy was ordained to the priesthood in 1871 and became parish priest in Macroom in 1897. He was a regular contributor to newspapers and other publications before he entered the Darwin debate in the 1880s with a series of articles attacking Darwinism, especially the Darwinism of *The descent of man*, the claims of which concerned him rather more than those of *Origin of species*. Murphy is interesting because he is an outright objector – in other words, he will have no truck with attempts to strike any kind of compromise between religion and the theory of evolution, especially as far as The origin of the human species is concerned. Murphy attacks Darwinism as if it were no more than a rival belief-system that is seeking to draw supporters away from a traditional religious belief-system based on revelation and scripture. He begins by trying to discredit Darwin's claim to belong to the community of scientists, arguing that fixity of species is the idea that is most generally accepted by the scientific community, that there is no evidence to support the notion of transmutation of species, that the evidence provided by experiments in artificial selection indicates that, while varieties can be cultivated within species, there is not a single case of artificial selection of a new species, that, in the natural world, the geological and fossil record supports fixity rather than transmutation of species, and that, as far as the notion of transmutation goes, the record is most defective precisely where it is most sadly needed.

As well as attempting to undermine Darwin's credentials as a scientist, Murphy also highlights the more fundamentally counter-intuitive nature of Darwin's theory. Murphy considers it contrary to good sense and good observation that Darwin should minimize the difference between man and ape. No superficial resemblance at the level of skeletal structure or anatomy can be taken to imply a resemblance at the level of mind and behaviour. There is not only a difference of kind rather than degree between man and ape, but in fact an enormous difference in kind between the appetites and instincts of the simian brute and the intellectual, creative, spiritual and moral faculties of the human being. It is contrary to experience itself to claim, as Darwin does, that the human faculties are merely a development out of pre-human brute capacities. Murphy goes on to list some of the faculties he has in mind, faculties for which there is no simian equivalent, no equivalent in any earlier form of life, even to the smallest degree:

> Man has surveyed the extent of the heavens and the ocean's abyss ... The fury of the storm, the darkness of night, time and distance are yielding to man's intellectual powers. And yet Darwin dares the audacious assertion that man's mental powers differ from those of the brute, not in kind but in degree! Surely every page of man's history stamps upon Darwin's degrading system a verdict of contemptuous condemnation.[15]

15 J. Murphy, 'Darwinism', *IER*, 3rd ser., 5 (Sept. 1884), 594.

Murphy has no doubt that Darwinism is essentially anathema to anyone who really believes in scripture. He disagrees fundamentally with those who claim that scripture can be reinterpreted in the light of new scientific thinking. Revelation is Revelation, as far as Murphy is concerned, and does not lend itself to convenient reinterpretations. New interpretations will merely undermine the traditional moral authority of a religion that has based itself in scripture, traditionally understood. Murphy published an article specifically criticizing one innovative attempt to bring scripture into line with Darwinism. The English zoologist and convert to Catholicism, St George Jackson Mivart, had suggested that the body of the first man – the evolutionary Adam – had evolved along the lines described by Darwin, that this first biological man was indeed produced by evolution from a lower animal, and that when the process of evolution had reached the desired level of perfection, the Creator had infused a distinctively personal soul into that first evolved man, and subsequently into all his descendents. In this way, wrote Mivart,

> we find a perfect harmony in the double nature of man, his rationality making use of and subsuming his animality; his soul arising from direct and immediate creation, and his body being formed at first ... by derivative or secondary creation, through natural laws.[16]

It was not necessary, according to Mivart, to believe that God had directly and immediately created Adam and Eve. It was possible, in Mivart's view, to take a figurative message from Genesis and to use science to fill in the details in a way that was consistent with the figurative message about God's creative intervention in the process.

This sort of compromising approach is repugnant to Murphy, for whom it is simply wrong to re-read the Genesis account as merely symbolic or figurative. To read it in such a way is to deprive it of its truth, moral authority and status as a divinely inspired communication:

> So direct, so precise ... is the scriptural account of man's creation, that, if the evolution theory were true, the sacred writers, if they intended to deceive us, could not have chosen language better calculated to effect that end.[17]

He refers to several passages that imply God's immediate formation of the bodies of Adam and Eve, passages that leave no room for an alternative meaning. In other words, if Darwin's theory is true, then the language of Genesis, which is clear and not at all obscure or figurative, would have to be seen as false, as misleading, as deceitful. Here we see Murphy having the courage of his convictions. He is prepared to stake his religious belief on a literal understanding of Genesis; prepared to set this literal understanding against everything that Darwinism can throw at it; prepared even to

---

16 St G.J. Mivart, *On the genesis of species* (New York, 1871), p. 305. **17** J. Murphy, 'Evolution and faith', *IER*, 3rd ser., 5 (Dec. 1884), 761.

say that if Darwinism should be verified in the future, then Genesis would have to be seen as untrue.

Of course, it was not merely leading members of the Catholic Church who reacted negatively to Darwinism. In all the other Christian churches in Ireland you find strong objectors to the new theory. One of the strongest objectors in the Church of Ireland was also in fact a scientist, and used scientific rather than religious language to express his objections.

Samuel Haughton, a fellow county-man of John Tyndall's, was born in the town of Carlow in 1821. He was ordained into the Church of Ireland, and became professor of geology at Trinity in 1851. Though he had no objection to a theory of evolution as such, he did have a very strong objection to the idea of natural selection and to the idea that one species could transmute, by small variations, into another. He has the distinction of being the earliest Irish critic of Darwinism, having published a very negative review of *Origin of species* in the *Natural History Review* in 1860. His main argument is that the study of animal anatomy reveals such a well-designed arrangement of bone, joint and muscle – such a well-designed arrangement of every feature of every part to the overall function of the animal – that any variation in any part of the organism would lead to a decrease in efficiency, and so the very idea of progress through variation is simply contrary to observed fact.[18]

THE ACCOMMODATORS

All the members of this group argue that evolutionary theory is consistent, after all, with religious belief. They are prepared to revise Darwin's conception of evolution to the point where it can allow for divine intervention, even if this intervention is very indirect and rather different from the kind of intervention described in scripture. They are also prepared to interpret scripture in such a way that it does not necessarily rule out an evolutionary account of the origin of species. The most impressive of the Irish accommodators was Joseph John Murphy, a Belfast-born businessman, the owner of a linen mill, who was greatly interested in both science and theology. The topic that most concerned Murphy was the relationship between science and religious belief. His own father had been a Quaker but he himself was drawn towards a more mainstream position and eventually became an active member of the Church of Ireland. Murphy produced a number of substantial works on the theme of the relationship between science and religion, but especially on the implications for faith of the claims of evolutionism, supposing these claims to be true. The most important of his books is his *Habit and intelligence*, of which there are two editions, and which has been described as 'the most considered and expansive appraisal of the new biology' to be published during the nineteenth century.[19]

18 See S. Haughton, 'Biogenesis', *Natural History Review*, 7 (1860), pp 23–32; repr. in D.L. Hull (ed.), *Darwin and his critics* (Chicago, 1973), pp 217–28.   19 D. Livingstone, 'Darwin in Belfast: the evolution debate' in J.W. Foster (ed.), *Nature in Ireland* (Dublin, 1997), p. 392.

Murphy goes a long way with Darwin – he accepts that species have not been separately created but have all been 'derived by descent, with modification and variation, from one, or at most a small number, of germs'.[20] At the same time, while being prepared to accept so much of the theory of evolution, Murphy declares that he is not a believer in Darwin's version. He refuses to accept that the purely mindless, mechanical principle of natural selection is enough to account for the whole complex process of modification whereby highly organized forms emerge from unorganized 'germs'. He maintains that there is an organizing intelligence at work in and through the process of modification, that this 'organizing intelligence co-exists and co-operates with the unintelligent forces through all life', and that this principle of intelligence 'is most dominant in the highest forms of life'.[21] He has no doubt that life, like matter or energy, has had its origins in the direct action of a creative intelligence – that, while all species are descended from a few original germs, these few germs 'were originally vitalized by Creative Power'.[22] He is equally convinced that the spiritual nature enjoyed by human beings was also a direct result of the same creative power. His argument exploits the scientific 'fact' that there is no significant *physical* difference between the human brain and the brain of the ape. The human brain shows no anatomical superiority over that of the highest apes, yet there is no doubting the great mental, intellectual and spiritual superiority of the human mind over that of the apes. This strongly suggests that superior human mentality must have a source other than the purely physical process of natural selection, which produces only the ape-like physical human brain. Considered as possessors of brains, there is no significant difference between ape and human; considered as possessors of minds, there is all the difference in the world. Brains may be the creatures of natural selection, but minds, despite their relationship to brains, must come into existence in accordance with the action of a different principle. He writes: 'I do not see any improbability in the belief that the same Creative Power which at the beginning created matter, and afterwards gave it life, finally ... completed the work by breathing into man a breath of higher and spiritual life'.[23]

Against Darwin, then, he argues that there is a guiding intelligence at work in and through the process of modification. This organizing intelligence is unconsciously immanent in all organic life, including plant life, emerging only into full consciousness in the highest form of life, such as we find it in the human species.[24] One of the most interesting points that Murphy makes is that there is no essential difference between conscious and unconscious intelligence, stating at one point that 'the instinctive intelligence which constructs the cells of the bee; and mental intelligence of man; are all fundamentally the same'.[25] There is an important sense in which intelligence was unconscious before it was conscious, and even that it was organic before it was instinctive or sentient. Wherever there is successful adaptation of means to ends, there is some degree or kind of intelligence at work:

20 J.J. Murphy, *Habit and intelligence*, 1 (London, 1869), p. 205. **21** Ibid., p. 337. **22** Ibid., p. 328. **23** Ibid., p. 331. **24** Ibid., p. 337. **25** Murphy, *Habit and intelligence*, 2 (London, 1869), p. 162.

> There is no more clear and definite instance of the adaptation of means to
> purpose in the whole organic creation than the structure of the iris, enabling
> it to contract, involuntarily and spontaneously, in order to protect the retina
> against too much light. The formation of the iris is a case of unconscious
> intelligence, and its action in closing against the light is a case of unconscious
> motor intelligence.[26]

What is interesting about Murphy's concept of an organizing intelligence is that he
does not always link it to an orthodox religious conception of divine power, but talks
about it as a force that might work in and through nature and life in any case. Even
when he uses the term 'Creative Power', it is not necessarily to be understood as
identical with the personal God of scripture. It is open to the reader to give it a
pantheistic interpretation, though Murphy dissociates himself from such an approach.
What is instructive about Murphy's attempt at accommodation is that it shows the
kind of price that has to be paid for sustaining religious belief in the face of
Darwinism. It means not only an adjustment in one's understanding of the supernatural but also in one's understanding of evolution. Something must give on either
side. Some critics of Murphy might say that he is compromised twice over, that he
falls between two stools, but he himself would have said that he has sought to
preserve the best of two worlds, the religious and the scientific, without having to
forsake one for the other.

THE COMPARTMENTALISTS

This group contains those who do not see a need to either modify religious belief in
the name of science or modify Darwinism in the name of religious belief. They
argue instead for the relative autonomy of the two provinces of human thought – the
religious and the scientific – and do not therefore see the need for any kind of
compromise or accommodation on either side, given the fact that each province
works with its own logic and within its own conceptual framework. An early effort
to offer a compartmentalist approach is to be found in *Science and revelation: their
distinct provinces*, a pamphlet published in 1874 by the Donegal-born Presbyterian
minister, Josiah Leslie Porter, in which he argues that the scientist, dealing with what
lies before him, cannot usefully address questions of ultimate origin, while the
theologian, for his part, 'does not attempt to intrude his dogmas into the field of
science'.[27] Revelation, he maintains, does not give a scientific cosmology or touch
on geology or 'enter into the mysteries of molecular physics, or the development of
the life-germ'; instead 'it reveals to the eye of faith that other world after which our
higher nature longs'.[28]

---

26 Ibid., p. 2.   **27** J.L. Porter, *Science and revelation: their distinct provinces* (Belfast, 1874), p.
35.   **28** Ibid., pp 35–6, 38.

One of the most intriguing of the Irish compartmentalists was the feminist campaigner and social reformer, Frances Power Cobbe, who criticized Darwinism from an ethical rather than from a defensively religious point of view. Cobbe was born at Newbridge House, Donabate, Co. Dublin, in 1822, but moved to London in the 1860s, where she took an active part in Victorian cultural life, becoming acquainted with John Stuart Mill, John Tyndall, Matthew Arnold and Charles Darwin. Her thought is dominated by her moral convictions; her objections to Darwinism are motivated by those convictions. In her autobiography, she tells a revealing story about a conversation and subsequent correspondence she had with Darwin. The story is that while Darwin was working on *The descent of man* he happened to mention to her that he was trying to formulate a view on the moral sense in the human species. She immediately advised him to read Immanuel Kant's *Groundwork of morals*. Although it seems that Darwin did not express any great interest in Kant's book, she nevertheless sent him a copy shortly after their conversation. On returning the book some time later, Darwin pointed out the contrast between Kant and himself: 'the one man a great philosopher looking exclusively into his own mind, the other a degraded wretch looking from the outside through apes and savages at the moral sense of mankind'.[29]

In her essay, 'Darwinism in morals', Cobbe draws on Darwin's self-humbling distinction in order to identify two great and mutually opposed schools of thinkers, namely, those who study human beings from the 'inside' and those who study them from the 'outside'. She opts to belong to the former school, insisting that a philosophy that dwells exclusively on the outer facts of anthropology, regardless of human consciousness, 'must be worse than imperfect and incomplete. It resembles a treatise on the Solar System which should omit to notice the Sun'.[30] For her, human consciousness is not only a fact in the world but also the greatest and most defining fact about human nature, one that it is scientifically and morally irresponsible to ignore or to approach reductively. Her quarrel with Darwin is that his approach is too reductive. Interestingly, she agrees with Darwin's theory of evolution, and even sings its praises. She declares that she is not only prepared to accept Darwin's 'fairy-tale of science' but says that she takes a degree of intellectual pleasure in its novelty and originality. She wonders why any 'free mind' should have purely religious objections to Darwin's views, and suggests that when the orthodox creationist account is compared with that of the slow evolution of order, life and intelligence from 'the immeasurable past of the primal nebula's "fiery cloud", we have no language to express how infinitely more religious is the story of modern science than that of ancient tradition'.[31] Nevertheless, she finds that Darwin's doctrines, considered from the ethical point of view, are 'the most dangerous which have ever been set forth since the days of Mandeville'.[32] Darwin's reduction of the moral sense to the level of

29 F.P. Cobbe, *Life of Frances Power Cobbe by herself*, 2nd ed. (London, 1894), pp 125–6.
30 F.P. Cobbe, *Darwinism in morals and other essays* (London, 1872), p. 126.   **31** Ibid., pp 2–3.
32 Ibid., p. 11.

social or sympathetic animal instincts fails to do justice to the fundamental, irre-
ducible and principled requirements of morality. The physiology of instincts cannot
begin to 'explain' the awe-inspiring imperatives of conscience or the tremendous
sentiments of repentance and remorse. The idea of right – that she calls 'the sacred
obligation of Rightfulness' – belongs to a category wholly distinct from that of either
social utility or animal instinct. Repentance and remorse have no ancestral precursors in the behaviour of even the higher non-human animals. The transition from an
instinctive social sense to a sense of moral obligation does not have a natural or evolutionary history. In *The descent of man*, Darwin had derived conscience from the
dissatisfaction that individual human beings experience when they act against their
social instincts:

> Hence after some temporary desire or passion has mastered man's social
> instincts, he will reflect and compare the now weakened impression of such
> past impulses, with the ever-present social instinct, and he will then feel that
> sense of dissatisfaction which all unsatisfied instincts leave behind them.
> Consequently, he resolves to act differently for the future – and this is
> conscience.[33]

It is just this sort of grounding of conscience in animal instinct that Cobbe rejects as
unacceptably and distortingly reductive.

It looks as if Cobbe has argued herself into a paradoxical situation here. On the
one hand, she accepts Darwin's theory of evolution, yet criticizes it on moral
grounds. If Darwin's theory is true, how can she have a moral objection to it, even if
it should have unpalatable implications? The apparent paradox is reduced if we interpret her as a compartmentalist with regard to the relationship between Darwinism
and ethics. It is perfectly clear that she has no difficulty with Darwin's theory of
evolution, considered as the best available scientific account of the origin of species,
including the human species. What she objects to is the intrusion of the scientific
method into an area where it has no business going – that is, into the kinds of human
relationships and interactions that are grounded in ethical values and that are best
understood from an ethical point of view rather than from the point of view of
biology or science in general. How we think when we are in human, ethical mode
is going to be different from the way we think when we are in objective, scientific
mode. To try to yoke the two modes together, or to try to derive the ethical from
the biological, is a mistake. The two areas are not continuous with each other. There
is separate work to be done in each area, using different language and concepts, and
applying different criteria.

Of all the positions examined so far, it is perhaps that of Cobbe that would
benefit most from being brought into contact with some contemporary philosophical perspectives. One contemporary perspective that seems potentially open to her

---

33 C. Darwin, *The descent of man, and selection in relation to sex* (Princeton, NJ, 1981), p. 392.

point of view, and that she in turn would, I think, have endorsed, is that of emergentism. In philosophy, emergentism is an alternative to reductionism. The reductionist sees even the most complex organism as no more than the sum of its evolutionary parts, while the emergentist will say that each new species of organism brings something irreducibly new into the world – new structures, new behaviour, new experiences, new styles of life, new ways of being in the world. Not everything can be traced back without remainder to an earlier form of life, or an earlier function; to be too mechanically reductive is contrary to the spirit of evolution, since the whole achievement of evolution is the trying out of new ways of doing things, new ways of surviving, new ways of living. In the case of human beings, this new way of surviving and being will include modes of consciousness, of experience, of response that are more than just complex variations on primitive precedents. Reference to such precedents is necessary to explain how things originated and subsequently developed to varying degrees, but it is not sufficient for a full understanding of what is really new about each late-comer to the natural world, including the late-comer that is the human species itself. At some point, differences of degree become differences of kind, and it is these differences that are recognized, in the case of human beings, in the development of an ethical discourse that is not reducible to the discourse of biology.

Another contemporary, and even more radical, perspective that is potentially congenial to Cobbe's position is that of internal realism, a philosophical perspective defended by the American philosopher, Hilary Putnam.[34] According to Putnam, it is not possible for human beings to have a purely or absolutely objective relationship to reality, or to arrive at one true description of reality. What counts as real, or as an object, or even as 'the world', is relative to, or internal to, one or other of the different conceptual frameworks that human beings have historically devised in the course of their attempts to provide answers to the different kinds of questions they find themselves asking. Since human beings are not all-seeing, all-knowing gods capable of an absolute standpoint outside reality, they should accept that they are capable only of constructing changing versions of reality from within their historical human situations, with no one version – the religious version, for example, or the scientific version – occupying a privileged position in relation to the others. Arguably, what Cobbe would have found congenial about internal realism is that it would have enabled her to argue that what really and truly matters within a scientific framework is different from what really and truly matters within an ethical or religious framework. In each case, the language is different, the mode of thinking is different, the conception of reality is different, and, ultimately, what counts as 'truth' is different.

34 See H. Putnam, *Reason, truth and history* (Cambridge, MA, 1981); H. Putnam, *Representation and reality* (Cambridge, MA, 1996), ch. 7.

Asserting medical identities in mid-nineteenth-century Ireland: the case of the water cure in Cork[1]

ELIZABETH NESWALD

The phenomenon of hydropathy, or the cold water cure, has been the subject of numerous studies since the 1980s. While straightforward accounts of its institutional history form the basis of early and recent histories of the hydropathic spa and leisure business,[2] several additional strands of investigation have emerged. Early studies of hydropathy focused on the water cure as a 'fringe', lay or oppositional practice on par with mesmerism, patent medicines and homeopathy, a product and casualty of battles for the professionalization of medicine.[3] More recent research into British hydropathy by James Bradley and Marguerite Dupree has questioned its fringe status, pointing out, as has often been noted, that it had numerous supporters among qualified physicians, and that the line of demarcation between orthodox and heterodox, regular and irregular practices and practitioners was at the time of hydropathy's emergence by no means settled.[4]

1 My thanks go to the Irish Research Council for the Humanities and Social Sciences, the Royal Irish Academy Third Sector Research Programme and the Humanities Research Institute of Brock University for their generous support. I thank Juliana Adelman and the anonymous referees for their insightful criticism and comments. 2 R. Metcalfe, *The rise and progress of hydropathy in England and Scotland* (London, 1912); A. Durie, 'The business of hydropathy in the North of England, c.1850–1930', *Northern History*, 39 (2002), 37–58; M. Dupree, A. Durie and J. Bradley, 'Taking the waters: the development of hydropathic establishments in Scotland, 1840–1940', *Business and Economic History*, 26 (1997), 426–37; K. Rees, 'Water as a commodity: hydropathy in Matlock' in R. Cooter (ed.), *Studies in the history of alternative medicine* (Houndsmills and London, 1988), pp 28–45. 3 L. Barrow, 'Why were most medical heretics at their most confident around the 1840s? (The other side of mid-Victorian medicine)' in R.K. French and A. Wear (eds), *British medicine in an age of reform* (New York and London, 1991), pp 165–85; R. Jütte, 'The paradox of professionalization: homeopathy and hydropathy as unorthodoxy in Germany in the 19th and early 20th century' in R. Jütte, G.B. Risse and J. Woodward (eds), *Culture, knowledge and healing: historical perspectives of homeopathic medicine in Europe and North America* (Sheffield, 1998), pp 65–88; R. Price, 'Hydropathy in England, 1840–70', *Medical History*, 25 (1981), 269–80. 4 J. Bradley, 'Medicine on the margins? Hydropathy and orthodoxy in Britain, 1840–60' in Waltraud Ernst (ed.), *Plural medicine: Orthodox & heterodox medicine in Western & colonial countries during the nineteenth & twentieth centuries* (Florence, KY, 2001), pp 19–39; M. Dupree and J. Bradley, 'A shadow of orthodoxy? An epistemology of British hydropathy, 1840–1858', *Medical History*, 47 (2003), 173–94; J. Bradley and M. Dupree, 'Opportunity on the edge of

Although water has long had its uses in medical practice, the cold water cure that swept through Europe in the 1840s proclaimed its origins in the authentic healing power of nature as discovered by the Silesian peasant Vincent Priessnitz. According to popular legend, Priessnitz had been injured in a farming accident but had cured himself by the application of cold, wet compresses and by drinking water. After perfecting his methods on animals and neighbours, he opened a treatment centre at Gräfenberg in Austria, which became a Mecca for the fashionable but ailing middle and upper classes of Europe. Although the cure itself was a demanding and uncomfortable regime of cold baths, boring food and teetotalism, it quickly became associated with the well-established spa culture and setting.[5]

Priessnitz did not develop a consistent medical theory himself, leaving it to his followers, most especially to the self-styled hydropathic missionary, 'Captain (R.T.) Claridge' to elaborate the basis of the cure. Cold water, inside and out, became part of a holistic physiological purification process that drew toxins, including those left by allopathic treatment, out of the organs, eliminated them through the skin and stimulated the body's self-healing capacities.[6] Medical practitioners expressed scepticism about this explanation, which carried an implicit criticism of standard medical practices. Nonetheless, the therapy attracted the attention not only of laymen, but also of many physicians, who sought to establish the physiological basis of the cure and who often refined Priessnitz's austere methods into a broad variety of treatments including wet sheet wraps, hot and cold showers of varying strength and baths for different parts of the body. From this uneasy status of hydropathy between lay traditions of natural healing and scientific explanation, Bradley and Dupree conclude that hydropathy had a dual existence:

> On the one hand it *was* a heterodox practice, supported by the radical underbelly of Victorian society; on the other, it was perched uncomfortably on the edge of orthodoxy, adhering to a received idea of pathology and physiology, but contesting the mode of therapeutic intervention advocated by most orthodox practitioners.[7]

English and Scottish hydropathy have been the subject of several studies, but the reception of the cold water cure in Ireland has received scanty attention.[8] Admittedly,

orthodoxy: medically qualified hydropathists in the era of reform, 1840–60', *Social History of Medicine*, 13:3 (2001), 417–37. Also noted by K. Rees, 'Water as a commodity: hydropathy in Matlock', p. 30. **5** See Durie, 'The business of hydropathy'. **6** R.T. Claridge, Esq., *Hydropathy; or, the cold water cure, as practised by Vincent Priessnitz, at Graefenberg, Silesia, Austria* (3rd ed. London, 1842), p. 74. Claridge was supposedly an asphalt contractor who was cured of his chronic diseases by Priessnitz at his spa in Gräfenberg. See Price, 'Hydropathy in England', p. 272. **7** Bradley and Dupree, 'Opportunities', p. 421. **8** Teresa Breathnach's essay deals mainly with the Turkish bath, a later modification of the cold water cure which added a hot steam bath. See T. Breathnach, 'For health and pleasure: the Turkish bath in Victorian Ireland', *Victorian Literature and Culture*, 32 (2004), 159–75.

Ireland produced few spas of note, with the exception of Dr Richard Barter's establishment, St Ann's, near Blarney, Co. Cork, which was popular with the Victorian
middle and upper middle class of Britain and Ireland. Nonetheless, Irish medical
practitioners and the Irish public were well aware of British debates and medical
trends and innovations, and local newspapers noted the cold water cure and its
controversies with interest. At the same time, Irish medical practitioners were
affected not only by the same laws and regulations governing the British medical
profession, but also by acts, regulations and pressures directed at them in particular.
In this situation, it is worthwhile to ask whether Irish hydropathic debates mirror
English and Scottish debates or whether factors specific to the Irish situation also
emerged. The fate of hydropathy and hydropathists in the case study of the provincial town of Cork offers the possibility of identifying some of the factors affecting
the reception of the cold water cure in Ireland.

SETTING THE SCENE: CAPTAIN CLARIDGE IN CORK

In 1843, Captain Claridge toured the south of Ireland, lecturing on the cold water
cure. He arrived in the town of Cork in mid-July, after having been warmly received
in Limerick, Kilrush and Killarney.[9] In Cork, Claridge was given use of the ballroom
of the Imperial Hotel without charge. Although entrance was free, the large audience (400–500) consisted nonetheless of townspeople of the better social classes,
including several medical practitioners.[10] Claridge's sojourn in Cork led to a flurry
of local activity. A few days after his lecture, a meeting was held in the rooms of the
Royal Cork Institution, the town's prestigious, incorporated science society. At one
time, this institution had aimed to emulate its London counterparts, the Royal
Society of London and the Royal Institution of Great Britain, but by the 1840s, it
had become a general upper-class meeting place rather than an institution with original scholarly ambitions. This meeting was attended by several local physicians as
well. Its immediate aim was to discuss the foundation of a water cure society in Cork,
similar to that which had been formed in London.[11] Despite its provincial situation,
Cork had a clearly metropolitan orientation.

Shortly afterward, a public meeting to discuss the cold water cure took place in
the Cork Court House. This gathering of medical practitioners and leading citizens
discussed a number of issues, many of them familiar to historians of British
hydropathy, including medical explanations of the physiological mechanisms of the
water cure, connections between hydropathy and temperance, the suitability of the
cure for a 'utilitarian' age, and witness reports of miraculous hydropathic restoration.

---

9 'Water cure', *Limerick Reporter*, 27 June 1843; 'Hydropathic Society', *LR*, 30 June 1843;
untitled, *LR*, 4 July 1843. **10** 'The water cure meeting at the Imperial Hotel: lecture of
Captain Claridge', *CE*, 14 July 1843. **11** 'Hydropathy: meeting at the Cork Institution',
CE, 19 July 1843.

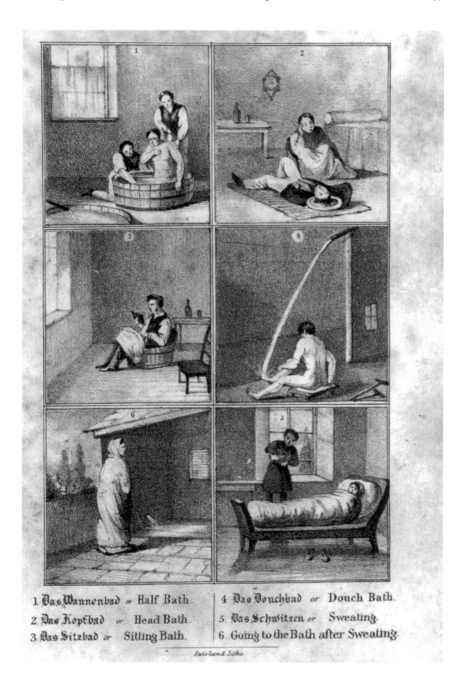

2.1 Frontispiece, R.T. Claridge, 'Hydropathy, or the cold water cure', London 1842. Reproduced with permission of the Wellcome Library, London.

More specific to the Irish situation, however, for some contemporaries the positive potential of the water cure was embedded within criticism of the medical care given to the poor through the medical charities system and criticism of the politics of dispensary and hospital appointments.[12] This position carried significant implications. While medical charity in Ireland relied primarily on voluntary donations and local government decisions, the early 1840s saw heated debates about British government proposals to remove the medical charities from this dependence on good will and intransparent appointment politics and place them under Poor Law Commission supervision.[13] In this context, criticism of the existing provision system was politically sensitive, whatever the intentions of the critic.

Two concrete plans of action emerged from this discussion. Firstly, Alderman Thomas Lyons suggested that the poor relief fund invest part of its reserves in a hydropathic project. This proposal was discussed some days later and will be elaborated more fully in the following section. Secondly, Dr James Richard Wherland, local physician, professor of anatomy and physiology and head of the Cork School of Anatomy, Medicine and Surgery, one of Cork's several medical preparatory schools, announced his intention of travelling to England to observe with his own eyes the methods of the cure. On his return, he stated, he intended to open a hydropathic establishment where he would treat the poor without charge. Although Dr Richard Barter, who was also present at this discussion, had previously expressed interest in water as a curative agent,[14] the motivation behind Wherland's turn to hydropathy is unknown. Whether he had prior interest in the cure, was converted through Claridge's presentation, or sensed a business opportunity and a way of distinguishing himself from the local medical competition in Cork, cannot be precisely known, but Wherland's actions following Claridge's visit may throw some light on this question.

The meeting closed with Claridge's thanks and flattering reminder 'of the discovery made by the French and Scotch philosophers, of the physical superiority of the Irish over the inhabitants of any other country'.[15] He left soon after to continue his tour of Munster, spreading the word in Youghal, Lismore, Waterford and Wexford, where his visit inspired further acolytes to further education travels and led to the establishment of a Hydropathic Society in the town of Enniscorthy, Co. Wexford, and several hydropathic establishments in the region.[16]

---

12 For a detailed study of the Irish medical charity and dispensary system, see L.M. Geary, *Medicine and charity in Ireland, 1718–1851* (Dublin, 2004). 13 'Report of the Poor Law Commissioners, to the secretary of state of the home department, on medical charities in Ireland' (1841); Geary, *Medicine and charity*, ch. 7. 14 'Barter, Richard', *Compendium of Irish biography* (1878), www.libraryireland.com/biography (accessed 5 Feb. 2010); M. Shifrin, 'Victorian Turkish baths', www.victorianturkishbath.org (accessed 5 Feb. 2010). 15 'The cold water cure: meeting of citizens', *CE*, 21 July 1843. 16 'Hydropathy', *Wexford Independent*, 13 Jan. 1844; 'Walsh's general bathing & hydropathic establishment', *CE*, 20 May 1844.

SITUATING HYDROPATHY WITHIN CORK MEDICAL POLITICS

Claridge's departure marked the beginning of hydropathic discussion and controversy in Cork. If his visit had taken place in an atmosphere of general curiosity and novelty, the debates that followed his stay illustrate the emergence of differences and the demarcation of specific interests and positions, both among physicians and among local inhabitants.

Immediately following his departure, the subscribers and trustees of the poor relief fund met to discuss Alderman Lyon's proposal to invest part of its funds in hydropathic research. This fund had, as a subscriber stated, been set up 'for the relief of actual destitution, and to provide against the scarcity and even famine which unhappily were so common to our country and our poor',[17] and the question of whether this mandate should be expanded to include the provision of medical care guided the discussion. Two points in particular were cited in support of their inclusion: cost considerations and humanitarian concerns. Supporters of the plan maintained on the one hand that it would be much more economical to treat the sick poor by wrapping them in cold, wet sheets than by giving them medicine, an assertion that was vehemently refuted by an anonymous contributor to the *Dublin Medical Press* shortly after.[18] On the other hand, they argued, the poor should be allowed to benefit from advancements in medical science, and the curative potential of hydropathy should not be withheld from those already disadvantaged by poverty.

Lyon's plan was not without its critics, but significantly the efficacy and legitimacy of hydropathy itself was not at stake, and none of the leading citizens and physicians involved in this discussion expressed outspoken opposition to the cure. Although subscribers could be divided into supporters of hydropathy and moderate sceptics, differences of opinion concerned the proper use of the subscribed poor relief funds, not hydropathy itself. While some trustees thought the potential benefits of the cure promising enough to warrant investing funds in investigating it, others considered such a use to be outside its mandate, since the monies had been donated for a different purpose. As a compromise, it was proposed to test the usefulness of the cure in the city's public hospitals and that those interested in testing the methods on the poor start their own, separate subscription.[19]

In addition, some subscribers, while disposed to support hydropathy, were uneasy with investing these funds in a therapeutic practice they deemed to be still experimental. As one cautiously approving sceptic expressed it,

> No one admired and appreciated the enthusiasm of Captain Claridge more than he did, but the citizens of Cork were not to take the as yet unsupported testimony of Captain Claridge, for that gentleman had himself declared that he had no scientific knowledge of the anatomy and physiology of man.[20]

17 'Hydropathy: meeting of subscribers to the poor relief fund', *CE*, 26 July 1843.   **18** Medicus, 'Hydropathy. To the editors of the Medical Press', *DMP*, 16 Aug. 1843, 107–10 at 110.   **19** There is no indication that this was attempted in a systematic manner.   **20** 'Hydropathy: meeting of subscribers to the poor relief fund', *CE*, 26 July 1843.

Instead, this sceptic recommended that they wait until the physicians had returned from their educational travels and let them be the judges of hydropathy's merits. Claridge's lack of medical credentials meant that his therapy and theory, as compelling as they might seem, needed expert confirmation.

Studies of the water cure frequently point out that, in contrast to assessments of hydropathy as a 'fringe' practice, most early hydropathists were medically qualified.[21] The Cork case study confirms these results. In total, three local physicians, two of them from competing medical schools, travelled to England to observe the practice of the water cure in various locations. Although little is known of the credentials and affiliations of Richard Barter,[22] his Cork colleagues, James Wherland and Timothy Curtin, were professionally unremarkable. Like many Irish practitioners, Wherland had received his medical degree from a Scottish university, the University of Glasgow. He was a licentiate of the Royal College of Surgeons in Ireland, member of the Cork Medical Society and professor at the Cork School of Anatomy, Medicine and Surgery, as well as physician at the South Lying-in Hospital and Dispensary for Women and Children. Curtin had likewise received his MD in Scotland, at the University of Edinburgh, and was a member of the Royal Medical Society of Edinburgh as well as professor of mid-wifery at the Cork Recognised School of Medicine, which had strong Scottish affiliations.[23] All three opened hydropathic establishments in Cork and its vicinity immediately or shortly after their return, although they followed differing business models. While Wherland and Curtin initially remained in the town and opened fairly utilitarian baths for medical treatment and hygiene, Barter was by far the most successful of the three. His medical resort at St Ann's with its extended gardens, indoor exercise corridors and comfortable, heated dining hall with food supplied from its own farms, attracted an enthusiastic middle- to upper-class clientele.[24]

None of these hydropathic physicians regarded themselves as dabbling on the fringe. In contrast, all sought to integrate the water cure into their professional arsenal of therapeutics, to make hydropathy a part of standard medical practice and to pull it

---

21 Bradley, 'Margins'; P.S. Brown, 'Social context and medical theory in the demarcation of nineteenth-century boundaries' in W.F. Bynum and R. Porter (eds), *Medical fringe and medical orthodoxy, 1750–1850* (London, 1987), pp 216–33 at p. 223. **22** The *Compendium of Irish biography* lists only his 'duties of his profession as a dispensary physician at Inniscarra, where he was elected honorary secretary of the County of Cork Agricultural Society, and contributed materially to improve the husbandry of the south of Ireland' www.libraryireland.com/biography/RichardBarter.php (accessed 5 Feb. 2010). **23** *The medical register 1860* (London, 1860), 83, 362; R. O'Rahilly, 'The pre-collegiate medical schools in Cork', *Irish Journal of Medical Science*, 23 (1958), 31–4. Most Irish practitioners were graduates of the Universities of Edinburgh and Glasgow and/or licentiates of the Dublin or London Colleges of Surgeons. Geary, *Medicine and charity*, p. 135. **24** For a contemporary description of the spa at St Ann's, see 'Hydropathy: Dr Barter's establishment in Blarney', *CE*, 16 Aug. 1844. Barter achieved further fame for being the first to introduce the Turkish (steam) bath and later the Turkish cattle bath to Ireland. See Breathnach, 'Health'; G.R., 'Dr Barter's cattle bath', *Ciba Symposia*, 1 (1939/40), 164.

away from the fringe and from empirics. Thus, like many of their medically qualified hydropathic contemporaries,[25] all emphasized that it was crucial that the cure be applied scientifically by a trained physician and warned in the direst terms not to attempt self-treatment. To be beneficial, it needed to be, as Wherland stated, 'judiciously and properly applied under medical advice'.[26] Barter as well emphasized that injudicious use of the water cure could be fatal. Indeed, already in September of 1843, only weeks after Claridge's visit, the first hydropathic fatality was reported in Lismore. A lay practitioner, a member of the Dean and Chapter of Lismore, had tested the method on an object of charity, an inmate of the Protestant Almshouse, with unsatisfactory results.[27]

Local disputes about the cure had already begun, however, and they took a different path than disagreement among the poor relief fund trustees. Whereas the subscribers had cited Claridge's lack of medical credentials as a reason to have the cure approved by trained physicians, that its efficacy was confirmed by physicians led to divisions within the Cork medical community. The first blows came from Dr John Murphy, member of the Royal College of Surgeons in Ireland who taught at least occasionally at Wherland's medical school.[28] Murphy concentrated on discrediting the doubtful personage of Claridge, and questioned Claridge's right to carry the title of 'Captain', since his name could not be found on Army or Navy lists. He then proceeded to discredit the knowledge of the Cork physicians, who 'formerly professing to understand and administer the curative resources of legitimate and scientific medicine',[29] had spent a week and a half travelling England to learn about the cure and now considered themselves to be experts on the subject. Murphy not only attacked them for approving the hydropathic system despite their credentials, but also questioned their claims that they had visited nine scattered hydropathic establishments within ten days. It was, he implied, a physical impossibility. With this veiled accusation of deception, he cast doubt on the characters of Barter and Wherland. Although Murphy did, eventually, dissect and ridicule Claridge's medical reasoning, his first line of attack was character, since, it implied, if the therapist was not respectable, the therapy could not be either.

This was a local dispute, and the chastisement from a peer did not prevent Wherland from opening his hydropathic establishment shortly after. It was left to the *Dublin Medical Press* to try to bring him to his senses. With the involvement of the *DMP*, however, the doings in Cork stopped being a mere local affair and became part of the wider Irish medical world, part of a conflict between metropolis and province about the organization of medicine and the process of professionalization.

---

25 Brown, 'Social context', p. 225. **26** 'Notice. Hydropathy or water cure', *CE*, 7 Aug. 1843. See also 'Hydropathy' (advertisement for Dr Curtin's establishment), *CE*, 11 Nov. 1846. **27** 'Progress of Hydropathy', *CE*, 20 Sept. 1843. **28** Surgeon Murphy, 'Hydropathy, or the cold water system. To the editor of the Cork Examiner', *CE*, 28 Aug. 1843; 'Lecture on surgery', *CE*, 1 Nov. 1844. **29** Ibid.

THE POLITICS OF PROFESSIONALIZATION:
THE LOCAL GOES NATIONAL

Hydropathy emerged at a particularly sensitive stage in the professionalization of medicine in Britain and in Ireland, situated between the Apothecaries' Act of 1815, which introduced regulations for the training, qualification and certification of apothecaries and surgeon-apothecaries, and the Medical Act of 1858, which laid out the educational qualifications and stipulated registration for physicians.[30] As Anne Digby notes, this drive for professionalization coincided with increasing competition on the medical market and aimed at least in part at restricting competition and reducing the number of practitioners.[31] Defining standard and acceptable medical practices was one way to control entrance into the profession. By excluding particular therapies as unorthodox, especially those that did not require initiation through learning an approved skill and knowledge set (that is, those therapies that could be practiced by laypeople), reforming physicians sought to solidify the status of their specialist knowledge.

The *Dublin Medical Press* was, like *The Lancet*, a metropolitan organ of professionalization. Founded in 1839, it both emulated *The Lancet* and reacted to it, or at least to Thomas Wakley's position on Irish medical politics.[32] It was, in addition, closely associated with the Royal College of Surgeons in Ireland, of which both Wherland and Murphy were members. It was part of a drive among the reform-oriented membership of the RCSI to unify the Irish medical profession, implement comprehensive reforms of medical education and licensing and define standards of professional behaviour.[33] It thus not only discussed the scientific aspects of medicine, physiology, medical theory and surgical techniques, but considered itself primarily a medico-political organ and covered a variety of debates and issues, such as the role of coroners, the vaccination and medical charities acts, dispensaries and the politics of positions, as well as all official debates and acts that could affect the body of medical practitioners that it was trying to whip into a medical profession. Politically, it was committed to medical reform. Professionally, it was committed to creating unity among Irish practitioners. In this regard, it was, like *The Lancet*, greatly interested in defining what constituted acceptable practice and it did this both by polemically condemning 'quack medicine' and by attempting to discipline provincial physicians, who were often open to heterodox therapeutic approaches, into metropolitan professionalism. Hydropathy was not the only front in its provincial battles. The *DMP* invested particular energy in

---

30 For a discussion of the goals and results of the Apothecaries' Act, see S.W.F. Holloway, 'The Apothecaries' Act, 1815: a reinterpretation', *Medical History*, 10 (1966), 107–29; 221–3. **31** A. Digby, *Making a medical living: doctors and patients in the English market for medicine, 1720–1911* (Cambridge, 1994), pp 42–3. **32** R.D. Cassell, 'Lessons in medical politics: Thomas Wakley and the Irish Medical Charities, 1827–39', *Medical History*, 34 (1990), 412–23 at 422. **33** R.J. Rowlette, *The Medical Press and Circular, 1839–1939: a hundred years in the life of a medical journal* (London, 1939), pp 16–17. Central figures were Arthur Jacob, Henry Maunsell (editors of the press) and Richard Carmichael.

condemning those provincial physicians who were prepared to let their names be connected to mesmerism, patent medicines or 'puffery' and was infamous for the rhetorical and polemical vehemence of its attacks.[34]

The hydropathic doings in Cork had not escaped the attention of the *DMP*. Only weeks after Claridge's first appearance in the city, notified by a disdainful medical student, they began their anti-hydropathic crusade. They singled out Wherland in particular for their condemnation, perhaps because he was a member of the RCSI.[35] As P.S. Brown remarks, 'the medical journals generally concentrated their attack on the medically qualified hydropaths, orthodoxy being less concerned about activity well outside the profession than about the breach of its own defences'.[36] Wherland, a leading Cork citizen and man of local standing, gave a feisty response. Like his colleague Barter, he took the position that hydropathy was not an illegitimate, quack practice, but constituted a further therapeutic weapon in the physician's arsenal. As Wherland defended himself, '*I have not laid aside one particle of information* I previously possessed for the water cure – no, far from it; I have merely taken it up in addition to my previous stock of remedies, as *a grand remedial adjunct* to medical science', one that must be administered by qualified physician.[37] Hydropathy thus did not constitute a threat to the profession, and resistance to its use, he implied, was merely the product of professional jealousy.

His response, however, was less a defence of the water cure per se than a stance against being dictated to at a distance by this self-declared voice of professional medicine. Wherland adopted the position of an insulted and maligned provincial practitioner being attacked by a metropolitan interest group and self-interested cartel. In essence, he told the editors of the *DMP*, who he viewed, not without reason, as representatives of the reforming RCSI, that his connection to hydropathy was none of their business. He further stated that he was not surprised at the attack made on him for, 'daring to have an opinion without the sanction of the learned editors of the medical press, who seem to have usurped to themselves a cathedral chair, as regards medical affairs in this country'.[38] Even worse, he accused the *DMP* and the physicians and surgeons associated with it of using the banner of medical reform to look after their own personal, 'place-hunting' interests. Wherland did not grant the *DMP* any legitimacy to speak for the medical profession or medical practitioners in general. With this, he was not alone, however. The College of Physicians and Trinity College were also prepared to question the legitimacy of the lower-status surgeons to speak for all.[39]

34 Rowlett, *Medical Press*, pp 22–4. **35** A medical student, Cork, 'Hydropathy. To the editors of the Medical Press', *DMP*, 10, 2 Aug. 1843, 77; Medicus, Skibereen, 'Hydropathy. To the editors of the Medical Press', *DMP*, 10, 16 Aug. 1843, 107–10; Anon., 'Water witches in Ireland', *DMP*, 10, 16 Aug. 1843, 110–11; Anon., 'Promoting the reputation, honour and dignity of a college', *DMP*, 10, 23 Aug. 1843, 126–7. **36** Brown, 'Social Context', p. 223. **37** Dr J. Wherland, 'To the editor of the Cork Examiner', *CE*, 4 Sept. 1843, emphasis in original. **38** Dr J. Wherland, 'To the editor of the Cork Examiner', *CE*, 4 Sept. 1843. **39** See Rowlette, *Medical Press*, pp 17–18.

The adversity, with which their attempt to establish the water cure as a thera-peutic practice was met, led to a radicalization among the three Cork hydropathic physicians. In 1847, despite two of them belonging to rival medical schools, they banded together to fend off attacks on their system.[40] In a petition made at a time when Cork had been hit by a fever epidemic, they took a more radical stance against what was now becoming medical orthodoxy. While pointing out the beneficial effects of the cure in treating fever, they distanced themselves from the extravagant claims made by the lay supporters of the hydropathic movement. The cure was, they stated, not an 'infallible remedy', but 'a splendid reform in the treatment of disease'.[41] While they positioned themselves as moderates against the lay hydropathists and their claims, they also positioned themselves as therapeutic reformers against mainstream medical opinion, stating that the cure had a '*decided superiority* over ordinary practice, being *always safe, and not calculated to injure*'. At the same time, they continued,

> we consider the Water Cure perfectly compatible with any medicines or medical appliances, that we deem essentially requisite; but *we repudiate all such systematic Drugging* as WE KNOW to be *conjectural, hazardous and not infre-quently destructive.*[42]

Continued opposition from the established medical mainstream had radicalized their approval of the water cure as an addition to their medical repertoire into a critique of mainstream therapeutic methods. If the *DMP* claimed to speak for medical reform in terms of careers and professionalization, the hydropathic physicians claimed for hydropathy and themselves the role of therapeutic reform and reformers.

Although all three hydropathic establishments remained open, through the persistent attacks hydropathy had lost much of its support among many former enthusiasts in Cork. In the mid-1840s it had been a popular topic for discussion in science societies. By 1847, a member of the Cork Literary and Scientific Society had to fend off attempts to have comments on the water cure censored from his essay presentation. Reporting on this incident, the editor of the *Cork Examiner* contrasted the public reaction to hydropathy on this occasion with the first enthusiastic response in the wake of Claridge's visit in 1843:

> It was clamorously contended that the subject of the essay was unfit for public discussion, although, on a former occasion, when the subject was new in Cork, and the public not so capable of estimating it, a medical gentleman [Barter, EN] read before the society an essay on hydropathy. On the present occasion, the water cure was denounced as a humbug, and its friends and advocates as fools and knaves.[43]

---

40 'Hydropathy, or the water cure', *CE*, 17 May 1847. **41** Ibid. **42** Ibid. Emphasis in original. **43** J. Gibbs, 'Cork Scientific and Literary Society: attempt to suppress an essay on the water cure', *The Water Cure Journal*, 1 (1847/8), 240–5.

THE ASCENDING DOUCHE.—"NOW SIR, DO SIT STILL".

Nº 11.

2.2 'The water cure illustrated in twelve subjects', London, 1869.
Reproduced with permission of the Wellcome Library, London.

Hydropathy did not disappear from Cork or from medical practice in the late 1840s, despite its loss in status and increasing marginalization by the medical community. It did become less a cause for excitement and controversy, however, perhaps because the dividing lines had become clearer, perhaps also because in Ireland during the Famine and its aftermath epidemics and deficiency diseases became more immediately relevant medical concerns. New hydros and Turkish baths were opened in the 1860s and later, but, as in other locations, the emphasis on spa culture, hygiene and general well-being became more prominent than specifically medical use.

Turning back to the early reception of hydropathy as a medical practice, the Cork case study seems to confirm much of what Marguerite Dupree and James Bradley have observed about hydropathy in Britain. Far from being a fringe practice from the outset, hydropathy fell into divisions among qualified medical practitioners about therapeutic methods. Cork's hydropathic physicians took a different view of the merits of hydropathy than lay practitioners, seeing in it an addition to their therapeutic repertoire and not as a replacement. Continuing attacks, however, led to a radicalization of their position into a critique of mainstream practices, as demonstrated by the Cork petition.

This case study also reveals an aspect in which hydropathy in Ireland adds a significant nuance to the British story. Studies on British hydropaths have often noted that the water cure was frequently supported by marginalized medical practitioners, who had not been able to secure lucrative hospital positions.[44] For these marginalized physicians, hydropathy functioned both as a source of income and as a means to distinguish themselves from a mainstream they felt ill-done by. The hydropathic physicians of Cork do not seem to be socially marginalized. Two taught at Cork's medical schools, one had a hospital appointment, and all were respected personalities, well integrated into local middle-class associational life, although they were almost certainly striving to distinguish themselves within Cork's competitive medical market. Marginalization need not be only individual, however, and the Cork case study adds to the dimension of individual social marginalization the aspect of provincial marginalization at a time when professionalization efforts came overwhelmingly from the metropolis. Criticism of hydropathy, like criticism of phrenology or mesmerism, was one way in which centralized metropolitan medical organs tried to name, shame and discipline provincial physicians into following the professionalization standards they were trying to establish. Provincial physicians, for their part, often resented this metropolitan intervention and defended their diversity of practices against the perceived self-interest of these organs of professionalization. As Alison Winter remarks in her study of mesmerism and popular culture, this divide 'was exploited by metropolitan and provincial reformers to promote their own individual projects [...]'. Provincial mesmerists, she concludes, 'would not, despite the assumptions of the Londoners and the efforts of the provincial professionals, allow themselves to be defined as the passive and ignorant objects of "reform"'.[45] A similar resistance can be found in Cork, where the metropolitan project of medical professionalization collided with the self-assertion of provincial practitioners.

Hydropathy's place in the conflict between metropolitan and provincial views of practices and professionalization in Cork is, of course, only one part of the story, and many open questions remain. Although the popularity of Barter's spa at St Ann among the British and Irish Victorian middle and upper middle classes is documented, and Curtin later (1858) also opened a spa bath,[46] less is known about the use of the water cure among other groups. Infrequent references to both successful cures and fatalities at charitable institutions indicate that hydropathy was at least on occasion practiced on the poor, but, despite Wherland's association with the

---

44 See especially Bradley and Dupree, 'Opportunity'.   **45** A. Winter, 'Mesmerism and popular culture in early Victorian England', *History of Science*, 32 (1994), 317–43 at 330–1. **46** For example, 'Hydropathy: Dr Barter's establishment in Blarney', *CE*, 16 Aug. 1844; 'Hydropathy: Mr Barter's institution for the restoration of health', *CE*, 1 Jan. 1845. For Curtin's spa establishment, see M. Shifrin, 'Victorian baths and family hotel and Dr Curtin's hydropathic establishment', www.victorianturkishbath.org (accessed 10 May 2010).   **47** For a cure by Barter, see 'Hydropathy: foundling hospital', *CE*, 26 Jan. 1844; for a hydropathic fatality, see 'Progress of hydropathy', *CE*, 29 Sept. 1843. According to Malcolm Shifrin, Barter did later open a bath for the destitute poor in the 1860s. M. Shifrin, 'Turkish baths for the destitute poor known as the people's Turkish bath', www.victorianturkishbath.org

South Lying-in Hospital, there is little evidence to suggest that it was applied system-atically as part of medical charity.[47] Even less is known about the clientele of the city hydropathic baths. Devoid of spa culture, they were more utilitarian in nature, but if a price list from an establishment in Youghal is any indication, only better-situated townspeople would have been able to afford some of its services.[48] Advertisements for Wherland's establishment in the 1840s vacillate between calling it a hydropathic establishment and referring to it simply as a 'bath', and indeed it may have been valued as much for its hygienic as for its medical utility among the town's population.

Finally, the relationship between the water cure and temperance deserves more attention. As Alastair Durie has shown, connections between hydropathy and temperance were strong in Scotland.[49] Certainly, Irish contemporaries noted their compatibility, and affinities in Ireland would be particularly intriguing due to connections between the mass temperance movement of the 1840s and the Repeal movement. Significantly, Durie begins his essay on hydropathy and temperance with a quote by a Dublin Unitarian convert, James Haughton. Haughton, who belonged to a wealthy Quaker family, was one of Ireland's leading temperance advocates, and a man strongly committed to Repeal, abolition and the education of the working classes.[50] Cork brush-maker Isaac Varian, as well, combined Irish nationalism, teeto-talism and hydropathy, while Father Mathew, charismatic leader of the 1840s Irish temperance movement, also expressed his support for hydropathy, sending a temper-ance medal to Priessnitz and to Claridge.[51] With water implying both internal and external purity in teetotalism and hydropathy, a connection between the two would not surprise. Nonetheless, these connections, which were so strong in Scotland, do not seem to have had an immediate counterpart in Ireland. At the current stage of research, explanations of this difference would be speculative at best, but two factors deserve consideration. Firstly, the Irish Temperance movement was at its strongest in the years between 1840 and 1843 and was ebbing as a mass movement just as the water cure was becoming well known in Ireland. Secondly, while the temperance movement was largely carried by Irish Catholics, there are some indications that

(accessed 10 May 2010). **48** 'Dr Curtin's hydropathic establishment', *CE*, 5 May 1845. Prices ranged from 4*d*. for a cold shower to 1*s*. 6*d*. for a hot douche bath or vapour bath at 'Walsh's general bathing & hydropathic establishment, Friar-Street, Youghal', *CE*, 20 May 1844. **49** A. Durie, 'Almost twins by birth: hydropathy, temperance and the Scottish churches, 1840–1914', Paper given at the Scottish Church History Society, Nov. 2001, www.schs.org.uk/samplepaper.htm (accessed 24 Nov. 2004). **50** See, for example, 'To Dr William Macleod from James Haughton', *The Water Cure Journal*, 2 (Dec. 1847), 188–91; J. Haughton, *On the connexion between intemperance and crime* (Dublin, 1849); Idem, *The use of alcoholic liquors: economically, socially and morally wrong* (Dublin, 1849). **51** For Varian's support of hydropathy and temperance, see 'Temperance institute', *CE*, 26 Sept. 1845; 'Excursion of the members of the Cork Temperance Institute to the Groves of Blarney, and to Dr Barter's hydropathic establishment', *The Irish Temperance Chronicle*, Sept. 1846; Durie, 'Almost twins', 1–2.

more interest in hydropathy was to be found among Irish Protestants. That support of medical (and scientific) theories can correlate with political and religious positions is well known. Whether this holds true in the case of hydropathy in Cork, or in Ireland in general, however, is a question that remains to be answered.

Grubbs of Dublin:
telescope makers to the world

IAN ELLIOTT

Although lacking a formal education in engineering, Thomas Grubb (1800–78) established a unique high-technology enterprise in Ireland. The Grubb instrument firm was continued by his son, Howard, and constructed many of the world's largest and best telescopes as well as producing a wide range of precision optical and mechanical instruments.[1] This paper examines the development of the Grubbs' reputation and successful business, a business that was aided by the support of prominent Irish astronomers such as Thomas Romney Robinson and William Parsons, third earl of Rosse. At the start of the twentieth century, Grubbs' business shifted towards the development of military technologies, as demand for large-scale telescopes in the British Isles and the empire declined. The long-standing relationship with the Parsons of Birr enabled yet another transformation of the business to Grubb-Parsons in 1925 and this company continued to manufacture telescopes until 1985.

THOMAS GRUBB

Thomas Grubb was born on 4 August 1800 near Portlaw in Co. Waterford, the son of William Grubb and his second wife, Eleanor Fayle, both members of the Society of Friends.[2] In 1826, Thomas married Sarah Palmer (1798–1883) in Kilkenny. As his wife was not a Quaker, he was immediately disowned by the Society of Friends.[3] Nothing is known about Thomas' education or how he became so knowledgeable about mechanical engineering. It is possible that he may have been employed at Malcolmson's cotton mill in Portlaw or in the shipyards that flourished in Waterford at the beginning of the nineteenth century.[4] Alternatively, he may have gained practical experience in some British engineering works.[5]

By 1832, Thomas Grubb (Fig. 3.1) had established an engineering works near Charlemont Bridge by the Grand Canal on the south side of Dublin.[6] He produced

1 C. Mollan, *Irish national inventory of historical scientific instruments* (Dublin, 1995), pp 481–3. 2 Uncatalogued archives, Dublin Friends Historical Library. 3 Disownment 312, Dublin Friends Historical Library. 4 B. Irish, *Shipbuilding in Waterford, 1820–1882* (Bray, 2001). 5 H. Andrews, 'Grubb, Thomas' in J. Maguire and J. Quinn (eds), *Dictionary of Irish Biography* (Cambridge, 2009) online ed. (dib.cambridge.org.elib.tcd.ie, accessed 15 Sept. 2010). 6 I.S. Glass, *Victorian telescope makers: the lives and letters of Thomas and Howard Grubb* (Bristol, 1997), p. 10.

3.1 Thomas Grubb (image courtesy of Charles Mollan).

small machine tools, telescopes and cast iron beds for billiard tables. He took up optics as a hobby and constructed a small observatory with a 9-inch reflecting telescope and a transit telescope; visitors were admitted for a charge of one shilling.[7] Grubb's reflector came to the attention of the Revd Thomas Romney Robinson (1792–1882) who was director of Armagh Observatory from 1823 until his death fifty-eight years later. Robinson was a mathematician and physicist with a keen interest in optical instruments; he was a fellow of Trinity College Dublin and well-established in Irish and British scientific circles.[8] He was well acquainted with William Parsons (1800–67), then Lord Oxmantown and later third earl of Rosse, who invented new techniques for making large speculum mirrors. By 1840, Parsons had constructed a 36-inch reflector and by March 1845 his famous 72-inch reflector, the Leviathan of Parsonstown, was bringing distant galaxies into view.

Robinson soon became responsible for Grubb's first major commission. About

---

7 D. Kelly, *Four roads to Dublin* (Dublin, 1955), p. 98. **8** J.A. Bennett, *Church, state and astronomy in Ireland: 200 years of Armagh Observatory* (Armagh, 1990), p. 85.

1831, Robinson learned that the largest refractor in existence had been erected at Markree Castle, near Sligo, in north-west Ireland.[9] The proud owner of this instrument was a wealthy landowner, Edward Joshua Cooper (1798–1863). Cooper had purchased the 13.3-inch objective lens from Robert-Aglaé Cauchoix in Paris.[10] However, the telescope did not perform well as it had been mounted on a temporary alt-azimuth stand of wood. Robinson persuaded Cooper to order a tube and equatorial mounting from Thomas Grubb. Both the tube and the sturdy mounting were made of cast iron and weighed 2,387kg. The telescope was erected in 1834 on a triangular pier of limestone blocks and the polar axis was driven by a clockwork mechanism. There was no dome but the lens was covered when not in use and the observer was protected from the wind by a circular wall sixteen feet high and thirty-six feet in diameter.

Work on the Markree telescope led Grubb to develop several innovations that would later be put to good use in other telescopes. As part of the preparations for making the Markree telescope, Grubb had constructed a trial equatorial mount; Robinson later purchased this mount to support a 15-inch clock-controlled Cassegrain reflector for Armagh Observatory. This was the first time that a large reflecting telescope had been given a proper equatorial mount with a clock drive. Another innovation was the use of a lever support system for the primary mirror whereby the supporting pressure was evenly distributed over the back surface of the mirror by eighteen support pads on three triangular plates, thereby avoiding strain on the mirror and consequent distortion of the image. This design feature was used by Lord Rosse for his 72-inch reflector, which had eighty-one support points and it has been adopted in various ways for large telescopes ever since. Grubb also supplied eyepieces and a micrometer for the 72-inch telescope.[11]

Grubb began to gain a reputation in scientific circles, which led to further commissions. The 1835 meeting of the British Association for the Advancement of Science in Dublin, when Thomas Grubb became a member, seems to have marked the beginning of his active engagement in the scientific life of the city. In 1836, he read a paper to the Royal Astronomical Society about a method for illuminating cross-wires in the field of a reflecting telescope to facilitate micrometer measurements.[12] About the same time, he received two important commissions for instruments from Trinity College Dublin. The first, from the mathematician Professor James MacCullagh (1809–47), was for an optical instrument to study the reflection of light from metals.[13] The second, from Prof. Humphrey Lloyd (1800–81), was for twenty sets of magnetometers for the global network of magnetic observatories then being established in the British colonies.[14] In 1839, Grubb was elected a

9 Glass, *Victorian telescope makers*, p. 13. **10** W.G. FitzGerald, *Strand Magazine*, 12 (1896), 369–81. **11** Glass, *Victorian telescope makers*, p. 28. **12** T. Grubb, 'On illuminating the wires of telescopes', *MNRAS*, 3 (1836), 177–9. **13** J. MacCullagh, 'On a new optical instrument', *PRIA*, 1 (1836–40, read 9 Apr. 1838), 158–60. **14** H. Lloyd, *Account of the magnetical observatory of Dublin, and of the instruments and methods of observations employed there* (Dublin, 1842).

member of the Royal Irish Academy on 14 January; this was a considerable honour as he did not have an academic background or formal education.

While Grubb achieved notable success in building scientific instruments, his main source of income arose from the commercial need for banknotes. About 1840, he became 'Engineer to the Bank of Ireland', where he was responsible for designing and constructing machinery for engraving, printing and numbering banknotes.[15] At that time, banknotes were usually produced manually from copper-plate engravings. After spreading ink over the plates, the surplus was removed to leave ink only in the grooves. Then the plates were pressed firmly against paper for the actual printing. Starting from the type of machine used by the Bank of England, Grubb introduced a number of cams to eliminate, as far as possible, the need for a human operator. He was employed by the Bank of Ireland until his death in 1878 when his son Henry took over his position. Several of Grubb's machines were still in use in the 1920s.

During the 1850s and 1860s, Grubb consolidated his reputation as Ireland's pre-eminent telescope manufacturer. He received numerous commissions for telescopes from the moderately sized 6.75-inch Sheepshanks refractor for the Royal Greenwich Observatory to the enormous Great Melbourne Telescope with its 4-foot speculum mirror. Grubb's position within the scientific community also became more significant and Robinson's support continued to be influential in his success.

In 1853, the Dublin Industrial Exhibition took place on the Leinster Lawn premises of the Royal Dublin Society and Grubb exhibited a 12-inch equatorial refractor; this telescope was exhibited also at the London exhibition of 1862. When Sir James South presented his 11.75-inch Cauchoix lens to Trinity College Dublin, Grubb mounted it on the equatorial and erected it at Dunsink Observatory in 1868 (Fig. 3.2). A novel feature of this telescope is the method adopted for reducing friction. For stability Grubb used large-diameter bearings on the polar axis and he reduced the friction on each bearing by applying sideways pressure with counterpoised rollers. This feature was used in the Melbourne and Vienna telescopes and became obsolete only when large roller bearings became available.[16]

Grubb's innovations in optics became a matter for scientific discourse as well as the basis of new instruments. During the 1850s, he published a series of papers in the *Proceedings of the Royal Irish Academy* and in the *Journal of the Royal Dublin Society* that demonstrate his ability to design optical systems. In a paper on spherical aberration in a microscope, he states that for several years he had been using ray tracing methods to gain insight into the effects of various combinations of optical components.[17] His ray-tracing diagrams were drawn on a scale ten times the actual size and he made measurements with a magnifier to 1/500th of an inch. By combining mathematical and practical approaches, he was able to estimate the overall aberrations of a lens

15 T. Grubb, 'Description of the banknote printing machine at the Bank of Ireland', *PIME* (1865), 166–78. 16 P.A. Wayman, *Dunsink Observatory, 1785–1985: a bicentennial history* (Dublin, 1987), pp 96–9. 17 T. Grubb, 'A new method of determining, approximately, the spherical aberration of a combination of lenses for microscopic purposes', *PRIA*, 6 (1853–7, read 27 Feb. 1854), 59–63.

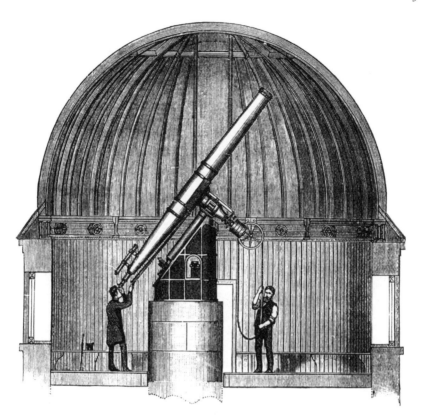

3.2 The James South 12-inch refractor at Dunsink Observatory
(from R.S. Ball, *The story of the heavens* (London, 1890), p. 13).

system. Other investigations led to his invention of a wide-angle achromatic portrait
lens which he patented and about which he read a paper at the Royal Dublin Society
in March 1858.[18]

THE GREAT MELBOURNE TELESCOPE

The success of Thomas Grubb in achieving a reputation as the preeminent scientific
telescope maker in the United Kingdom during the nineteenth century is demonstrated by the story of the Great Melbourne Telescope. The influence of Robinson
and Lord Rosse was paramount. In the late 1840s, efforts were made by Sir Edward
Sabine, Robinson and others to persuade the British government to fund a large
astronomical telescope in the southern hemisphere. These suggestions were chan-

18 T. Grubb, 'On a new patent compound view lens for photographic cameras', *JRDS*, 2
(1858), 27–9.

GREAT MELBOURNE TELESCOPE.
MIRROR, 4 FEET IN DIAMETER.
CONSTRUCTED FOR THE GOVERNMENT OF VICTORIA, N.S.W.

3.3 The Great Melbourne Telescope (from Grubb Catalogue (1880), p. 14).

nelled through the British Association and later, the Royal Society of which Lord Rosse was then president. In 1852, the Royal Society set up the Southern Telescope Committee which included G.B. Airy, T.R. Robinson, J.C. Adams, Lord Rosse, J. Nasmyth, E.J. Cooper and J. Herschel. In July 1853, the committee agreed to ask the government for funds to enable Thomas Grubb to construct a 4-foot reflector. However, the Crimean War caused the proposal to be put aside until 1862, when a proposal for a large telescope came from the University of Melbourne. Despite the fact that J.B.L. Foucault (1819–68) had demonstrated the feasibility of silver-on-glass mirrors, it was decided that a metal mirror would be the safest option (Fig. 3.3).[19]

Grubb received the order for the telescope in February 1866 and immediately withdrew his youngest son Howard (Fig. 3.4) from Trinity College Dublin, where he was a third-year student of engineering. Grubb senior bought a piece of land in

19 T. Grubb and T.R. Robinson, 'Description of the Great Melbourne Telescope', *PTRS*, 159 (1869), 127–61.

3.4 Howard Grubb at 35 (Mary Lea Shane Archives of the Lick Observatory).

Rathmines and erected workshops, machinery and furnaces suitable for casting a 4-foot speculum mirror.[20] The procedure for casting two speculum mirrors followed closely that pioneered by the third earl of Rosse at Parsonstown. The Great Melbourne Telescope was completed in February 1868 and shipped to Australia (see Fig. 3.3 and jacket). Regular observing started in August 1869 but, despite its acclaim as a technical triumph, it became an embarrassing failure. The main reason for the failure was the lack of adequate expertise in Melbourne to maintain the surfaces of the speculum mirrors.[21]

Despite its failings, the construction of the Great Melbourne Telescope brought the Grubbs international recognition. Thomas Grubb's achievements were recognized in 1864 by his election as a Fellow of the Royal Society. He developed further scientific contacts, including Sligo-born George Gabriel Stokes (1819–1903), Lucasian Professor of Mathematics at Cambridge and great-grandson of Gabriel Stokes, a Dublin instrument maker. Stokes, who had married Robinson's daughter in 1859, gave the Grubbs advice on theoretical optics over many years.[22]

The Great Melbourne Telescope also marked a turning point in the Grubb business. From 1868, the firm was run as a partnership of father and son and renamed 'Messrs Grubb & Son (formerly Thomas Grubb)'. Howard adopted a more empir-

20 H.C. King, *The history of the telescope* (Dover, 1955), pp 264–7. **21** T. Grubb, *The Great Melbourne Telescope: an examination of and reply to the official reports from Melbourne respecting the instrument, its erection at Melbourne etc. etc.* (Dublin, 1870). **22** Glass, *Victorian telescope makers*, p. 64.

3.5 The casting of the speculum for the Great Melbourne Telescope
(from W.G. Fitzgerald, Howard Grubb et al., *Strand Magazine* (1896), 369–81).

ical approach to design than his father and took advantage of the latest advances in precision measurement. By 1873, the elderly Thomas appears to have withdrawn from the business and the firm was called 'Howard Grubb (late Grubb & Son)'. In 1871, Howard Grubb married Mary Hester Walker, who was born in 1854 in New Orleans of Irish parents. Her father, George Hamilton Walker, was born in Kells, Co. Meath. Howard and Mary had six children, of whom four survived to adulthood. The youngest surviving son was named Romney Robinson, an indication of the high regard of the Grubbs for the Armagh astronomer.[23]

In April 1869, Grubbs received an important order from the Royal Society, whose president was then the Dublin-born Sir Edward Sabine. In order to promote the new field of astronomical spectroscopy that had been pursued very successfully by William Huggins of Tulse Hill in London, and his neighbour, the chemist W. Allen Miller, the society decided to equip Huggins with a Grubb 15-inch refractor and an 18-inch reflector. In 1871, Grubbs supplied Huggins with a multi-prism spectrograph for solar work.[24] Howard Grubb also introduced Huggins to Margaret Lindsay Murray of Dublin, a young woman nearly twenty-five years his junior who became his wife and skilled collaborator. It remained a standing joke between the two men that however correctly they settled their business accounts, Huggins still remained indebted to Grubb for introducing him to the future Mrs Huggins.[25]

23 Glass, *Victorian telescope makers*, p. 69. **24** H. Grubb, 'Automatic spectroscope for Dr Huggins' sun observations', *MNRAS*, 31 (1871), 36–8. **25** C.E. Mills and C.F. Brook, *A*

3.6 Completion of Grubb's optical and mechanical works in 1875 (image courtesy of the Department of Astronomy, University of Vienna, Austria).

THE GREAT VIENNA TELESCOPE

Howard Grubb, now fully in charge of the firm, benefited from the reputation that his father had established. In 1873, Howard received an enquiry from Vienna Observatory about supplying a large refractor for a new observatory to be built on high ground 5km from the centre of Vienna. The observatory was to be a very large building in the shape of a cross with a 45-foot dome at the centre and three smaller domes on each of the arms. After a representative of Vienna Observatory had examined observatories and engineering works in Europe and America, he recommended that Grubb should be asked to build the telescope and four domes. In June 1875, Howard Grubb signed a contract with the Austro-Hungarian government for a 27-inch refractor and the four domes at a cost of £8,000. To build the largest refracting telescope in the world was quite a challenge for a man only thirty years old.[26]

Howard Grubb immediately rebuilt the engineering works in Rathmines. The new building had a large twelve-sided central hall 42 feet wide and 42 feet high (Fig. 3.6). The hall was surrounded by workshops containing machinery for grinding and polishing lenses and for constructing the components of the telescopes and the domes. The factory was known as 'The Optical and Mechanical Works, Rathmines' and was situated on Observatory Lane, which exists to this day.[27]

sketch of the life of Sir William Huggins, KCB, OM (London, 1936). **26** H. Grubb, 'Grubbs equatorial telescope', *Engineering*, 28 (1879), 278; H. Grubb, 'The Vienna Equatorial', *Engineering*, 29 (1880), 114–16, 199–202, 309–11, 391, 409, 467–9; 30 (1880), 314–15, 424–8. **27** H. Grubb, 'Sir Howard Grubb's works, Dublin', *Engineering*, 46 (1888), 571–3.

A local committee, including many of the Grubbs' scientific contacts, was set up to monitor the building of the telescope. It consisted of Prof. R.S. Ball, the earl of Crawford, W. Higgins, Prof. J.E. Reynolds, the earl of Rosse, Prof. G.G. Stokes, Dr G.J. Stoney and Mr Richard Walsh, the Austrian consul in Dublin. The telescope was to be delivered within three years of the delivery of the lens blanks. The mechanical work on the telescope and mounting progressed rapidly. The forty-five-foot dome had a double skin of riveted steel plates for stiffness and to keep the temperature of the interior constant. The total weight of the dome was fifteen tons, yet a force of only 70 pounds was required to move it. The domes were sent to Vienna and erected at the end of 1878.[28]

The Vienna Telescope was completed towards the end of 1880 and was ready for testing on the stars. It was approved by the local committee in March 1881 and was declared 'a splendid success'. Despite governmental red tape, which delayed the delivery of the telescope, it was commissioned and in full working order by the end of 1883, just ten years after it was first conceived. The Vienna Telescope was briefly the largest refractor in the world until one of 30-inch aperture was completed for Pulkovo Observatory in 1885.[29]

Howard Grubb continued in the tradition of his father by maintaining contacts in the scientific community through the Royal Dublin Society and the British Association for the Advancement of Science. He had strong interactions with his customers, especially David Gill of the Royal Observatory, Cape of Good Hope. He received recognition from Trinity College Dublin in 1876, when he was awarded the honorary degree of Master of Engineering. In 1883, he was elected a Fellow of the Royal Society and in 1887 he was knighted.

HECTIC TIMES

During the 1880s and 1890s, Howard Grubb extended and enhanced the international reputation that his father had built, by building telescopes for countries beyond Europe and the British Empire. By 1888, he was employing between thirty-five and forty men at the Rathmines works. He made about ninety objective lenses ranging from five to twenty-eight inches in diameter and most of the required mountings and controls. The countries to which he exported telescopes included South Africa, India, the USA, Germany, Mexico, Australia, Spain, Venezuela, Belgium, Bulgaria, New Zealand and Turkey, and many telescopes were also sold in Ireland, England and Scotland. It was said that Grubbs exported to every continent except Antarctica.[30]

The Rathmines works frequently accommodated overseas visitors who were considering ordering a telescope. Among these, in February 1875, was Simon Newcomb of the US Naval Observatory in Washington DC. Newcomb was scien-

28 H. Grubb, 'The Great Vienna Telescope', *Nature*, 24 (1881), 11–14. **29** Glass, *Victorian telescope makers*, p. 93. **30** W.G. FitzGerald, *Strand Magazine*, 12 (1896), 369–81.

tific advisor to the board of trustees of the Lick Observatory to be established at Mount Hamilton in California. At the end of a tour of European optical workshops, Newcomb judged that Howard Grubb was the only person outside the United States who had any chance of successfully building the instruments for Lick Observatory.[31]

Grubb had ambitious plans for the new Lick Observatory. He envisaged a 40-inch refractor in a dome 70 feet in diameter, a 72-inch reflector with a special sliding roof as well as a meridian room with a meridian circle and a transit instrument. One important feature was the provision of a rising floor, controlled hydraulically. He presented a plaster model of the proposed scheme to the Lick trustees.[32]

Grubb's chief competitor was the firm of Alvan Clark and Sons of Cambridge, Massachusetts, then widely regarded as the best lens makers in the world. However, Clark did not undertake mechanical work. Alvan Graham Clark visited Grubb in 1879 and the two men debated the pros and cons of refractors and reflectors. Clark believed that his refractors were superior to reflectors double their aperture and Grubb tried to convince him of the benefits of reflectors. In December 1880, the Lick trustees awarded the contract for a 36-inch lens to Alvan Clark at a cost of $50,000 and Grubb, despite his disappointment, offered to build a tube and mounting. The project was delayed for want of suitable glass blanks, which were not available until December 1885.[33]

In April 1886, Grubb delivered a lecture at the Royal Institution in London on 'Telescope Objectives and Mirrors, their Preparation and Testing', in which he described his plans for Lick Observatory.[34] An important feature of his design was that despite the size of a large telescope in a seventy-foot dome, he could arrange for it to be operated single-handed by the observer. In the end, the Lick trustees awarded the contract for an equatorial mount and dome to Warner and Swasey of Cleveland, Ohio. The design incorporated Grubb's idea of a hydraulically operated rising floor and he was compensated by the payment of $600.

In 1882, David Gill, Her Majesty's Astronomer at the Royal Observatory, Cape of Good Hope, attached an ordinary portrait camera to his six-inch equatorial telescope to take photographs on the new 'dry plates' of the great comet then visible. With exposures up to one or two hours duration, he obtained fine photographs not only of the comet but of the background stars. He realized that it would be possible to use photography to make star maps free from personal errors and avoiding the great labour of observing by eye. He obtained an f/9 lens of six-inch aperture from Dallmeyer and began a sky survey known as the *Cape Photographic Durchmusterung*.[35]

The potential of photography for recording star positions was also recognized by the Henry brothers, opticians at Paris Observatory. They built a special photographic refractor and the successful trials of this telescope led Admiral Mouchez, director of

31 Glass, *Victorian telescope makers*, p. 96. **32** Glass, *Victorian telescope makers*, p. 100. **33** Glass, *Victorian telescope makers*, p. 110. **34** H. Grubb, 'Telescope objectives and mirrors; their preparation and testing', *PRI*, 11 (1887), 413–32. **35** D. Gill, *Cape Photographic Durchmusterung*, 1, ix.

3.7 Grubb's 13-inch astrographic telescope (from Grubb Catalogue (1899)).

Paris Observatory, and Gill to organize an international congress in Paris in April 1887.[36] Fifty-six astronomers from nineteen countries attended the congress and a permanent commission was set up to promote the *Carte du Ciel* (Map of the Sky). The plan was to make a photographic map of the sky showing stars to the fourteenth magnitude and, by measuring the photographs, to make a precise catalogue of stars to the eleventh magnitude. It would require exposing over 10,000 plates and would give rise to a catalogue of over four million star positions; in the event, it was not completed until 1964. Each of the eighteen participating observatories mapped a particular declination zone. The Henrys' telescope was chosen as the standard instrument for the survey; with an aperture of 33 centimetres and a focal length of 343 centimetres, it gave a plate scale of one minute of arc per millimetre.[37]

36 Glass, *Victorian telescope makers*, p. 133.   **37** H.H. Turner, *The great star map, being a brief*

While continental observatories chose to order their astrographic telescopes from the Henrys, British institutions preferred to deal with Howard Grubb, and he obtained orders for seven telescopes (Fig. 3.7). Designing lenses for photographic use raised new problems and Grubb had to carry out much experimental work before he was in a position to manufacture the telescopes. As the early dry plates were most sensitive to the violet and ultra-violet region of the spectrum, the lenses had to be in focus for these wavelengths. Grubb sent his lenses to Oxford Observatory for testing on the stars and the list of defects guided him in making corrections. The work progressed slowly but surely and by 1889, the first telescope had been completed.[38]

In constructing the drives for the astrographic telescopes, Grubb had to pay special attention to avoid periodic errors in the worm screws which transmitted the driving torque. He devised a new machine especially for cutting these screws. For cutting the teeth of the driving sectors he used a dividing engine and as each tooth was cut it was watched under a microscope. He also devised a precise sidereal drive that was locked to the beats of a seconds pendulum. It was in effect a phase-locked clock drive and was provided with all his photographic telescopes after 1888.[39]

The seven observatories that Grubb supplied with astrographic telescopes were Oxford, Sydney (lens only), Melbourne, Tacubaya (Mexico), Greenwich, Cape of Good Hope and Perth. Some of these instruments were later used for some very important observations. In 1919, Arthur Eddington organized expeditions to observe a total eclipse of the Sun at Principe Island off the coast of West Africa and at Sobral in north Brazil. The objective of the Oxford astrographic telescope was used at Principe and the Greenwich one was used at Sobral. With these and with a long-focus lens and an eight-inch coelostat made by Grubb and owned by the Royal Irish Academy, Eddington and Dyson confirmed the bending of starlight as predicted by Einstein's general theory of relativity and overnight Albert Einstein became an icon of science.[40]

A NEW CENTURY AND NEW TECHNOLOGIES

In the early years of the twentieth century, Howard Grubb turned his attention to military and surveying instruments. This change in direction may have been caused by the declining economy of Britain and Ireland and the rising prosperity of the United States, where there were prosperous benefactors willing to fund large tele-

general account of the international project known as the astrographic chart (London, 1912). **38** H. Grubb, 'The construction of telescopic object-glasses for the international photographic survey of the heavens', *TRDS*, 4 (1891), 475–80. **39** H. Grubb, 'On the latest improvements in the clock-driving apparatus of astronomical telescopes', *PIME* (1888), 308–16. **40** F.W. Dyson et al., 'A determination of the deflection of light by the sun's gravitational field, from observations made at the total eclipse of May 29, 1919', *PTRS*, 220 (1920), 291–333.

scopes. In Europe, telescope-making came to be dominated by the Schott glassworks and by the firm of Carl Zeiss of Jena in Germany.

The last big refractors made by Grubb were ordered before the First World War but were not delivered until long after it ended. In 1909, the Transvaal Observatory in Johannesburg ordered a 26.5-inch refractor and the Chilean National Astronomical Observatory ordered a 24-inch refractor. These instruments incorporated several improvements in design. Instead of sectors that had to be rewound every few hours, the telescopes had continuous circular worm wheels. Apart from the advantage of avoiding interruption to the observations, the wear on the gears was more uniform. In addition, ball bearings were used in the friction relief systems for the first time. These changes may have been due to Cyril Young (1875–1949) who joined the Dublin firm in 1910. A delay in obtaining blanks for lenses was extended by the outbreak of the First World War and work on the telescopes ceased in 1914.[41]

Even before the outbreak of war, Howard Grubb seems to have recognized a new market for his skills in the development of military devices. Between 1900 and 1916, Howard Grubb filed a score of patents items such as periscopes, gun-sights and range finders. A 1901 patent shows drawings for a periscope and the first effective submarine periscope was made by Grubb in Dublin. Initially, there was some difficulty in making the early periscopes watertight but successful trials were reported to the British Admiralty in 1902. Grubb supplied most of the periscopes for the British submarines in the First World War. These were made at first at the Rathmines and Charlemont Bridge works. However, for security reasons, the Admiralty insisted on moving production to St Albans, some twenty miles north of London. The thirty-foot steel tubes for the periscopes were made at Vickers works in the north of England and had to be transported across the Irish Sea. In addition, growing political unrest in Ireland put the Rathmines works at risk and it had to be guarded night and day by the military.[42]

The end of the war created considerable turmoil for Howard Grubb's business. In November 1918, the move to St Albans was only partially completed, yet it was impossible to reverse it. By March 1919, some three hundred tons of machinery still had to be moved across the Irish Sea. Moreover, wages had risen by a factor of two or three and many workers were on strike.[43]

Howard Grubb tried to complete the telescopes that had been ordered before the war, but ran into great difficulties from the rising wages and the lack of glass blanks. Eventually, in January 1925, the firm went into liquidation. However, by April the same year it was rescued by Sir Charles Parsons and re-established as 'Sir Howard Grubb, Parsons and Co.' at Heaton, Newcastle-on-Tyne in north-east England. Charles Parsons (1865–1931), inventor of the steam turbine, was the youngest son of the third earl of Rosse, who had been associated with Thomas Grubb many years before.[44]

41 Glass, *Victorian telescope makers*, p. 211.   42 Glass, *Victorian telescope makers*, p. 213.   43 Glass, *Victorian telescope makers*, p. 214.   44 G.M. Sisson, 'Sir Howard Grubb, Parsons and Company', *PRS*, Series A, 230 (1955), 147–57.

After the St Albans works closed, Sir Howard Grubb retired to Monkstown in south Dublin where he lived in a house overlooking the sea. Lady Grubb died in April 1931 and Sir Howard died only a few months later on 16 September 1931 at the age of 87.

The firm of Grubb-Parsons went on to build many large astronomical telescopes. These included the 74-inch reflectors at Pretoria Observatory in South Africa, Helwan Observatory in Egypt and Mount Stromlo Observatory in Australia. The firm also supplied the tube and optics of the Anglo-Australian Telescope and the UK Schmidt at Siding Spring in New South Wales. Grubb-Parsons telescopes at the Spanish observatory on La Palma in the Canary Islands include the Carlsberg Automatic Transit Circle, the 1-metre Jacobus Kapteyn Telescope, the 2.5-metre Isaac Newton Telescope (originally erected in 1967 in England) and the 4.2-metre William Herschel Telescope. The firm of Sir Howard Grubb, Parsons & Co. finally closed in 1985.

CONCLUSION

It seems probable that few Dublin citizens appreciated the achievements of the high-precision engineering firm at the end of Observatory Lane in Rathmines. Yet the quality of design and construction gained a worldwide reputation for Thomas and Howard and enabled them to sustain a high level of employment at their works. Indeed, it is only with hindsight that we can see the impact that their innovative ideas had on the general progress of telescope technology in the nineteenth and twentieth centuries. Grubb telescopes were characterized by sturdy mechanical design, precision optics, reliable tracking and ease of use. It is still not widely known that the crucial test of Einstein's General Theory of Relativity in 1919 relied on optical components made entirely by Grubbs. Around the world, many Grubb telescopes continue to scan the heavens and help astronomers probe the secrets of the universe.

Representing the imagination: a topographical history of Dublin's Monto from Ordnance Survey maps and related materials

TADHG O'KEEFFE & PATRICK RYAN

The main aim of this paper is to present an account of the topographical spaces of Dublin's 'Monto', the city's notorious red-light district of the late 1800s and early 1900s. Monto has had its historians already,[1] and parts of what we present here are familiar to readers of that literature, but our version differs from these by virtue of its concentration on its spaces – the linear spaces of streets, the nuclear spaces of concealed courtyards – and their histories. The main source for reading and reconstructing the histories of topographies of nineteenth-century Ireland is the Ordnance Survey map, a product that engaged technology in both its assembling of data and its production or publication. Here, we use the testimony of Ordnance Survey (hereafter OS) maps of the Monto area, as well as street directory and rateable valuation materials (which themselves used OS records), to guide us towards mental reconstructions. This strategy reflects the origin of our interest in Monto: a multi-disciplinary project on the heritage of the recent past in inner-city Dublin, funded by the Heritage Council, for which we selected the site of Monto as a case-study.[2]

An additional aim of the paper is to draw attention, even briefly, to the gap

1 J.J. Finegan, *The story of Monto* (Cork, 1978); T. Fagan, *Monto: madams, murder and black coddle* (Dublin, 2000); M. Luddy, *Prostitution and Irish Society, 1800–1940* (Cambridge, 2007).
2 T. O'Keeffe (ed.), *Placing voices, voicing places: community, diversity and heritage in Dublin city* (Dublin, 2010); see also T. O'Keeffe, 'Landscape and memory: historiography, theory, methodology' in N. Moore & Y. Whelan (eds), *Heritage, memory and the politics of space: new perspectives on the cultural landscape* (Aldershot, 2007), pp 3–18; T. O'Keeffe & P. Ryan, 'A landscape at the world's end: the rise and fall of Monto, Dublin's notorious red-light district', *Landscapes*, 10 (2009), 21–38; The research on which this paper is based was conducted as part of a larger research project on inner-city archaeology and heritage, generously funded by Heritage Council's INSTAR programme, 2008. Our thanks to our colleagues on this project: Pat Cooke, Alice Feldman and Ian Russell of UCD, Cormac O'Donnell of Dublin City Council, and Sarah Tuck of CREATE, and to Michael Brown, the project photographer. Our sincere thanks also to Terry Fagan of the North Inner City Folklore Project for providing valuable data, including Figure 4.7, and the Old Dublin Society for permission to reproduce from the Frank Murphy Collection the image in Figure 4.10.

between the OS cartographic representations (or imaginations, even) of the streets that are remembered as being 'of Monto', and Monto itself as an imaginary/imagined place in late Victorian and Edwardian Dublin. In this respect, our interest is less in the OS maps as conveyors of information about places than as media through which places were created in the past and are recreated in the present, an interpretation of maps now well established.[3] Monto is but one reading of what is depicted on the detailed street maps of the district of Dublin under review, and we contend that it can be no more than one reading: the place that was named Monto was one of many places – places communally imagined at one moment in time, places individually experienced at another, places known intimately at another, places vaguely remembered at yet another – which were imbricated in the Cartesian details of the nineteenth- and early twentieth-century maps. The maps themselves were no more real than any of these places: the surveyors extracted spatial nuts and bolts from complex, palimpsested, and often alien and dangerous streetscapes, and then sent them on to the engravers for a further translation into the wholly abstract forms that we see on the maps. This paper demonstrates both the value and the limitations of the OS in recovering cultural and social phenomena, especially activities that were illegal and often seen as shameful. The empiricism of Victorian scientific endeavour has enabled our reconstruction of Monto by providing a wealth of data, yet the same ethos was to underly the eventual suppression of prostitution in the area.

MONTO'S HISTORY

Monto – named after Montgomery Street, one of its thoroughfares – enjoys a posthumous reputation inversely proportionate to its original geographical extent. Contemporary reports indicating that it was a league-topper among Europe's turn-of-the-century red-light districts create an impression today that it occupied quite an extensive area within Dublin, comparable perhaps with Amsterdam's present-day red-light district. The reality was, however, different. The space that Dubliners of the decades around 1900 knew as Monto was geographically quite small. OS maps showing the core area are reproduced in Figures 4.1–4.6. As we will discuss below, the 1847 and 1864 maps show the area prior to Monto's emergence, the 1871 map dates from around the time that prostitution was concentrating locally, the 1889 and 1907 maps date from the period of its peak, and the 1936 map post-dates Monto, but not prostitution, in the area.

No attempt is made here to mark an actual boundary on any of these maps, so where exactly in these maps *was* Monto? At its largest it was defined by part of Mabbot Street (later Corporation Street, now James Joyce Street) to the west, by the eastern or 'Lower' half of Mecklinburgh Street (later Tyrone Street Lower, now Railway Street) to the north, and by Montgomery Street (now Foley Street) to the

---

3 D.E. Cosgrove, *Social formation and symbolic landscape* (2nd ed., Madison, WI, 1998).

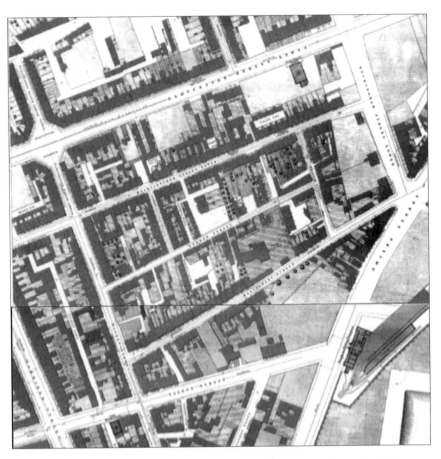

4.1 The Monto district in 1847 (reproduced with permission from the OSI).

south, and it contained two smaller streets, Beaver Street (still extant and still so-named) and Purdon Street (built-over but with its line maintained in the present built-topography). As well as these main streets there were many house-lined small lanes, most of which were linear cul-de-sacs, and small courtyards, again lined with houses. The names of some of these tiny streets and courts were recorded on Ordnance Survey maps, but, for the full complement of names, we need to use material in Thom's *Directory* (hereafter TD) over many years and in Griffith's Valuation of 1854 (hereafter GV).[4] Although these are not OS sources themselves, they drew on OS source material.

4 In the research, Thom's *Directory* was consulted in general ten-year intervals, the years lined up to be close in date to years of issued maps and censuses: 1847, 1861, 1872, 1881, 1891, 1900, 1911, 1921, 1931, 1941, 1951, 1961, 1971, 1981, 1990 and 2001. Of course, even with this tight control on dates, the *Directory* needs to be used with a degree of caution: as a source for Dublin's history, it ostensibly offers a series of annual snapshots, but in the context of

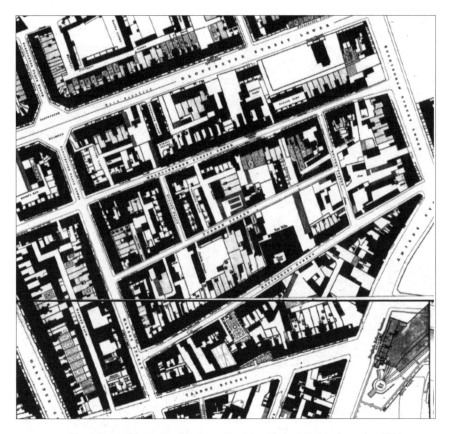

4.2 The Monto district in 1864 (reproduced with permission from the OSI).

Although the entire area described above is popularly imagined today as having been an area of prostitution, within it were parts of streets, whole back-lanes and whole off-street courtyards where there was probably little or no such activity at any stage; on Mecklinburgh Street, for example, there was a known concentration of brothels between numbers 78 and 89 (including the house of Bela Cohen, which features in *Ulysses*), but there is no evidence to suggest that the houses beside or opposite this block were similarly used.[5] Moreover, as our street-by-street review below suggests, by the last quarter of the nineteenth century some of the smaller alleys and courtyards off the big streets of the area *may* have had derelict rather than tenemented properties, and so may have been fairly empty of people; they certainly appear to have been empty when the census enumeration was being carried out in

Monto, as elsewhere in the city, its coverage of the streets and their properties is sufficiently inconsistent, and its details occasionally at odds with other sources, for us to query the regularity and accuracy of its updating. **5** O'Keeffe & Ryan, 'A landscape at the world's end', Fig. 7.

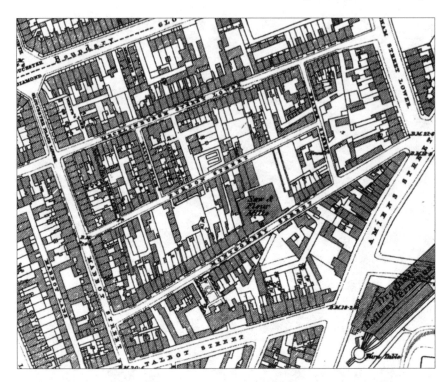

4.3 The Monto district in 1871 (reproduced with permission from the OSI).

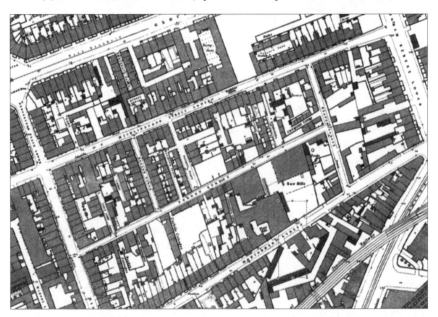

4.4 The Monto district in 1889 (reproduced with permission from the OSI).

4.5 The Monto district in 1907 (reproduced with permission from the OSI).

1911, although one cannot rule out the possibility that many people did not return details, or that enumerators thought better of venturing into some of the more secluded of the district's spaces. If Monto is remembered as being bigger than it actually was, perhaps it was a combination of things – the larger-than-life personas of the madams,[6] a voyeurism to counterbalance the city's strong Catholic ethos, the mythologizing of it as Nighttown by James Joyce – that magnified it.

Cartographic evidence indicates that the Montgomery Street area really only developed in the 1760s and 1770s. Some of the streets had been laid out by 1750, including Mabbot Street,[7] but few of them had names and housing on them was rather scattered. In 1765, Great Martin's Lane, marked on John Rocque's map of 1756,

---

6 Fagan, *Monto*, passim. **7** This is marked on Charles Brooking's map of Dublin, 1728; Gilbert Mabbot was official licenser of the press during the English Civil War, and he moved to Dublin after the Restoration.

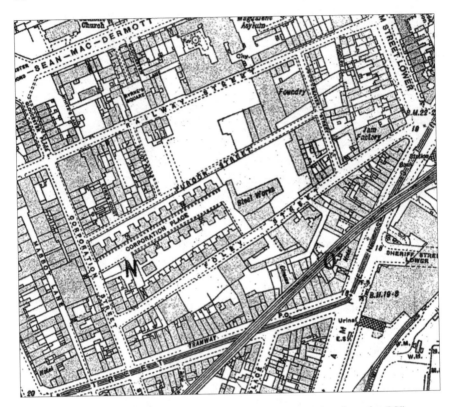

4.6 The Monto district in 1936 (reproduced with permission from the OSI).

was renamed Mecklenburgh (later rendered Mecklinburgh) Street, honouring Princess Charlotte of Mecklenburgh, who had married George III in 1761, while in 1776 World's End Lane, also on Rocque's map, was renamed Montgomery Street, honouring Elizabeth Montgomery, wife of Luke Gardiner, scion of one of Dublin's great land-owning families.[8] It was probably around the time of these particular re-namings that short terraces of classic 'Georgian' houses began to be erected on these streets. Shortly afterwards, between 1792 and 1798, Lord Aldborough, a well-connected peer, built a very fine mansion at the edge of the area, a sign perhaps that the area was up-and-coming. The Act of Union, which profoundly affected Dublin's prosperity by changing its status from a capital city to a provincial city, was only a few years in the future, but there was a certain prescience in the immediate fate of Aldborough's mansion: his wife refused to move in, he himself died in 1801, and the place lay idle for more than a decade before becoming a school and eventually, from the time of the Crimean War, an army barracks.[9]

---

8 C.T. M[c]Cready, *Dublin street names: dated and explained* (Dublin, 1892), no page numbers.
9 A. O'Boyle, 'Aldborough House, Dublin: a construction history', *Irish Architectural and*

At the start of the nineteenth century, the eastern part of Gloucester Street (the part suffixed 'Lower'), which was later to delimit Monto to the north, was still very incomplete. So too was Buckingham Street, which later delimited Monto on the east side. Mecklinburgh Street itself was almost fully developed by 1800 (fig. 4. 7) apart from a small part at the eastern end, but only the north side of Montgomery Street was developed. Purdon Street[10] originated as a 'stable lane' between the rears of Mecklinburgh and Montgomery Streets in the later 1700s.[11] Its particular transformation from a service lane to a street of small two-storey houses by 1847, coupled with cartographic evidence that other small courtyards and alleys were simultaneously developing as small residential islands behind the street fronts of Mecklinburgh and Montgomery, places the peak of the area's topographical development in the first half of the nineteenth century.

The start-date of Monto as a red-light district is uncertain. The existence of a Magdalen Asylum on Mecklinburgh Street from 1822[12] suggests the presence of prostitutes in the early 1800s, a time when much of the area's building stock was less than half-a-century old. Moreover, there are revealing references in 1837 in the Ordnance Survey name book, a valuable textual accompaniment to the first-edition maps: 'destitute', poor, 'dissolute and depraved characters' were noted in Purdon Street, one of the notorious streets of the later Monto.[13] It is probable, then, that the Montgomery Street district had a reputation within the early nineteenth-century city as an impoverished locale in which immoral practices were ubiquitous, but it would not have been the only part of Dublin so regarded. Its reputation as the city's premier district for prostitution was possibly only achieved, or maybe only secured, around the 1870s.[14]

Anti-prostitution measures across the city by the local constabulary around that time, nourished perhaps by those same concerns for health and morality as inspired the Contagious Diseases Acts, may help explain why women engaged in prostitution were drawn to one discrete, fairly self-contained, place within the city.[15] The same constabulary must, of course, have turned a blind eye to this process of centralizing vice, as did the constabularies in contemporary British cities.[16] They must have reasoned that prostitution was unlikely ever to be eliminated from Dublin and was therefore best contained within a restricted zone. Three factors gave the

Decorative Studies, 4 (2001), 102–41. **10** Named as 'Purdens Street' on the Pool and cash map of Dublin, 1780. **11** Dublin City Archive: WSC/Maps/230: 'A survey of holdings in Montgomery Street Dublin the estate of Viscount Mountjoy' (undated). **12** C. Casey, *Dublin* (London and New Haven, 2005), p. 140. **13** *Name book, Dublin city: notes concerning the city of Dublin compiled during the progress of the Ordnance Survey in 1837*, typewritten MS, UCD School of Irish, Celtic Studies, Irish Folklore & Linguistics, 215 (69); see also Fagan, *Monto*, p. 30. We are grateful to Críostóir Mac Cárthaigh, UCD, for giving us easy access to the *Name book*. **14** O'Keeffe & Ryan, 'A landscape at the world's end'. **15** Luddy, *Prostitution and Irish society*, pp 33–4. **16** P. Howell, D. Beckingham & F. Moore, 'Managed zones for sex workers in Liverpool: contemporary proposals, Victorian parallels', *Transactions of the Institute of British Geographers*, 33:2 (2008), 233–50.

4.7 Georgian houses, no longer extant, on Lower Tyrone Street (formerly
Mecklinburgh Street, now Railway Street), photographed in the early 1900s (image
reproduced courtesy of Terry Fagan and the North Inner City Folklore Project).

Montgomery Street area a strong advantage over others in this unofficial but toler-
ated reorganization of Dublin's spaces of prostitution. First, it was almost entirely
tenemented from the mid-1800s, so rents were very low. Second, it was close to
Dublin port (with its supply of sailors), the Great Northern railway station at Amiens
Street (with its supply of country girls, many in desperate need) and the barracks that
was Aldborough House (with its supply of soldiers). Third, it was sufficiently distant
from Dublin's better shopping streets for the city's middle-class not to notice it, be
offended by it, and complain about it to the police or to the press.[17] Thus, the
Montgomery Street area was 'othered' within the city: 'Monto', as it became known,
was physically within Dublin, but in other respects it was outside Dublin, a district
created by the blind-eye of officialdom and cordoned off in the imagination from
Victorian and Edwardian middle-class sensibilities. Indeed, when we speak of Monto
today, we speak not really of the Montgomery Street area at all but of this 'other' place
that shared that same space as it, hovering over it and imbricated with it but never
being the same as it; a place of 'otherness'. Monto is not unique in this regard: the

---

17 It may be that, in Dublin, as in the States (see N. Shumsky, 'Tacit acceptance: respectable
Americans and segregated prostitution, 1870–1910', *Journal of Social History*, 19 (1986), 665–
79) there was middle-class acceptance of prostitution provided it stayed within its area.

Little Lon district of Melbourne, for example, another (in)famous nineteenth-century red-light district, similarly existed as place of otherness.[18]

This virtual cordon allowed Monto to develop its own rules in accordance with its 'otherness', and those rules were often reversals of the rules of conventional civic society and civic space in the official city: madams rather than men ran Monto, the district's back-lanes and hidden spaces were among its places of commerce (even, and perhaps especially, when largely unoccupied and therefore most secretive), and the spaces and activities of greatest privacy and intimacy in the city outside Monto were the spaces and activities that were most public and least intimate inside it. And when the official city of Dublin slept, the small urban enclave of Monto came to life. Joyce captured this perfectly when describing it as Nighttown.

While Monto prostitutes were removed from the gaze of the day-time city, they were equally, and paradoxically, among the defining or quintessential spectacles of urban life, figures to whom a culture of voyeurism attached but in whom were simultaneously condensed general civic anxieties about poverty, disease and moral decay;[19] Katherine Mullin has described the prostitute and the slum as the 'twin urban spectacles for a fascinated yet repulsed urban bourgeois gaze' and has contended that Monto was made compelling in the late nineteenth- and early twentieth-century imagination by this very combination of prostitute and slum-as-home.[20] The women who worked as prostitutes in Monto were thus positioned where civic society was fascinated by them but not bothered with their welfare. In that exposed and yet concealed place, we imagine that they experienced a very personal othering: violence, venereal disease and especially chronic alcoholism,[21] even more than poverty, must have distorted their views of themselves and of their world, othering them by depriving them of the agency that they presumably possessed in their earlier lives.

It was only when religious purity movements like the White Cross Vigilance Association and the Legion of Mary penetrated the cordon of Monto in the late 1800s and early 1900s, involving themselves directly in the fate of these women, that Monto's terminal decline began. It was the intervention of the latter, famously, that brought about the demise of Monto: following much agitation on the ground and much mobilizing of public opinion by the Legion, a large police raid in spring 1925 saw the arrest of significant numbers of madams, prostitutes and customers. The problem of Monto, an embarrassment to the capital of the new Free State, was regarded as solved. Although prostitution did remain a feature of the streets of the area for some time afterwards,[22] it was the steady clearing-away of those streets in the second quarter of the twentieth century that finally brought closure to the area's

18 A. Mayne & S. Lawrence, 'An ethnography of place: imagining "Little Lon"', *Journal of Australian Studies*, 57 (1998), 93–107. **19** J. Walkowitz, *City of dreadful delight: narratives of sexual danger in late-Victorian London* (Chicago, 1992), pp 15–39; O'Keeffe & Ryan, 'A landscape at the world's end', p. 25. **20** K. Mullin, *James Joyce, sexuality and social purity* (Cambridge, 2003), p. 177. **21** Luddy, *Prostitution and Irish society*, pp 250–1. **22** Fagan, *Monto*, p. 28.

almost industrial-scale prostitution problem. Thus, the technological project of
mapping the city was also a social project of designating certain spaces as problematic and paving the way for their future destruction.

MONTO IN THE ORDNANCE SURVEY

Although we assert that 'Monto' and the actual place to which the moniker was
attached must be regarded as fundamentally different places, our best means today of
visualizing the former is through the records of the latter. Given the paucity of
graphic material,[23] we are reliant on OS records, along with the 1911 census returns,
the street directories and rateable-valuation materials, and published oral recollections.[24] The first OS map of the area of interest to us had its survey conducted in
1837 and was then published with some revisions and new contours in 1847. It was
published with further revisions in 1864, 1871, 1889 and 1907. The 1847 edition of
the map had house or lot numbers, but, regrettably, numbers did not appear on the
later revision in 1864. Unfortunately, also, the street numbering system changed regularly and it is quite a challenge to match the numbers given in TD and GV with
properties marked on the maps.[25]

Although it lies beyond the scope of this essay, it is possible with respect to some
Monto streets to reconstruct graphically how the buildings appeared prior to their
mid-twentieth-century demolition. The evidence comes mainly from the shapes of
the properties on the OS maps themselves; their shapes can be compared with houses
of late eighteenth- and nineteenth-century date that are still standing in other parts
of the city. The 1911 census, which classifies houses, is the other informative source.
The reconstruction sketch of part of the south side of Mecklinburgh (then Tyrone)
Street *c.*1910, as shown in Figure 4. 8, captures the sheer diversity of house-types
attested to in these sources. Railway/Mecklinburgh is actually the one street of
Monto for which this type of reconstruction drawing is possible; we have the same
supply of information pertaining to properties on Foley Street (formerly
Montgomery Street), but matching 1911 census descriptions to the properties is more
difficult here.

23 Fagan, *Monto*, passim; some images are shown in C. Corlett, *Darkest Dublin: the story of
the Church Street disaster and a pictorial account of the slums of Dublin in 1913* (Bray, 2008).
24 For oral recollections, see Fagan, *Monto*. **25** For example, from Mulgrave Place
westwards to the Gloucester Diamond the numbers on the 1847 OS map run from 141 to
149, but TD for the same date suggests that the sequence runs to 150/151, which on the map
are clearly shown as being on the *opposite* side of the intersection; GV, on the other hand,
lists 149 and allocates numbers 149a, 149b & 149c to the additional buildings on the south-
eastern corner of the Gloucester Diamond (still officially part of the Gloucester Street
Lower), and TD later (1861) adjusted its numbering scheme to reflect Griffith's.

4.8 Conjectural sketch reconstruction of the façades of numbers 36 (right-hand-side) to 48 (left-hand-side) on the south side of Lower Tyrone Street (formerly Mecklinburgh Street, now Railway Street), as they might have appeared *c.*1910. The house on the far left was at the corner of this street and Beaver Street, and the arched passageway in the centre of the drawing was the entrance to Uxbridge, one of the many small alleys off the street. Note that the plan of the street shown here (see also Fig. 4.9), on which the properties are highlighted, is inverted (north facing downwards).

MECKLINBURGH STREET LOWER (NOW RAILWAY STREET)

Female penitents retreat. St Thomas' parochial school & widows house. Street rather narrow & dirty paved & macadamized paved footways lighted. Houses of various description from 3 to 4 storeys high with stabling in the rere. Inhabitants private families, spirit dealers, artists, huxters, marble yards &c. &c. &c.[26]

The former Mecklinburgh Street Lower (renamed Tyrone Street Lower in 1888 and Railway Street in 1911) has changed much since the Monto years. The north side of Railway Street between Gloucester Place Lower and Gloucester Lane is dominated by the flats block containing St Mary's Mansions. The remaining part of the street eastwards from there to Buckingham Street Lower, with the exception of a small section at the very east end of the street, is taken up by 'convent lands', all scheduled for redevelopment. The south side of the street has effectively been redeveloped several times, with Liberty House, a flats complex, dominating the street as far as James Joyce Street.

Central to the history of this street since the 1800s has been the Magdalen Asylum, so a brief history of its appearance in our sources is appropriate. Founded in

26 *Name book, Dublin city* (1837), 212 (41).

1822,[27] the 1830 valuation – a pre-GV valuation – names this house, no. 106 at that date, as a 'Female Penitentiary' with a valuation of £40, and describes it as '3 stories, with yard'. The 'Magdalene Asylum' is given a different property number – 76 – on the street on the 1847 OS map. TD describes this establishment in 1847 as the 'Female Penitents' Retreat', under the control of a Mrs Eliza Doyle, titled Matron; GV describes the occupiers as the 'Trustees of the Female Penitentiary', with Revd James Laphan as the immediate lessor, and puts an annual rateable valuation of £44 on the property. The 1864 revision of the OS map does not indicate any significant change in the street topography in the immediate vicinity between the late 1840s and early 1860s. Within a decade of that map revision, however, the no. 72 address had become the 'Back entrance to Female Penitents Retreat' (TD), reflecting the construction of the new Sisters of Charity Convent on Gloucester Street, while the Female Penitents' Retreat itself had expanded (and changed its name to St Mary's Penitent Retreat), to include the next plot to the west on Mecklinburgh Street, no. 77 (TD). From *c*.1880 to the turn of the century, the combined Gloucester Street-Mecklinburgh Street site continued to expand gradually to the north, east and west, consuming various small residential courts and lanes in the process. By 1900, the complex included plot numbers 68 to 80 inclusive on the renamed Tyrone Street Lower. The complex continued to expand in the early 1900s, with the last major expansion occurring in the late 1930s, when some of the remaining properties to the west of the old asylum site, some of them having houses associated with prostitution, were demolished and the space was occupied by an extended laundry facility.

We noted above a row of contiguous brothels on the north side of Mecklinburgh Street around 1900. Indeed, this very street probably had the lion's share of Monto brothels, although one imagines – and here we are conscious of importing a modern-day perception into the Victorian and Edwardian city – that many of Monto's prostitutes lived and worked in the small lanes, courtyards and 'places' off Mecklinburgh (Fig. 4.9); two for which this statement is certainly true are Faithful Place and Elliott Place, both now gone. The former had two parts, Faithful Place West and Faithful Place East, named as such only in GV. However, TD records only the latter of these, with 'nine small houses in tenements' ranging from £6 to £12 in value in 1847. By 1861, the directory was including the more modest properties in Faithful Place West in the enumeration, and the number of properties was therefore larger: 'nineteen small houses in tenements'. This figure continued to be given for Faithful Place until 1872, when the street disappeared completely from TD records. Forty years later (1911), Faithful Place was back in the directory, with eight houses recorded, although the contemporary 1911 census lists twelve buildings, eight of them heavily overcrowded houses and four of them 'stores'. That census confirms the presence of prostitution on Faithfull Place: in one house (no. 1) were two females, Lily Thompson, a 'laundress' from Blackrock, and Maggie Boylan, a boarder from Co. Meath, whose occupation was recorded on the census form as 'Pros.' Whether this was entered by Lily Thompson or the enumerator is not clear, as Maggie Boylan

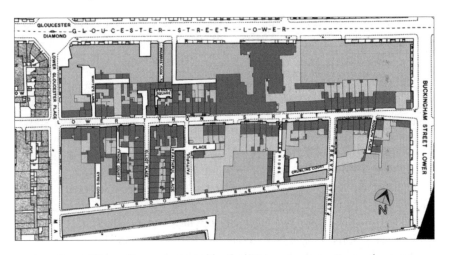

4.9 Lower Tyrone Street as captured by the OS in 1907; properties on the street and properties accessible directly from the street are highlighted here, showing (a) how many small alleys and courtyards were connected to the street, and (b) how this street was linked to Purdon Street, also part of Monto, rather than Gloucester Street Lower (now part of Sean McDermott Street), which was outside Monto (reproduced with the permission of the OSI).

herself could neither read nor write. She is one of only two women in the entire area recorded as prostitutes in the census. Lily may, of course, have been another, as 'laundress' may have been a euphemism.[28]

Elliott Place was also known for prostitution. In 1837, it was not an unrespectable place to live or visit.[29] When first mapped in 1847, it contained nineteen houses, four of them in tenements according to TD. Their valuations at that time ranged from £10 to £4, but these values had reduced – revealingly, perhaps – by approximately 20 per cent by the time of GV in 1854, with the number of tenements increased to seven. Moreover, the occupants named in 1854 are not the same as those named seven years earlier. Elliott Place was omitted from TD from the 1880s to 1911, when its reappearance (as an entirely tenemented street) coincides with the census. That census again

---

28 One wonders if the 'Laundry women' recorded by the OS as living in the rented houses of Brewery Yard, 'an irregular dirty st. or yard not paved without footways and not lighted' which was located between Gloucester Street and Mecklinburgh Street and accessible from both, were prostitutes: *Name book, Dublin city* (1837), 60 (45). But we do need to be cautious: it was not uncommon in the nineteenth century for working-class women to earn income at home, sometimes by taking in lodgers, sometimes by doing work in the domestic space for an industry – the garment industry in particular – which would allow work from home, and sometimes by running illegal drinking dens; see S. Deutsch, *Women and the city: gender, space and power in Boston, 1870–1940* (New York, 2000). **29** 'Place ordinary breath paved no footways lighted with gas. Houses good with small yards let in single tenements. Inhabitants nearly all respectable mechanics, artists, clerks, huxters shops': *Name book, Dublin city* (1837), 65 (76).

informs us of heavy overcrowding, with between two and four family units in seventeen of the nineteen small houses. In one room in one house (no. 15) lived 28-year-old Maud Hamilton. The census forms record that she could read and write. Under the heading 'occupation' was the word 'unfortunate', but inserted under this in another hand is '(Prostitute)'. This house may be typical of a back-street Monto brothel: three other young women occupied the second room in the house, and all are described – again, euphemistically? – as domestic or general servants, while the third room was occupied by a single, 40-year-old, female of unstated occupation. Both census enumerators and residents consistently demonstrate a reluctance to use the designation 'prostitute', further distancing social reality from its empirical reckoning.

None of the other lanes and courtyards off Mecklinburgh acquired the same reputation as Faithfull Place and Elliott Place. White's Lane, named after its owner, existed in 1830, when it had two tenements; this increased to eight by 1847 (TD) but reduced again to five by 1854 (GV). From the 1870s, it no longer features in TD but it was not cleared away until the 1930s. Byrne's Square, named after a John Byrne (GV), had six tenements of a total value of £42 in 1847, but this figure was revised down to £22 in 1861, when only four tenements were recorded (TD). It too disappeared from the TD in the 1870s but remained to the 1930s. The evocatively named Nickleby [Court], with no more than two well-valued houses recorded in any source at any stage, remained in TD until 1875 but survived until gobbled up by the Magdalen Asylum before 1907. Similarly short-lived were Palace Yard, Uxbridge and Breen's Court. Palace Yard had between three and four tenements between the 1840s and 1870s (TD). There was a dispensary here – 'St Thomas' Parish Dispensary' – in 1847 (TD) and it was marked as still-extant on the 1864 OS map, but its site was listed as a tenement in 1854 (GV) and 1861 (TD). Indeed, it continued to be listed as such until c.1900, when it was recorded as part of St Mary's Penitent Retreat. Uxbridge was a fairly new development in 1837.[30] There were four well-valued houses here in 1847 (TD), and they were still here, but with different occupiers, in 1854 (RV). Breen's Court, or Tyrone Court from c.1900 to c.1930, was not named on the 1847 or 1864 OS maps but was recorded by GV with six houses.

PURDON STREET

> Institution for worm complaints for the poor. Street narrow & dirty paved middle footways lighted. Houses of various qualities with dirty reres. Inhabitants provision dealers, huxters, a great number of destitute poor, dissolute & depraved characters in both sex, labourers.[31]

30 'Street irregular in breadth *not yet finished*, covered entranceway from Mecklinburgh St., not lighted, no footways. Houses good two stories high, with confined reres. Inhabitants private families, clerks, artists': *Name book, Dublin city* (1837), 123 (9); emphasis added. **31** *Name book, Dublin city* (1837), 215 (69).

Purdon Street no longer exists but its line survives in the entrance to Liberty House Flats on James Joyce Street, as well as in other boundaries. The letters suggest a bustling, if narrow and grotty, backstreet around 1840, and the presence of an 'institute' to treat parasitic worms is suitably Dickensian, but information about Purdon dries up quickly thereafter. In 1847, for example, we know of fifty houses in tenements, valued at between £1 and £10 each, but we have no details, while in 1872 only one person is mentioned by name ('Ryan, Michael, marine stores'), with the number of his residence or shop not given (TD). Discrepancies between the numbers attached to properties in the various sources are not inconsistent with its backstreet, out-of-sight, character. Between 1872 and 1911, Purdon is not listed at all in TD, even though it still existed and had a nineteenth-century building stock: its houses seem from 1930s photographs[32] to have been no more than small two-storey buildings, with single rooms to the front beside the hall doors. When the street reappears in the record around 1911, its buildings 1 to 39 are listed as 'Corporation Buildings', which was actually the development on and to the rear of Foley Street to the south. This cryptic record in TD continues up to the 1950s, before the street disappears from the record for a second and final time, having been demolished in 1958.

There were several small lanes or courtyards leading off Purdon Street, but few of them seem to have been still occupied by the time of Monto. Their histories, insofar as we can say anything about them, sum up the nature of the entire area. Fox's Lane was the name given to a narrow alley recorded in TD in 1847; the same accessway is described in GV (1854) as being 'in rere' between two properties, suggesting that this was merely a lane leading to the back of a couple of properties, and possibly one of the accessways from which the Ordnance Surveyors could see that the reres of the houses were 'dirty'. White's Court, or Carlisle Place as it was named on the 1864 OS map, had eleven houses and/or sheds in 1854 (GV), but by 1861 all that remained were four low-valuation tenements recorded by TD. By 1907, it had been gobbled up by the redevelopment of Foley Street. Similarly, Connolly's Court, described by the surveyors in 1837,[33] was recorded as having only four tenemented houses with lodgers from 1854 to 1872, and was also gone by 1907.[34] GV records Mitchell's Court, with three small houses, although this court is not mentioned at all in TD. Beaver Court is also mentioned in GV, with five houses (with named occupants); TD mentions 'Three houses in tenements' here in 1861, after which it ceases to be mentioned. There was also a courtyard known as Ayer's Court or Eyre's Court, but confusion between the various recorders about its location and proper spelling seems to have resulted in two courtyards – the original one and another, hitherto unnamed one – carrying one of these names each. Whatever its original name, the original

---

32 Fagan, *Monto*, pp 30, 39. **33** 'Court narrow and dirty has a covered entrance paved but not lighted no footways. Houses indifferent let in single apartments. Inhabitants labouring poor chiefly in great poverty': *Name book, Dublin city* (1837), 62 (63). **34** It was located at the east end of what for a period was Corporation Place, where it became part of the entrance to the Corporation Buildings complex from Foley Street.

court seems to have been on the north side of Purdon in 1847. GV records five
houses there, the three larger ones having 'lodgers'. TD for 1847 complicates matters
by locating 'Ayre's Court' on the opposite side of the street, apparently in a space not
recognized as a court by the OS; the directory then gives separate entries to each
court after 1847! Finally, there was a Supple's Court (sometimes recorded as Purdon's
Court or Ryan's Court). In 1847, it had '1 to 7 tenements', with various valuations
between £2 and £4 in 1847. In 1861 and 1872, this number was reduced to 'four
houses in tenements' with valuations of £3 10s. The court ceased to be recorded in
TD after 1875, but it remained on OS maps (as Ryan's Court) into the early 1900s.

MONTGOMERY STREET (NOW FOLEY STREET)

> Paving house depot. Street narrow and rather dirty macadamized lighted
> paved gravelled & flagged footways. Houses, some good and others indifferent
> 2 & 3 stories high let in single tenements. Inhabitants private families, small
> retail shopkeepers, spirit dealers, destitute poor, cars and float drivers.[35]

Today, very little remains of the original fabric of the eponymous Montgomery
Street, other than some cobblestones. At the intersection with James Joyce Street on
the north side of the street is Liberty House, located on the site of Phil Shanahan's
public house (no. 134), well-remembered in the area's folklore.[36] To the east again is
a large tree-lined, grassed, recreational area with playgrounds and tennis courts,
replacing what once was the site of Corporation Buildings, a large complex of public
flats that was begun after the demolition of houses in 1901, was finished in 1905 and
was pulled down around 1980.[37] 'The Steelworks', a major apartment and office-
building complex occupying the remainder of the block as far as Beaver Street,
occupies a site with a long history of industrial or commercial activity. The block
from Beaver Street to Buckingham Street Lower is now taken up with a Bord Gais
building. The south side of Foley Street has, from east to west, a public house (Lloyds,
established 1893), some remnants of old buildings (including a dilapidated wooden
shop-front bearing the name of John Mullett), some new apartment buildings called
Montgomery Court, and a variety of commercial buildings, sites under construction,
and a hotel.

Perusal of the maps indicates that the whole street, in both its original
Montgomery Street and later Foley Street configurations, was never fully developed
(notwithstanding the construction of Corporation Buildings), and this suggests in
turn that some of the very long plots on the south side of the street in the early 1900s
were survivals of the mid-eighteenth-century street. Given this relative underdevelopment, we suggest that Montgomery Street gave its name to the place of

---

35 *Name book, Dublin city* (1837), 213 (47).   **36** Fagan, *Monto*, p. 74.   **37** J.V. O'Brien, *Dear,
dirty Dublin: a city in distress, 1899–1916* (Berkeley, 1982), pp 193–4.

prostitution – Monto – not because it was lined with more brothels than any other street of the district but because much of the prostitute-seeking traffic into the area came through it.

As with the Mecklinburgh and the other main streets, there were several small lanes and courts off Montgomery/Foley, such as Nugent's Court and Brady's Cottages, the former a small development listed in TD up to the 1880s but about which we know little, and the latter a development of seven small, low-valuation, houses originally belonging to and rented out by one Daniel Brady (GV); 'Brady's Cottages' disappeared at the start of the 1900s, when it was wrapped up by the new Corporation Buildings development, but the space it occupied survived as a walkway from Foley Street into this new development.

MABBOT STREET (NOW JAMES JOYCE STREET)

> Street rather narrow paved and broken stone dirty footways flagged and lighted. Houses good from 2 to 4 stories high, a great part let to room keepers and lodgers. Inhabitants, respectable private families, gentlemen master artists, spirit dealers & grocers, provision dealers, vintners, boarding schools.[38]

The oldest street in the area, this is now called James Joyce Street, having previously been known as Corporation Street and, before that, Mabbot Street. It has been almost completely redeveloped over the past twenty years. James Joyce referred to 'the Mabbott Street entrance to Nighttown', thus securing the street's association with prostitution, but there is little evidence that prostitutes actually operated here. Its houses were quite substantial in the early 1800s, as reflected by rateable valuations in 1847 of £30, £20 and £25 for numbers 9, 10 and 11 respectively (TD), and indeed Hugh Byrne, the city architect of the day, lived in no. 10. In GV, the valuations for these three houses alone are lower, as one finds is the case in many instances, but they are not significantly lower: £22, £15 and £24 respectively. The level of tementation on the street in the 1880s, 1890s and 1910s matches that of the other streets of the district.

Parallel to James Joyce Street today, but to the west, is Mabbott Lane, known as Mabbot Court in TD but named as O'Loughlin's Court on the OS maps of 1847 and 1864. As in the case of so many of the minor spaces around the area, its residential profile is really known to us in the mid-1800s only, when it had low-value 'stables and tenements' (TD, 1847).

---

38 *Name book, Dublin city* (1837), 210 (33).

BEAVER STREET

Street narrow and dirty part paved and part macadamized paved footways, lighted with gas. Houses some good others of inferior quality generally 2 stories. Inhabitants purposes a few private families a number of poor tradesmen, huxters and retailers of vegetables.[39]

Today, this street has been redeveloped, with the exception of a small area on the east side (where there are remains of a premises of the 1940s of one James Daly, a brush manufacturer). Its history of tenementation in the later 1800s matches that of the other main streets, and in the 1880s and 1890s it is absent completely from TD. Again, like the other streets, there were several small lanes and courts off Beaver. Ring's Court had 'three houses in tenements' valued at £20 in 1847 (TD). Seven years later (GV) it had eight houses with a cumulatively lower valuation, all rented out by the 'Trustees of Simpson's Hospital'. By 1861, this court was recorded as 'Ruins' (TD), and the later maps show an open space. In the 1900s, it was redeveloped a couple of times. Wood's Court had 'two houses in tenements' with a £6 valuation between the mid-1840s and the mid-1860s, but GV records 'lodgers' in four houses here. In any case, from the 1860s it was in 'Ruins' (TD). Marr's Court is one of a number of courts not named by the OS, but GV identifies its site and records five lowly-valued houses, all leased by a John Marr. Cromwell's Court, another short-lived development, had eight small houses and small yards in the 1840s (TD).

MONTO AND THE URBAN IMAGINARY

The best-known, even iconic, photograph from Monto shows two women, both assumed to be prostitutes, standing beside a lamp-post at the junction of Elliott Place and Purdon Street (Fig. 4.10). One wonders if the photograph was staged, given its careful composition and the fact that the women make no attempt to conceal their identities, but it does at least correspond with the published testimonies of local people: this particular lamp-post was a place at which prostitutes were known to gather, and the windows of houses close by were indeed boarded-up to prevent children witnessing the gestures and transactions of such public solicitation.[40]

The photograph's date is as interesting as its content. It was taken during the 1930s; the exact details are not recorded. A decade earlier, as we have seen, a concerted constabulary effort to deal with prostitution in Monto had resulted in many arrests, and this led in turn to a common perception of prostitution as a problem solved, at least in the north inner-city area. The photograph suggests otherwise: the 'open brothel' that was Monto may have been 'closed down' in the mid-1920s, but women were still openly scouting for business in the area in the

39 *Name book, Dublin city* (1837), 59 (41).   **40** Fagan, *Monto*, pp 28–9.

4.10 Two women stand at a lamp-post in the former Monto, 1930s (image reproduced courtesy of the Old Dublin Society: Frank Murphy Collection).

second quarter of the twentieth century. What is striking, even remarkable, is the fact that we depend on a photograph from as late as the 1930s to get some visual sense of the area and its principal, illicit, industry. In the late nineteenth century, glass-plate photography had revolutionized the concept of representation, and by extension the ways in which people perceived the world, and by the time of Monto's official 'closure', Dublin was a well-photographed city, with its slums (including those around Monto) especially well recorded.[41] But if photographs were taken of turn-of-century Monto in its red-light incarnation, none seems to have survived. The likelihood is, surely, that few if any images were ever captured, leaving us bereft of the sort of informative and evocative record of the place that contemporary technology was capable of generating. It is only in our imaginations, then, that we can now visu-

41 Corlett, *Darkest Dublin*.

alize Monto as it must have been in the later 1800s, when it acquired its reputation as one of the world's most infamous red-light districts, or even in the early 1900s, when some Christian organizations actively campaigned against the brothel owners.

Moreover, while the great information-gathering exercises of the 1800s – by the Ordnance Survey, by the Valuation Office and even by the commercial publishers of street directories – together captured the character of the district, especially the steady declines in both the quality of the built-fabric and the quality of life during the last quarter of the century, they captured little or nothing of the place's notorious red-light character. The individual brothels were ordinary houses, or were spaces inside ordinary houses, and so were recorded only as houses. The madams were primarily landladies, and were recorded as such (if they were recorded by name at all). And, critically, the trade in sex was both furtive, which meant that it occupied no fixed or permanently demarcated space, and illegal, which excluded it anyway from representation in some of the compilations of data – maps, gazetteers – that were then in the public domain.

This essay has highlighted the possibilities and difficulties for recovering such hidden activity using major historical sources of the 1800s. The lack of information in some of these sources is as regrettable as the lack of photographic coverage, but it should probably not surprise us. There is no reason to think that records of areas like Monto were always compiled assiduously and kept up-to-date for dissemination purposes, or even that census returns were always accurate. On the contrary, synchronic and diachronic inconsistencies within and between sources for Monto's topography, as well as for its permanent and tenant populations, suggest both a lack of rigour in the giving of information by those within the area and a lack of accuracy in the collecting of information by those from outside the area. This project reminds us of the social attitudes reflected in scientific projects such as the OS and the census: surveyors and enumerators expressed their disapproval of the illicit activities of Monto by failing to record them and thereby preventing them from entering the official record. The OS maps do inspire confidence as accurate snapshots of Monto, but these are maps of spaces, not maps of people, and it was the specific activities of people within Monto's topographical spaces that marked it as a special place within the city.

A microscopic look at Mary Ward: gender, science and religion in nineteenth-century Ireland

ÉADAOIN AGNEW

Robert Young claims that at the 'heart of science we find a culture's values';[1] this has certainly been the case since the Victorian era, when the relationship between contemporary science and culture began to develop, a connection that is confirmed by Mary Ward's science writing. With the aid of optical equipment, Ward set out to reveal to her readers new worlds and new ways of seeing. However, what is actually unveiled in her writing is a careful negotiation and affirmation of conservative Victorian values.

Scholars have long acknowledged that science writing can be made to act in support of individual and cultural preconceptions; as Eveleen Richards demonstrates, despite the ground-breaking developments offered by Charles Darwin, his scientific theories also provided sustenance for Victorian male chauvinism:[2]

> The chief distinction in the intellectual powers of the two sexes is shown by man's attaining to a higher eminence in whatever he takes up, than can woman – whether requiring deep thought, reason or imagination, or merely the use of the senses or hands.[3]

In *The descent of man* (1871), Darwin purports that man is ultimately biologically superior to woman, thereby authorizing a white male supremacy through an apparently scientific conception of female nature. In this way, science was used to deny women's full participation in intellectual disciplines, particularly during the Victorian period, as women began to encroach upon male-dominated science disciplines.[4]

Although it may have seemed that, for the most part, the natural sciences were becoming a new way of defining and organizing the moral and social order of the nineteenth century, in many respects these scientific disciplines simply underlined traditional ideologies in relation to race, class and gender. In this way, those aspects of intelligence attributed to women – intuition, perception and imitation – were

---

1 B. Lightman, 'Introduction' in B. Lightman (ed.), *Victorian science in context* (Chicago, 1997), pp 3–8. **2** E. Richards, 'Redrawing the boundaries: Darwinian science and Victorian women intellectuals' in Lightman, *Victorian science in context*, pp 119–43. **3** C. Darwin, *The descent of man and selection in relation to sex*, 2 vols (London, 1871), 2, p. 326. **4** Lightman, 'Introduction', p. 8.

simply dismissed by Darwin as being characteristic of the lower races. In other words, they were viewed as evidence of a lesser state of civilization.[5] Unsurprisingly, several other leading scientists, such as Francis Galton (1822–1911) and Patrick Geddes (1854–1932), followed Darwin's direction; together, these intellectuals forged a formidable body of biological determinist theory that purported to show that women were inherently different from men and could never expect to match the intellectual and cultural achievements of their male counterparts.[6] Thus, science could be made to devalue women's ability to produce quality work in these areas. At the same time, the move to the professionalization of science led to bifurcations in science practices and increasingly pushed women to the periphery, granting them a supporting role but rarely enabling them to become forerunners in their field.

Nonetheless, as Ann B. Shteir has shown, nineteenth-century women were an important part of the broader map of Victorian science, operating as readers, writers, investigators and helpmeets.[7] It would seem that despite the institutional and cultural changes that sought to resist women's participation in scientific disciplines, women continued to produce work, albeit textually and discursively restricted. What is of particular interest here is how Ward negotiates such gender constraints in order to contribute to scientific knowledge; in fact, in many ways, science is the means through which Ward is able to resist the role of the archetypal Victorian female. At the same time, this close textual analysis will illustrate how, for Ward, science also confirmed certain preconceived ideas about the world in which she lived. By considering the formal, discursive and visual negotiations of Ward's science writing, it will be argued that while she cautiously disrupts gender discourses, she leaves other narratives, such as religion, firmly intact.

Although Ward has been largely overlooked by literary scholars, in recent years she has received some recognition from historians of science. For example, Owen Harry's invaluable recuperative work has demonstrated how Ward's family background played a major part in awakening and encouraging her interest in science.[8] She was born on 24 April 1827 to Revd Henry King and his wife Harriett, who was sister to Alice, the mother of William the third earl of Rosse, a relative who was to have a profound impact on Ward's life and career. The family home was a spacious mansion called Ballylin in Co. Offaly; it was the hub of a large estate close to and incorporating the town of Ferbane. While residing in the parental home, Ward's upper-middle-class background ensured that she had sufficient leisure time to investigate the natural world around her; and although she was typically restricted in terms of her education and her mobility, her parents encouraged her early interest in science. The fact that her father inscribed for her a copy of Buffon's *Natural history*,

5 Richards, 'Redrawing the boundaries', p. 119.   6 Ibid., p. 120.   7 A.B. Shteir, 'Elegant recreations? Configuring science writing for women' in Lightman, *Victorian science in context*, p. 236.   8 Ward's biographical information is largely drawn from Owen Harry's invaluable article, 'The Hon. Mrs Ward (1827–1869); a wife, mother, microscopist and astronomer in Ireland, 1854–1869' in J. Nudds, N. McMillan, D. Weaire & S. McKenna-Lawlor (eds), *Science in Ireland, 1800–1930: tradition and reform* (Dublin, 1988).

a present on her seventh birthday, perhaps indicates the level of her curiosity.[9] Throughout her childhood, she plundered whatever books, newspapers and periodicals she could lay her hands on in the vast library at Ballylin. Gradually, she began to assemble her own collection of books about astronomy, the microscope, entomology and zoology.[10] But, perhaps even more influential than her reading habits was her social circle. As noted above, her cousin was William Parsons (1800–67), the third earl of Rosse and the inventor of the famous 58ft Leviathan Telescope, an instrument that was to remain the world's largest telescope for over fifty years. Living nearby, Ward was a regular visitor to Birr Castle, where her cousin lived, and he involved her closely in the consultations leading up to the completion of his instrument. In fact, between 1840 and 1845, Ward chronicled the building of the Leviathan and she was among the first to mount its gantries and galleries to view a world unavailable to the naked eye, evidence of which can be found in the photographs taken by William's wife Mary.[11] Clearly her cousin had a profound impact on Ward by inspiring and encouraging her interest in astronomy, a fact she acknowledges in her dedication to him in *Telescope teachings* (1859).[12]

It was also through William that Mary Ward and her sisters had the opportunity to meet many of the most celebrated men of science at this time, including Sir James South (1785–1867), Sir William Rowan Hamilton (1805–65) and Sir David Brewster (1781–1868), for whom Ward illustrated several books and articles and who assisted her search for scientific papers and specimens.[13] Brewster in particular was impressed by Mary's keen powers of observation and her ability to record natural objects in an accurate and artistic manner. As a result, the illustrations of Newton's telescope and both aspects of Lord Rosse's telescope in Brewster's *Memoirs of the life, writings and discoveries of Sir Isaac Newton* (1855) were produced by Ward.[14]

In 1854, at the age of 27, Mary married Henry William Crosbie Ward (1828–1911) of Castle Ward, Northern Ireland. This was a union which provoked a rather telling comment from Henry's mother, Lady Bangor, who wrote in a letter to a friend that her new daughter-in-law was 'A most *independent* young woman, but very pleasant'.[15] Henry Ward had served in the Crimea but resigned his commission in 1855 and had no regular employment thereafter; this brought great domestic and financial difficulty during the period when their family was growing – Mary conceived eleven times between 1855 and 1867, giving birth to eight live infants. Amazingly, during this period of childbirth and childrearing, Ward managed to study and to write, perhaps out of necessity. Her initial public effort was a home-printed article entitled 'A windfall of the microscope' (1856), which was a careful, detailed description of her investigation of caddis flies. Prefiguring her later texts, the article

9 S. McKenna-Lawlor, *Whatever shines should be observed* (Dordrecht, 2003), p. 21. **10** For a full list of titles, please refer to Harry, 'The Hon. Mrs Ward', p. 190. **11** D.H. Davison, *Impressions of an Irish countess: the photographs of Mary, Countess of Rosse, 1813–1885* (Birr, 1989). **12** M. Ward. *Telescope teaching* (London, 1859), p. iii. **13** Harry, 'The Hon. Mrs Ward', p. 187. **14** D. Brewster, *Memoirs of the life, writings and discoveries of Sir Isaac Newton* (Edinburgh, 1855). **15** Harry, 'The Hon. Mrs Ward', p. 191.

was lively, enthusiastically told and nicely illustrated.[16] Her first book was published in 1857 when she commissioned Shields, the local printer and stationer in Parsonstown to reproduce a collection of short letters which had been written to a friend some years earlier. The letters examined the structure of common objects suitable for scrutiny under the microscope.[17] Ward had completed drawings to exemplify her instruction and she lithographed the plates before arranging them to be hand-coloured by a Dublin engraver. The plates and the text were then bound together into *Sketches with the microscope*, which she sold by private subscription. It was a great success. By the end of the year, she had sold all the copies and had a waiting list for the reprint. The book was eventually taken to London by a relative and shown to the publisher Groombridge and Sons, who published it under the name *A world of wonders revealed by the microscope*. It went through a number of print-runs between 1858 and 1864, when it was extensively revised and expanded into *Microscope teachings*, the companion volume to *Telescope teachings*, which Ward had produced in 1859. These books are probably her best-known scientific writings. With their combination of easy style and attractive illustrations they quickly became established as popular and accessible studies of microscopic and telescopic objects.

From 1859 to 1869, Ward wrote on a number of subjects: toads in Ireland; hummingbird moths; insect development; and astronomy. Consequently, she became well-respected for her scientific work. This is evident from the fact that Sir William Rowan Hamilton requested the Royal Astronomical Society to include her on its list of eminent people and institutions entitled to receive its monthly notices.[18] Ward was one of only three women to achieve this honour, holding rather esteemed company with Queen Victoria (1819–1901) and Mrs Mary Somerville (1780–1872). In a further groundbreaking move, she was allowed entry to Greenwich Observatory, despite their strict rule against women. Taken together, these accolades clearly signal the esteem in which her work was held by her contemporaries.

Despite such apparent respect from individual male scientists and the fact that the growth of popular scientific culture during the eighteenth century had shaped an audience of women and children who participated in home-based scientific education and experiments, nineteenth-century women such as Ward generally found it difficult to engage in the increasingly professionalized world of science. For many scientific professionals, such as Huxley, women were ipso facto amateurs, clearly out of place in a masculine arena where their very presence seemed to threaten the mid-century establishment of Darwinian expertise and status.[19] Accordingly, they were excluded from learned societies and formal education. In a series of knock-on effects from such beliefs and practices, women's lack of formal education in certain areas was cited as a reason for refusing to accept their entrance into professional circles, and yet

---

16 M. and T. Creese, *Ladies in the laboratory 2: western women in science, 1800–1900* (Oxford, 2004), p. 41.   **17** Harry, 'The Hon. Mrs Ward', p. 194.   **18** He also helped Mary obtain particulars of the most recent developments in science in books and articles to which it was difficult for her to gain access. See Harry, 'The Hon. Mrs Ward', pp 194–5.   **19** Richards, 'Redrawing the boundaries', p. 126.

they found it extremely difficult to gain access to those learned institutions that would provide the necessary preparation for admittance to these professional institutions and societies. On the whole, Ward's experience was no different: she had not received any recognized training, but she was fortunate to have parents who nurtured her early interest in natural history. As Owen Harry outlines, in 1845 when Sir James South was visiting the house, he observed her making drawings of small objects seen through a single lens magnifying glass and noted her ability; he suggested to her parents that she should be provided with a quality microscope capable of higher magnification and better resolution. An instrument by Andrew Ross, one of the best then available in London, was ordered immediately;[20] her debt to this piece of equipment is exemplified by the prominence it is afforded as the frontispiece of all the editions of her microscope books.

Furthermore, despite Ward's exclusion from libraries and laboratories, through her cousin she was fortunate to be brought into an intellectual community where she could participate and engage in scholarly debates and discussions with leading scientists of the time. Nonetheless, the gender bias of Victorian culture meant that not everyone was readily convinced of her scientific ardour; she wrote:

> It was easy to ask Professor Owen about the deer in Richmond Park and on that lead to tell him how exceedingly common red deer's remains are in the beds of Irish rivers, and moreover, how I had myself scraped together a good number of bones of one of them; on which he began to think I was not merely pretending to care for natural history.[21]

It seems that in order to distinguish themselves from numerous female counterparts who enjoyed the natural sciences as a middle-class past-time, those women scientists fortunate enough to encounter experts in their field had to prove the seriousness of their interest. In addition, they had to be careful not to step on any intellectual toes, finding it hard to voice dissent or disagreement, particularly with the scientific heavyweights of the Victorian period. Such difficulties are exemplified in a scrapbook of Brewster's articles that Ward compiled. She includes his address to the Edinburgh Philosophical Society on 11 November 1851 that attempts to reconcile fundamental Christian beliefs with the new theories and discoveries of science, especially astronomy. He relates new ideas about the formation of asteroids between Mars and Jupiter. On an additional scrap of paper, Ward has written: 'The above is not to be depended on, as it is not in my power to *give my authority*. But it is what I should *say* were I asked'.[22] But, of course, generally women were not asked.

For many women who wished to pursue a career in science, it was necessary to find a niche, a way to produce scientific knowledge without really appearing to do so. For Ward, this meant positioning herself as an adjunct to male writing on science, as she does in this letter to the *Irish Times*:

20 Harry, 'The Hon. Mrs Ward', p. 192. **21** Ibid. **22** Ibid., p. 193.

Sir, —As I happen to have obtained a good view of the meteors this morning from 12am till their subsidence at 3.30am, I beg to send you an account of what I saw, thinking it may supplement the far more precise and scientific reports which are likely to appear in your columns.[23]

As this letter exemplifies, like many other women of the time, Ward exercises a textual sleight of hand that self-effacingly sets her up as a necessary mediator. She continually positions herself as someone who can move between the worlds of professional masculine science and more plebeian neophyte explanations of the natural world and 'heavenly bodies'.[24] It is by assuming this conciliatory role that Ward leaves the myth of masculine authority intact while simultaneously dismantling the notion of separate intellectual spheres. In this way, women scientists took care to differentiate themselves from the masculinized persona of the knowledge-giver; this determined that their publications were, ostensibly at least, aimed at a readership derived from the broader public rather than from scientific circles as Barbara Gates has previously explored.[25] In Ward's writing, this intention is iterated by the fact that she dedicates and directs her texts to younger readers and other amateurs, often specifically cited as women, such as her mother and her friend Emily.

During the early and mid-Victorian years, science writing directed explicitly to women and children was a particularly productive labour, as it found a place on the lists of many publishers.[26] At this time, the audience for educational books was expanding quickly and affordable instruments were available, making microscopy and astronomy fashionable hobbies,[27] a fact that Ward herself notes.[28] Considering the financial difficulties faced by her family, it is not surprising that Ward wished to avail of the popularity of texts written for so-called amateurs; in this way, she markets her texts by setting up a particularly gentle form of pedagogy, as seen in *Entomology in sport*:

> The following pages are intended, not so much for the scientific, as for the young or the comparatively uninstructed reader. The authors have therefore aimed at making them entertaining, rather than complete or systematic; an agreeable bait, in short, by means of which unwary youth may find themselves caught in the meshes of science, while seeking only for amusement.[29]

In this text, Ward assumes a rather maternal role, acting as a gentle guide who will lead others through the elementary stages of scientific learning; this can be read as a quasi-feminist move that seeks to democratize science by making it available to other

23 M. Ward, correspondence to the *Irish Times*. Clipping in Ward's scrapbook held in Castle Ward. Dated 15 Nov. 1866. **24** Ward, *Telescope teachings*, p. v. **25** B. Gates, *Kindred nature: Victorian and Edwardian women embrace the living world* (Chicago, 1998). **26** Shteir, 'Elegant recreations', p. 244. **27** Creese, *Ladies in the laboratory 2*, p. 41. **28** Ward, *Microscope teachings*, p. vii. **29** M. Ward, 'Preface' in *Entomology in sport; and entomology in earnest* (London, 1859).

women similarly excluded from gaining access to such information. At the same time, such sidestepping also suggests a discursive negotiation that deliberately disguises any aspirations of professionalism or expertise and denies the disruption of separate intellectual spheres. Accordingly, academic science is largely absent from the first half of *Entomology in sport*, which is written in rhyming couplets and decorated with playful illustrations of anthropomorphized insects. However, the amateur approach is somewhat reconstituted in the second part of the text, entitled *Entomology in earnest*. Although this section is written as a friendly dialogue between the two characters, Sylvius and Eugenius, it is full of detailed information and helpful hints for studying entomology.

Graeme Gooday argues that, by the mid-century, conversational structures in science writing had largely disappeared.[30] Stylistically, the use of dialogue had been common practice in narratives of science, particularly within those texts that incorporated some degree of natural theology or were introductory works of informal education, such as those by Jane Marcet.[31] Furthermore, moral and spiritual topics were typically given authority through writing that conventionally took the form of educational conversations or letters. But, by the mid-century, this formal strategy was considered old-fashioned and feminine;[32] therefore it is significant that Ward, whose avid reading of science writing would certainly suggest an awareness of textual development, chooses to present her information in such an anachronistic manner. Thus, this structure can be seen to act as a buffer for the level of scientific knowledge contained within, a stylistic move also adopted in *Sketches with the microscope*.

In the first edition of Ward's best-selling text about microscopy, personal ambition is deflected as a motive for her scientific writing; she claims that she writes because of the desires of others, specifically a female other:

> My dear Emily,
> You have expressed a wish to receive tidings from the world of wonders which surround us, and which is revealed only by the microscope.[33]

However, by 1859, Ward has eschewed the epistolary structure, a literary format that was used by women writing in various masculinized genres in order to create a distance from the more academic and authoritative tones assumed by their male counterparts. Thus, while *Microscope teachings* and *Telescope teachings* are clearly marketed to an amateur readership, Ward seems to have established herself sufficiently to no longer need to couch her work in the same way. At the same time, it remains necessary for her to stress the accuracy of her information by invoking the male

30 G. Gooday, 'Instrumentation and interpretation: managing and representing the working environments of Victorian experimental science' in A.B. Shteir and B. Lightman (eds), *Figuring it out* (London, 2006), p. 249.   31 A. Shteir, 'Articulating the mimosa' in A. Fyfe and B. Lightman (eds), *Science in the marketplace* (London, 2007), p. 172.   32 Shteir, 'Elegant Recreations', p. 247.   33 M. Ward, *Sketches with the microscope* (Parsonstown, Co. Offaly, 1857), p. 1.

authorities in the various disciplines she refers to, such as Paley (1743–1805), Linnaeus (1707–78), Kirby (1759–1850), Spence (1783–1860) and Herschel (1738–1822), and by asserting that her knowledge is received through keen observational skills, a fact she proves through her use of accurate illustration.

In Ward's texts, alongside the light-hearted characters that appear as frontispieces and the various colourful distractions, there are a number of highly precise drawings, a feature of her work that Lightman and Shteir have noted the importance of:

> At a time when T.H. Huxley and his allies were trying to force women out of scientific societies, it was of paramount importance for women engaged in writing popular science, like Ward, who worked to construct the narrative of natural history, to present in their works visual images that bolstered their authority as interpreters of nature.[34]

By supporting her texts with visual representations, Ward could demonstrate clearly the power and acuity of her observations. And yet, simultaneously, illustration was seen as a definitely feminine activity. Many female would-be scientists had to satisfy themselves with illustrating the works of their male counterparts rather than producing new knowledge themselves. As Lorraine Kooistra explores, the relationship between the visual and the written reflects the gender politics of the time: the visual (the feminine) being viewed as secondary to the written word (the masculine) for most of the nineteenth century.[35] In this way, Ward's accompanying illustrations can be seen to feminize texts that were verging on a masculinized epistemological approach. At the same time, the illustrations can be seen to authorize Ward's populist texts. It seems that in her work, Ward strives to strike a balance between the two modes of expression: professional and populist. Thus, her illustrations are meant to delight as well as instruct, to have aesthetic as well as pedagogical purposes.[36] It is this dual motive that we see most apparently at work in *Entomology in sport* and its companion piece *Entomology in earnest*. Taken together, there is an equilibrium achieved between the light-hearted introduction to the insect world and the more advanced consideration of life beneath a lens. Even Ward's choice of scientific disciplines reflects the symbiosis she is striving to achieve in her work. Ultimately, the microscope and the telescope enabled Ward to undertake scientific activities within the domestic setting, which meant they could be made to fit around her female duties of wife and mother. At the same time, it was precisely these activities that propelled her beyond the role of the angel of the house. In a sense, the new technology offered, in more ways than one, a world beyond that which was immediately available to a middle-class nineteenth-century woman.

34 A.B. Shteir and B. Lightman, *Figuring it out: science, gender and visual culture* (London, 2006), p. 232. **35** L. Kooistra, *The artist as critic: bitextuality in fin-de-siècle illustrated books* (Aldershot, 1995). **36** B. Gates, 'Those who drew and those who wrote' in Shteir and Lightman, *Figuring it out*, p. 192.

As Kate Flint has argued, the Victorians wanted to make the world visible, to make things available to the eye and ready for interpretation, and this inclination can be linked to the rise in ophthalmic inventions.[37] Technological innovations enabled and encouraged many budding scientists to look at things from different perspectives and to see the apparent truths of the natural world. Ward writes: 'The most important thing in managing a microscope is to place the object in the clearest light, or else we cannot find out the truth about them'.[38] Lightman explains that the Victorians were driven by a quest for clarity in an effort to escape vagueness and inaccuracy, and that they were fascinated by new worlds.[39] Certainly, Ward seems to see the ophthalmic equipment as a means of fulfilling this pursuit for transparency and discovery:

> With a suitable instrument, and a little leisure time at command, how happily is the observer brought face to face with the minuter parts of God's creation, and how easy it seems at once to enjoy and to learn. It is like visiting a rich, but hitherto undiscovered region – like opening a page, hitherto unread, or a treasured volume.[40]

By breaking up domestic routine and offering greater visibility, the instruments appeared to open up a new world. But, what Ward ultimately revealed about the world was largely a confirmation of her preconceived value-system, particularly in relation to religion:

> We are enabled, with the microscope –
> *To trace in Nature's most minute design*
> *The signature and stamp of power divine.*[41]

For many during the Victorian period, science did not so much explain away the mysteries of the earth as reinforce the very idea that there was so much more to life than what met the eye, thereby providing evidence of God's work. Undoubtedly, in Ward's writing there is a fundamentally Christian attitude. However, it is pertinent to question the extent to which religion is employed as yet another discursive negotiation. This is not to suggest that Ward was not religious, her family background would dispute that, but it could be argued that in her more informative texts, she may have felt the need to stress her religiosity in order to counter the epistemological.

For many women encroaching onto the masculine world of scientific writing, a religious explanation for the world's natural sciences was often asserted, even after the Darwinian watershed, because for them it provided an acceptable motive for their

37 K. Flint, *The Victorians and the visual imagination* (Cambridge, 2000), p. 8. **38** Ward, *Sketches with the microscope*, p. 9. **39** B. Lightman, 'Introduction' in B. Lightman (ed.), *Victorian science in context* (Chicago, 1997), pp 1–2. **40** Ward, *Microscope teaching*, p. ix. **41** Ward, *Sketches with the microscope*, p. 8.

interest in scientific knowledge. At this time, middle- and upper-class women were largely regarded as the moral and religious centres of their society; therefore, it was generally perceived that they were the providers of the Christian well-being of those within their homes and communities, whereas their male counterparts were seen to provide the intellectual, economic and political ideals. By citing religion as the motivating force behind their scientific interest, they remained within the demarcated gendered spheres; they placed themselves beyond criticisms of personal and intellectual ambition. For example, Margaret Gatty's work on seaweed is contextualized and authorized by claiming that an educational and evangelizing Christianity motivates her publications. She situates her scientific work within the context of teaching about God's wonders and encourages other mothers to pass this same message along to their children. Gatty further reinforces her familial concerns by asserting that the publication of her work is necessary for the financial welfare of her own family. Through these discursive constructs, Gatty evokes the image of a mother of nature, extending her normalized role of domestic carer to the natural world. Therefore, by negotiating the representation of scientific knowledge, it could remain a comfortably 'feminine' topic. However, this led to some peculiar configurations: Mrs E. Perkins actually went to the extent of censoring the botanical classification system because it referred to the reproductive organs of plants, which was simply inappropriate for her female readers. Perkins' text is dedicated to the newly crowned Queen Victoria, and in her effort to comply with the ideals of the middle-class virginal Madonna emblematized by the young queen, she excises those references that she believes are 'peculiarly unsuited for the perusal of female youth'.[42] Like Perkins, numerous Victorian women writers melded scientific information and religious conviction, writing with an eye to shaping the values of their chosen audiences. But not all women wrote with an evangelical mission. Because discussions of moral and spiritual topics were an acceptable mode of expertise, other female authors, such as Ward, adopted a religious tone as a way to balance more academic information rather than necessarily as a means of spiritual persuasion.

Therefore, it can be argued that Ward's Christian doctrine works in the same way as her art: both allow her to push at the gender constraints enforced by nineteenth-century culture and society and to engage in the increasingly exclusive world of science. Thus, although the main texts of *Microscope teaching* and *Telescope teaching* are largely devoid of natural theology, there are occasional gestures toward a spiritual approach to science, most notably in the Prefaces, which end with a definite acknowledgment of God's role in science and nature. Significantly, in the latter, Ward closes her introduction by quoting from Herschel's *Treatise on astronomy*, which is followed by Psalm cxlvii, 3, 4: 'He healeth the broken in heart, and bindeth up their wounds. He telleth the number of the stars; he calleth them ALL by their names'.[43]

---

42 Mrs E.S. Perkins, *The elements of botany, with illustrations* (London, 1837), p. xxi.   **43** Ward, *Telescope teachings*, p. vii.

In this way, her text is astutely bolstered by the authority of the Bible and a male scientist.

Nonetheless, it would seem that for Ward, religion is more than merely a textual negotiation. For her, science and religion are totally compatible and complementary. While in some instances her Christian beliefs may be employed to couch certain modes of representation, religion, like science, seemed to open up another way of seeing. In both cases, the lesson to be learned is that there is so much more than what meets the eye, that 'we must not judge by outward appearance'.[44] Thus, Ward comes to the conclusion that 'certainly no entomologist can be an atheist'.[45]

Under the guise of correcting the problems of the naked eye and the limitations of what it saw, Ward used the microscope and the telescope. Yet, as we have seen, even with this technological aid the gaze is never innocent; it is always imbued with the cultural, political and subjective persuasions of the viewer.[46] For Ward, the new optical inventions of the nineteenth century may have enabled her to penetrate further into the very heart of life itself, confirming her religious convictions, but they also worked to counter the cultural myopia that saw women as intellectually inferior. However, although new technology enabled Ward to push at the boundaries of her nineteenth-century life, it was unfortunately also to be the cause of her death.

In the summer of 1869, she and Henry went on an ill-fated trip to Birr Castle to visit the widowed Lady Rosse and her sons. On 31 August she went with Henry to visit the tomb in the grounds of the old churchyard to pay her last respects. That afternoon, she went with Henry and Clare and Charles Parsons on a steam road locomotive designed and built by Lord Rosse. When turning a sharp corner she was thrown from her seat and killed, giving her the dubious honour of being the first person to be killed in a car accident. To mark the 150th anniversary of her death, in 2009 the Birr Estate mounted a commemorative plaque. While it is certainly appropriate to acknowledge the death of this pioneering woman, we must take care not to forget how she lived. She may have been unable to move beyond her personal religious beliefs, but she certainly pushed at the boundaries of gender constraints through textual, visual and discursive negotiations that produced interesting, enlightening and inspiring texts for many budding female science writers.

44 Ward, *Entomology in earnest*, p. 38.   **45** Ibid., p. 42.   **46** D. Spurr, *The rhetoric of empire* (London, 1993).

'Pilf'ring from the first creation': Dáibhí de Barra's *Parliament of weavers*

SEÁN Ó DUINNSHLÉIBHE

INTRODUCTION

Párliment na bhFíodóirí (*The parliament of weavers* hereafter) was composed by east Cork scribe and writer Dáibhí de Barra (1757/8–1851). In common with a great number of his Gaelic-speaking contemporaries, the author was educated locally at a hedge-school. Our knowledge of his life and career is scant: we have only a dozen or so surviving manuscripts in his hand and a small amount of correspondence between him and local antiquarians from which to piece together a biography.[1] Records show that by 1833 de Barra was farming a small holding of twenty-nine acres in Carrigtwohill, which he had inherited. His circumstances were accordingly modest and not infrequently quite difficult. As far as we can tell, he never travelled widely or left his home for any extended periods. His literary works also offer occasional insights into his life. The author was unusual in that at a time when the flow of Gaelic writing – prose writing in particular – was petering out, his own output was reasonably substantial. His surviving writings, comprising well in excess of 150 poems, over a dozen translations (all from English) and two original prose works, reveal a continuing preoccupation with the social and political issues of his day.[2] Varied topics and themes emerge in the work: reflections on the transience of human existence (a concern with mortality recurs) and the consequences of one's actions in life are the focus of several of his devotional poems;[3] in other works, nationalistic

---

1 For a short biographical account in English of Dáibhí de Barra's life, see *Dictionary of Irish biography* (Dublin, 2009), s.n. The most comprehensive account of de Barra's life and work can be found in B. Ó Conchúir, *Scríobhaithe Chorcaí* (Dublin, 1983), pp 8–13. I should like to thank my colleague, Dr Pádraigín Riggs, who read an earlier draft of this article and suggested several helpful amendments. I would also like to acknowledge the support of the Irish Research Council for the Humanities and Social Sciences, which funded this research.
2 Regarding his poetic output, almost 160 compositions alone are attributed to Dáibhí de Barra (the majority of these being in his own hand) in the catalogue description of the Irish-language manuscripts held in St Colman's College, Fermoy, see P. Ó Fiannachta, *Clár lámhscríbhinní Gaeilge: leabharlanna na cléire agus mionchnuasaigh – fascúl II* (Dublin, 1980), pp 108–12. For an account of his translations, see S. Ó Duinnshléibhe, 'Mar is fánach mac a' teacht go cruinn mar ' athair: Dáibhí de Barra's surviving translations' in C. Breathnach and C. Lawless (eds), *Visual, material and print culture in nineteenth-century Ireland* (Dublin, 2010), pp 257–70.   3 De Barra's devotional verse was collected together by the author in the form of an anthology in 1835; this manuscript (Fermoy MS F PB 6) is now held in St Colman's

sentiments are often to the fore as is a firm denunciation of the Protestant clergy – the Second Reformation, for instance, and the spread of proselytizing bible societies were an especial source of antipathy, as was the extortion of tithes by the Established church, and the two subjects feature in a cluster of poems that advert to the contemporary position of the oppressed Catholic underclass.

The parliament of weavers, likewise prompted by events in contemporary life, is primarily important because of its literary representation of the artisan and his craft and, to this end, it draws heavily both on Gaelic literary tradition and on a store of general stereotyped descriptions. The work was inspired in part by developments in the local industrial milieu (itself characterized by unrest and distress) which not only received widespread attention in local press but were also a source of much public comment and concern far beyond Cork and its hinterland. Contemporary prose accounts in Irish from the post-classical period (*c.*1650–1850) of events of the day are comparatively rare. For this reason, the *Parliament*, still largely unexamined,[4] is important because of its distinctive portrayal – highly-coloured and satirical as it may be – of the various actors and viewpoints involved. The evolution of the relevant textile industries in Cork and their respective adaptation (or lack thereof) to new technologies pioneered elsewhere have been charted in great detail by Andy Bielenberg.[5] De Barra's *Parliament* reflects particular aspects of the situation of weavers in the final quarter of the eighteenth century and the first quarter of the nineteenth, and the final part of the work, in particular, prefigures the severe industrial decline locally that would gather pace soon after. Cornelius Buttimer in his study of Gaelic life and literature in Cork in the pre-Famine period has demonstrated how native scribes and writers in the region did not operate within 'an isolated and introspective Irish-speaking community',[6] as once imagined, but sought to articulate in their works local reactions to specific events much further afield such as the Seven Years War as well as more general developments in Revolutionary and Napoleonic Europe. These writings also sometimes offer a window into the subject of communal

College, Fermoy. He called the work his 'Book of pious miscellanies' and it contains almost 190 pages of religious poetry, some of which (although unacknowledged) are translations into Irish of poetry in English.   **4** For a useful summary discussion of the work and an overview of the relevant scribal and intellectual milieu, see C.G. Buttimer, 'Gaelic literature and contemporary life in Cork, 1700–1840' in P. O'Flanagan and C.G. Buttimer (eds), *Cork history and society: interdisciplinary essays on the history of an Irish county* (Dublin, 1993), pp 585–654 [621–3]. The present author is preparing a critical edition of *The parliament of weavers*, which will be published in 2011.   **5** A. Bielenberg, *Cork's industrial revolution, 1780–1880: development or decline?* (Cork, 1991), pp 8–40. Dr Bielenberg has outlined the development of the textile industries in a broader national context in the following publications: A. Bielenberg, 'British competition and the vicissitudes of the Irish woollen industry, 1785–1923' *Textile History*, 31:2 (2000), 202–21; A. Bielenberg and P. Solar, 'The Irish cotton industry from the industrial revolution to partition', *Irish Economic and Social History*, 34 (2007), 1–28 and A. Bielenberg, *Ireland and the industrial revolution: the impact of industrial revolution on Irish industry, 1801–1922* (London, 2009), pp 11–51.   **6** Buttimer, 'Gaelic literature and contemporary life in Cork, 1700–1840', p. 588.

tension within their authors' community: in his article, Buttimer, for instance, cites two examples of *barántais* (a literary genre, taking the form of a parody of certain conventions of English law, in which individuals are brought to book for misdemeanours committed)[7] that deal with the contentious issues of landholding prices and labourers' wages. Turning his attention to *The parliament of weavers*, he contends quite rightly that this work allows us to observe similar 'communal stress [...] in full measure',[8] albeit that such stress pertains in this instance to matters primarily affecting the weaving fraternity. In the case of the *Parliament*, the result is not reportage of real-life events; rather de Barra reflects the contemporary circumstances of weavers through the prism of his native literary tradition in a comic and engaging manner. A mock-heroic register is employed regularly throughout, in particular in his description of the solemn parliamentary debates, which are given over to quite trivial and self-serving concerns. Further, the influence of medieval romance tales is in evidence at the beginning and end of the work, where the tone is set and reinforced respectively as well as in the occasionally archaic and alliterative style that the author adopts. Owing to its pervasive influence, and because of the need for careful attention to the literary features of the text, it is to the Gaelic tradition and analogues, rather than to the historical context, that I shall first turn.

THE LITERARY BACKGROUND: 'A TALE OF TWO PARLIAMENTS'

De Barra's work falls into two parts, each of which describes an imaginary parliament of weavers. The first of these assemblies has as its *locale* the author's neighbourhood of Carrigtwohill and is set towards the end of the eighteenth century (1790), while the second book, although situated in the same location, was composed over twenty-five years later and is set at the time of writing in 1826. The two books share a broadly similar plot structure, which can be summarized as follows: the weavers are summoned by their leader to assemble on an appointed date for the purpose of discussing the recent decline in their circumstances. Soon afterwards, the tradesmen gather in a local pub and proceed to elect a speaker, crier and committee, and the members remove themselves from the gathering in order to consider the state of the trade. The chief aim of their discussion is the enactment of a series of resolutions intended to revive their fortunes. After some debate and deliberation, the resulting acts are delivered to the assembly where they meet with enthusiastic approval. These acts or regulations consist of a variety of unpromising and deceitful measures (mostly

---

7 The name of this literary genre derives from Anglo-Norman and is equivalent to 'warrant' in English. For a discussion of the function of the *barántas* in the native tradition, see D. Kiberd, 'Dying acts: Ó Rathaille and others', *Irish classics* (London, 2000), pp 49–53 and N. Buttimer, 'Images of law in pre-Famine Gaelic Ireland' in G. Hofmann (ed.), *Figures of law: studies in the interference of law and literature* (Tübingen & Basel, 2007), pp 222–5. **8** Buttimer, 'Gaelic literature and contemporary life in Cork, 1700–1840', p. 621.

aimed at short-term advancement) which seem certain to drive the weavers further out of favour with their customers. A dissenting voice rises from the crowd, prevailing on them to see sense and to abandon the proposed decrees. At this juncture, a riotous debate ensues before the leader restores some order and instructs all present to return home, but not without first cautioning the weavers to enact the measures in full.

This general outline of events clearly recalls another literary work in Irish, *Pairlement Chloinne Tomáis* (*The parliament of Clan Thomas* hereafter), the most famous example of the parliament genre in the Gaelic literary tradition.[9] In order to demonstrate the degree to which *The parliament of weavers* is indebted to the earlier work, I offer the following brief description of the precursor text and its background. *The parliament of Clan Thomas* was written in the seventeenth century, in part to satirize the lower orders (known as *Clan Thomas* in the text) of a fragmenting Gaelic society whose opportunism may have resulted in its authors' reduced state. As the editor of the definitive edition of *The parliament of Clan Thomas* has shown, the work in its best versions falls into two books, the first of which (PCT I) consists of 'a cruel and sometimes bawdy satire on the rural labourers of south-west Munster in the early seventeenth century'. The second part, an imitation of PCT I written approximately fifty years later by another author, 'describes a similar imaginary parliament of labourers, small tenants and minor tradespeople from Leinster and eastern Munster, that sat near Mullingar at some time during the Commonwealth'.[10] The work proved to be immensely popular and was copied by generations of native scribes. As well as being frequently transcribed by Gaelic copyists, *The parliament of Clan Thomas* was often imitated by later authors. In point of fact, the work gave rise to a long literary progeny in Irish which was initiated in the mid-seventeenth century, and among the various targets satirized in these works were the native clergy and social climbers of one kind or another. *The parliament of weavers* is the last known example of the genre in the post-classical period and is one of the last works from this period to have come under the influence of *The parliament of Clan Thomas*.

De Barra's work not only copies the general structure of the earlier *Parliament*, which likewise consists of two parts, but also borrows motifs from it, most notably that of giving certain of his characters mocking sobriquets and surnames, in order to lampoon the weavers. Examples include the humorous surnames: Ó *Glugaráin*, Ó *Preicealláin* and Ó *Smulcacháin*, all of which are patterned on the common Gaelic surname form containing the patronymic Ó (grandson or descendant), but which stem in these instances from frivolous and insulting epithets: *Glugarán* can be

---

9 Relatively few parliament texts in Irish have come down to us. Of the four examples of the genre known to have survived, none was written before the seventeenth century. For a brief discussion of the subject, see B. Ó Cuív, *Párliament na mBan* (Dublin, 1952), p. xxxiv. A short summary of the main forms of the parliament genre as well as a discussion of some examples in Irish are given by A. Titley in 'Scéal bleachtaireachta', *Eiriceachtaí agus scéalta eile* (Dublin, 1987), 104–5. **10** N.J.A. Williams, *Pairlement Chloinne Tomáis* (Dublin, 1981), p. xi.

rendered as 'prattler';[11] *Preiceallán* as 'double-chinned one'[12] and *Smulcachán* can be variously translated as 'one having a prominent or ugly nose' or as 'a surly-looking person'.[13] De Barra sometimes adapts this motif to his subject matter and so, as well as referring to unfavourable attributes, the sobriquets are on occasion linked to the trade or its accoutrements, instances of which include *Diarmuid na Sumóg* and *Rághnall na Srangán*. The former can be translated approximately as 'Dermot of the rags or clouts'[14] (a rag was often used in the application of a weaver's size), while the latter can be rendered as 'Reginald of the twines or cords' (*srangán* may be a reference to the [hempen] cords that run from the laths at the top of the loom to the treadles at its base). Other motifs borrowed from *The parliament of Clan Thomas* are similarly adapted in line with the author's intention and thus the taking of oaths, which occurs frequently in the earlier *Parliament*, also appears in de Barra's work but in a manner more in keeping with the object of the satire; accordingly, the weavers swear fervently and with great gusto on their treadles, on the cross straps of their aprons and on their heddles. In a few instances, de Barra makes so bold as to incorporate into the weavers' remarks occasional sentences or short snatches of speech paraphrased from Clan Thomas' pronouncements. These remarks invariably consist of gibberish and are clearly intended to reinforce the comparison he is making. In a handful of cases, the mocking epithets assigned to the weavers so nearly resemble humorous epithets and surnames from the earlier *Parliament* that there can be no gainsaying the parallels; the weavers *Maonas na Feime* and *Domhnall an Díoscáin*, for example, plainly recall *Raghnall na Fime* (PCT II, l. 1394) and *Donnchadh Drochbhéasach Ó Díosgáin* (PCT I, ll. 99–100) of Clan Thomas respectively. In one instance, the same character, *Cormac Ó hAlpacháin* (PCT II, ll. 1384, 1672), appears in both works, although de Barra adds the epithet 'speisialta' to the character in his work as a means, perhaps, of lessening the act of appropriation. With these further echoes and repetitions, the association with Clan Thomas and their uncouth, self-serving ways is emphasized for the benefit of more 'knowing' readers/listeners familiar with the precursor text.[15] Interestingly, in both books of *The parliament of weavers*, flesh-

---

11 This substantive is based on the noun *gliogar*, see Revd P.S. Dinneen, *Foclóir Gaedhilge agus Béarla* (Dublin, 1927) and N. Ó Dónaill, *Foclóir Gaeilge-Béarla* (Dublin, 1977), s.v. 12 See Dinneen, *Foclóir Gaedhilge agus Béarla* and Ó Dónaill, *Foclóir Gaeilge-Béarla*, s.v. *preiceall*. 13 See Dinneen, *Foclóir Gaedhilge agus Béarla*, s.v. *smulchachán* and Ó Dónaill, *Foclóir Gaeilge-Béarla*, s.v. *smuilceachán*. 14 See Dinneen, *Foclóir Gaedhilge agus Béarla*, s.v. *somóg*. 15 Although de Barra's scribal activities involved the transcription of a range of earlier native works, no copy of *The parliament of Clan Thomas* has come down to us among the transcripts made by him of traditional material. Nicholas Williams has shown that the text itself was subject to frequent change as received versions of the *Parliament* were gradually revised in the eighteenth century by subsequent generations of scribes. This series of changes occasioned a shorter composite version of PCT, which predominated in the textual tradition in successive decades, see N.J.A. Williams, 'Nótaí éagsúla ar Phairlement Chloinne Tomáis', *Studia Hibernica*, 16 (1976), 76–7. The preponderance of literary borrowings and echoes between *The parliament of Clan Thomas* and *The parliament of weavers* strongly suggests that de Barra was acquainted with such a composite version when he set

and-blood characters exist alongside the aforementioned literary incarnations, some of whom we know from historical records (Tithe Applotment Books and Griffith's *Valuation*) to have been neighbours of de Barra's; although described as weavers in the *Parliament*, I have been unable to uncover any direct links between the trade and the individuals mentioned.[16] In lampooning the greed of contemporary weavers through satire and in overlaying his work with frequent and sometimes elaborate allusions to Clan Thomas, de Barra raises the subject of the *Parliament* beyond the level of a mere *querelle de clocher* to a work of broader appeal. Ironically, this also proves to be a short-coming. In the final analysis, what denies *The parliament of weavers* any claim to high literary merit is an over-reliance on *The parliament of Clan Thomas*; interesting and ingenious as some of de Barra's borrowings are, the reader feels at times that his work owes too much to the earlier satire.[17]

SOCIO-ECONOMIC CONTEXT TO *THE PARLIAMENT OF WEAVERS*

It is the enactments themselves and the debates surrounding them that provide the primary focus for much of what happens in *The parliament of weavers*. In de Barra's work, the weavers are consistently portrayed as an opportunistic and greedy set, bent on extracting money from their unwitting customers at all costs. These resolutions, presented in burlesque fashion, deal, inter alia, with matters relating to the retention of yarn for the weavers' own use, the administering of false measures, the inflation of prices of substandard cloth and the fixing of apprenticeship fees. The more elaborate the deception involved, the greater the weavers' approval of the enactments. In both books of *The parliament of weavers*, contributors to the debate take great pains to convince those assembled of the merits of the proposed course of action and of the benefits that will accrue to them in the long term. The following example, taken from the second book of the *Parliament*, is typical of the resolutions they are intent on enforcing:

> Muna mbeidh slinn is úim cheart agaibh is é an t-acht déinig meabhla,
> is bainíge roinnt chéadta do leataobh an tslabhra.
> Má bhíd na mná a' cannrán ná a' gearán gur cúng é,
> glaofam air fi an *huckabag* is glacfa' siad an ciúineas.
> Ó ardaíodh an pá dhúinn, gach lá beam a' famaíol;

about writing his own work. However, in the absence of any copies of the earlier work among his surviving manuscripts, internal testimony remains our most compelling evidence of this connection. **16** For the most part, the cast of characters who participate in the parliamentary assemblies changes from the first book to the second and so, for instance, in the latter book, a new leader and committee are elected to guide the weavers. **17** A similar criticism was levelled by Seán Ó Tuama at Aogán Ó Rathaille's satire, *Eachtra Thaidhg Dhuibh Uí Chróinín*, another of *The parliament of Clan Thomas'* literary progeny, see S. Ó Tuama, *Filí faoi sceimhle* (Dublin, 1978), p. 98.

is bíodh poitín a' bhracháin againn lán do gach dramhaíol.
Más tanaí é an t-éadach an tan dhéanfam é smearadh;
beidh tiugh, deighscéimheach nó go ndéinid é ghlanadh.
Ag sin díbh na dlithe, a shlua chliste na seoltha;
is ná brisige tríotha, nó díolfa' sibh as an rósta.[18]

If you are without proper reed or heddles, treachery is the course of action
    I decree,
Take several hundreds [of thread] from one end of the chain [= warp].
If housewives grumble or complain that [the cloth] is narrow,
We will call it a 'huckabag' weave and quieten they will.
Since our pay has been raised, we will pass every day going about idly;[19]
And let us have the dressing pot full of all kinds of dross.
[So that] if the cloth is thin when being smeared by us;
It will 'appear' thick [= closely-woven] and beautiful until they wash it.
These are the laws for you, o clever host of the looms,
And do not infringe them, or you will 'pay for the roast'.

The foregoing reference to the production of cloth for housewives along with several other similar references elsewhere in the text suggests that the artisans described in the *Parliament* were working at household level and that their textiles were intended for local consumption. The frequent use throughout of the terms *bannlá* ('bandle', a measure for homemade cloth usually twenty-four inches in length) and *slat* ('yard') to quantify their ware would seem to corroborate this interpretation.[20] On the whole, the false and deceitful devices that de Barra catalogues in the text are aimed at unsuspecting individual customers and, in most cases, the weavers attempt to justify this treachery by reference to their reduced circumstances, although there is also an implicit suggestion of *caveat emptor*. The fraud involving a 'huckabag' weave

18 NLI MS G 656:161. The spelling in the original here (and elsewhere) has been normalized in order to render quotations more intelligible to contemporary readers, but only insofar as the linguistic integrity of the extracts is not compromised. **19** Brenda Collins, Irish Linen Centre and Lisburn Museum, Lisburn, reminds me that the practice described in this line was one which 'Industrial Revolution employers' generally tried hard to end (pers. comm., Apr. 2010). I should like to thank Ms Collins very sincerely for her advice on matters of a technical nature. **20** The term *dosaein* ('hank') is used on a handful of occasions in the second book of the text, but this measure relates only to the manner in which cloth was spun. It should be stated that the exact nature of the weavers' dealings with their customers is not clearly outlined. What is more, there is no compelling evidence in the Parliament to imply the existence of a formal 'putting out' system between weavers and merchants or of other proto-industrial arrangements (current at the time of writing) between artisans and capitalized middlemen. For a description of the 'putting out' system, see W.H. Crawford, *Domestic industry in Ireland: the experience of the linen industry* (Dublin, 1972), pp 39 and 44–6 and David Dickson, *Old world colony: Cork and south Munster, 1630–1830* (Cork, 2005), pp 396ff.

mentioned above underlines the weavers' technical knowledge and ingenuity in this regard. 'Huckabag' is defined in the *Oxford English Dictionary* as follows: 'a stout linen fabric, with the weft threads thrown alternately up so as to form a rough surface, used for towelling and the like'.[21] This particular weave was especially suited to the kind of deception alluded to above for the reason that, being a form of twill weave with an uneven number of warp threads to weft threads, it was possible to remove some of the warp threads more easily from one side of the chain; that is, a number of threads [hundreds] could be more readily taken out of the reed that aligns them. This would make the appearance of the woven cloth structure seem different at one side, perhaps denser or tighter. As a huckaback weave is tight, and the web produced thereof is absorbent, a cloth could be represented as 'huckaback' for a use with which the housewife would be familiar, while the weaver would have got away with using an inappropriate reed or harness.[22] Incidental benefits of a corresponding kind are mentioned earlier in the text, for instance in the following decree taken from the first book:

> achtaímíd easnamh do bheith ar abhras gach mná
> gan faíonna ná fuíollach chur abhaile go brách.[23]

> we decree that there be a 'deficiency' in every housewife's yarn
> and never to hand back the [resultant] thrums or remnants.

As is clear from the quotation, the enactment proscribes the return to their rightful owner (a housewife in this instance) of any thrums or remnants left over after weaving; this does not refer, however, to the usual surplus but rather to additional leavings arising most probably from a deliberate adjustment of the ratio of the number of warp threads to weft threads. This is, I believe, the deficiency in the web to which de Barra is referring. Other examples of deliberate fraud are found in the text, but to list all instances would be to labour the point.

Although a trade society of weavers is not mentioned by name in the *Parliament*, the manner in which the dimensions and prices of cloth are set out in the form of legislative decrees carries undeniable overtones of a regulatory body.[24] Moreover, a

---

21 *Oxford English Dictionary*, vol. vii *Hat-Intervacuum* (Oxford, 1989, first ed. 1927), s.v. *huckaback*. **22** Personal communication by email from Brenda Collins, Irish Linen Centre and Lisburn Museum (Mar. 2004). **23** NLI MS G 656:140. **24** It is worth noting that the text contains no explicit references to either journeymen or masters. Reference is made, however, in the second book, to the conditions under which apprentices would be accepted for work, see NLI MS G 656:162–3. Apart from individual guilds and trade societies, other regulatory bodies came into existence during the eighteenth and nineteenth centuries. The most famous regulatory body of the time was the Linen board, which was set up in 1711 and dissolved in 1828, and whose primary function was 'to regulate and subsidise the growing industry', W.H. Crawford, *Domestic industry in Ireland: the experience of the linen industry* (Dublin, 1972), p. 3.

small number of motifs in de Barra's work echoes practices common to contemporary trade societies. The choice of a public house as a setting for both books, the taking of oaths during the two assemblies, as well as the reference in the second book to the need to keep their activities away from the attention of the local peelers and constabulary imply a definite degree of illegality. The meeting of tradesmen in public houses in order to force those in attendance to swear agreement to various conditions of work and to price rates was widespread; a series of acts of parliament outlawing these practices had been passed during the eighteenth century, the last of which came into effect in 1792.[25] In addition, an ironic reference to 'intermarriage' can be found in the decree below and the lines in question, although satirical in tone, are reminiscent of contemporary endogamous patterns of marriage found not infrequently among families working in the trade:

> Achtaímíd gach fiodóir ag a mbeidh scóiléad iníne
> dá tabhairt do mhac fiodóra chum ná saileofaí an síreach.[26]

> We decree that every weaver possessed of a slovenly daughter
> give her over to [another] weaver's son so as not to contaminate the line.

Given that women were typically responsible for the spinning of cloth, the virtue of this decree under normal circumstances might be the resultant pooling of skills. In this instance, however, the reference to 'scóiléad iníne' ('a slovenly daughter') is obviously satirical and implies the passing on of a liability rather than any increase in expertise. Earlier in the text it is mentioned, in the initial debate on the worthiness of individual decrees, that weavers' daughters should be married only to men of their own 'class' and not to fullers, tailors, shoemakers or any other category of worker, thereby improving the material situation of the couple and the trade.[27] This exclusivism is, at the very least, suggestive of the discriminatory pooling of skills found in many trade societies, albeit that such exclusivism consisted of restricting entrance to the trade to weavers' (members') sons. The tendency to limit entry to the trade in this way was often lambasted by outsiders as being unjustly restrictive and an impediment to the natural flow of supply and demand.[28]

---

25 John W. Boyle refers to these acts in his book, *The Irish labor movement in the nineteenth century* (Washington, DC, 1998), p. 8. An interesting account of an illicit gathering of a small group of wool-combers (who were subsequently tried for their actions), which took place around the time of writing of the second book of *The parliament of weavers*, can be found in the *Southern Reporter*, 6 Nov. 1826. Incidentally, wool-combers were the only branch of the textile industry in Cork at the time still to have an active society. **26** NLI MS G 656:140. Of further interest is the fact that, in the course of proceedings, two of the offices of the imaginary parliaments (that of speaker in the first book, and supreme chief of deliberations in the second) are given to the respective sons of the two leaders of the tradesmen, see NLI MS G 656:134 and 153 respectively. **27** NLI MS G 656:138. **28** M. Cronin, 'Work and workers in Cork city and county, 1880–1900' in C.G. Buttimer and P. O'Flanagan (eds), *Cork*

More generally, the act of assembling privately for the purpose of regulating prices, wages, fees etc., as described in detail in de Barra's composition, calls to mind the actual practice of combination, which was prevalent among many trade societies in Ireland in the eighteenth and nineteenth centuries. This practice has been commented on and described in great detail by historians such as Seán Daly and Maura Cronin in the case of Cork, by Brian Henry in respect of Dublin and in a more general context by John Boyle.[29] Combinations were widespread in Cork throughout the eighteenth century and continued to be so well into the nineteenth. Such was the prevalence of the practice in Cork that two separate anti-combination acts were passed – the first in 1764 (3 Geo. III, c. 17) and the second in 1772 (11 & 12, Geo. III, c. 18) – both of which pertained specifically to the region.[30] It is not clear in all cases exactly when a particular trade society came into existence, but we do know that weavers in Cork had established theirs some time before 1768, although no record of the specific date for the founding of the society has survived.[31] The sixties, seventies and eighties were turbulent and extremely unstable decades for local weavers, as individual branches of the industry enjoyed mixed fortunes. The woollen industry in Cork suffered a slow but steady decline for most of the second half of the century;[32] the linen industry in the south, forever overshadowed by the zenith of linen production and demand in the thirties, experienced a serious depression during the period 1771–3,[33] while the cotton industry in the region was only just beginning to establish itself. As a result, members of the trade were frequently active in clubbing together and, in some cases, were responsible for violent behaviour and the destruction of property as a consequence of their gatherings and enactments.[34] By then, a pattern had been set as industrial disturbance increased or declined throughout the second half of the eighteenth century in response to the prevailing, though not always unfavourable, economic conditions (the situation of the linen and cotton industries would improve somewhat during the final decades before beginning to fail towards the end of the century).[35] For instance, combinations among weavers in Cork were still taking place in the 1780s and early 1790s, due in a

history and society: interdisciplinary essays in the history of an Irish county (Dublin, 1993), pp 721–58 [727]. **29** S. Daly, *Cork: a city in crisis* (Cork, 1978); M. Cronin, *Country, class or craft? The politicisation of the skilled artisan in nineteenth-century Cork* (Cork, 1994); M. Cronin, 'Work and workers in Cork city and county, 1880–1900', pp 721–58; B. Henry, 'Industrial violence, combinations and the law in late eighteenth-century Dublin', *Saothar*, 18 (1993), 19–34; B. Henry, *Dublin hanged: crime, law-enforcement and punishment in late eighteenth-century Dublin* (Dublin, 1994); Boyle, *The Irish labor movement in the nineteenth century.* **30** With respect to the two anti-combination acts, see Daly, *Cork: a city in crisis*, pp 264 and 269 respectively. **31** Ibid., pp 253–4. **32** Bielenberg, *Cork's industrial revolution, 1780–1880: development or decline?*, p. 32. **33** See L.M. Cullen, *An economic history of Ireland since 1660* (London, 1972), p. 53; C. Rynne, *The industrial archaeology of Cork city and its environs* (Dublin, 1999), p. 15. **34** Daly outlines many of these disturbances in his work *Cork: a city in crisis*, see in particular, Appendix A, pp 253–314. **35** See Bielenberg, *Cork's industrial revolution, 1780–1880*, pp 8–40, for a detailed description of the fortunes of the relevant branches of the industry during this period.

number of cases to the fact that woollen operatives in the city had suffered great misfortune in the 1780s; 1784 proved to be something of an *annus horribilis* for the branch, with many of its workers being consequently forced on to the streets to protest.[36] In June 1791, not long after the time of writing (1790) of the first book of *The parliament of weavers*, a series of accusations was traded in the local newspaper, *Cork Hibernian Chronicle*, between cotton and linen weavers on the one side, and worsted weavers on the other, focusing on claims that respective sides had been combining for a number of years in the city to the detriment of the industry in general.[37] All of these disturbances form part of the pattern that had begun mid-century and it is against this backdrop of industrial unrest that de Barra composed the first part of his satire.

Ironically, by the time he set about writing the second book in 1826, combinations among weavers in Cork had all but ceased and the trade generally was so depressed that the weavers' ability to organize and unionize themselves effectively had virtually deserted them.[38] Many of the city's trade societies, prompted perhaps by the supposed Union of Trades, had been active in organized protest and violent disruption in the early twenties, but weavers had had no hand in these activities.[39] Notwithstanding the weavers' weakened position, the work seems to indicate strongly anti-unionization sentiments on de Barra's part. Without the benefit of hindsight, the author could not have fully appreciated the extent of the depression the industry was experiencing nor could he have known that the effective organization of the trade and its society would diminish significantly soon after. 1826, the year in which *The parliament of weavers* was completed, is a particularly significant one in the history of the industry. In fact, the second half of the 1820s along with subsequent decades proved to be a truly devastating period, resulting in famine and hardship for many involved with the trade. Dissatisfaction among the tradesmen of Cork (as elsewhere) was compounded by the assimilation in 1826 of the Irish and English currencies and the resultant decrease in the nominal value of wages.[40] Such was the depressed state of the trade in the mid-1820s that relief schemes were set up in Dublin and Cork in order to afford weavers temporary respite. The *Southern Reporter* (16 May 1826) describes a gathering of some 5,000 people in Cork city

36 Ibid., p. 32. An account of the march undertaken by weavers through the streets of Cork can be found in the *Cork Hibernian Chronicle*, 8 Apr. 1784. The years 1776–83 had brought short-lived respite to the industry because of wartime demand for woollen clothing. **37** The initial accounts given on both sides can be found in the *Cork Hibernian Chronicle*, 20 June 1791 and 23 June 1791 respectively. The calamitous effects of the rise of the cotton industry on woollen manufacture are alluded to by the worsted weavers in their contribution to the newspaper. **38** Combinations did persist among weavers in Bandon as late as the 1830s, owing to the profound set-back the town's cotton industry had suffered in the previous decade, see M. Cronin, 'The role of organized labour in the political and economic life of Cork city, 1820–1920' (PhD, U Leicester, 1979), p. 15. **39** Some scholars doubt whether such a union ever existed. The vexed question of the historicity of the union is discussed by Cronin, *Country, class or craft?*, pp 219–20. **40** Ibid., pp 36, 206; see also Daly, *Cork: a city in crisis*, p. 310.

centre, consisting for the most part of the wives and children of weavers from Blackpool and surrounding areas. The 'ragged procession', as it was described, made its way to the Mansion House bearing placards that read 'we want employment – ourselves and our families are starving'. While the protest was mostly peaceful (apart from a minor scuffle), the intention of the newspaper account was clearly to draw attention to the severe privations being suffered by weavers and their families. A related account can be found in the same newspaper a month or so later.[41] It retails an appeal submitted by the operative woollen, cotton and linen weavers, and wool-combers of the city of Cork, who were seeking relief employment at an allowance of one shilling per day in the hope of improving their circumstances. The support they received was short-lived, however, as relief funds soon dwindled. Maura Cronin gives the following summary of the state of the trade in the ensuing years:

> By 1827, journeymen weavers' wages had fallen to between four and six shillings, and a scheme of relief payments and subsidized emigration to England failed to substantially remedy the condition of the trade. By the early 1830s the situation had declined still further: subsidized emigration schemes were continued but unemployment still rose, and by February 1830, of the city's 160-plus cotton weavers, from 100 to 150 were idle.[42]

By the time de Barra had finished writing his *Parliament*, the industry's fate in the region was effectively sealed: the end of the Napoleonic Wars in 1815 and the accompanying reduction in demand for cloth production (primarily army clothing, coarse woollens and linen), the removal of the remaining protective duties in 1824 (a condition of the earlier Union of Ireland and Great Britain) and a general lack of mechanization had left weavers in Cork in a highly vulnerable position and they were no longer able to compete with their counterparts in Britain. The industry in the south would never recover its former importance thereafter. In view of this, by choosing to close the *Parliament* with a comment on the pointlessness of the gathering(s) and on the subsequent abandonment of the artisans by their customers, the author strikes a firmer and more final chord with readers in retrospect than was perhaps ever intended by him when completing his work.

SOCIAL, LITERARY AND FOLK STEREOTYPES OF THE WEAVER

The portrayal of the artisan and his craft in *The parliament of weavers* can be appreciated and the satirical thrust of the text enjoyed without a thoroughgoing knowledge of *The parliament of Clan Thomas* or of the socio-economic conditions obtaining at the time of writing. The various descriptions of the weavers as a greedy, dirty set,

41 *Southern Reporter*, 15 June 1826. **42** Cronin, 'The role of organized labour in the political and economic life of Cork city, 1820–1920', p. 31.

given in turn to improvidence and laziness, and to gambling and drinking, have parallels in contemporary accounts produced by travel writers and sundry officials, as well as in descriptions in folklore and literary genres. For this reason, it could be argued that parts of de Barra's work owe their inspiration as much to the store of common stereotyped descriptions that can be found in many of the foregoing sources as other parts of the *Parliament* do to the contexts already outlined. Weavers were always known for their resourcefulness and cunning in extracting better prices for their produce. Because workers were often paid according to the length of the web, the Congested Districts Board – as late as 1900, and possibly later – was forced to address the custom among weavers in Donegal of stretching tweeds between two donkeys in order to add measure to the cloth![43] To take an example closer to the time in which *The parliament of weavers* was composed, Cesar Otway in his submission to *Report of the Royal Commission on the hand loom weavers* (1840) frequently refers to the dishonesty of the fraternity.[44] It was his view that the frauds perpetrated by weavers had brought the profession into serious disrepute. He claimed that the embezzlement and detention of yarn were common among practically every category of weaver he encountered on his travels in Ireland; only the silk weavers of Dublin, according to him, did not engage in the practice.[45] The following is an illustrative account from the same source of a local trial in Co. Down, which indicates the extent of the fraudulence prevalent among weavers of the locality (in a factory context):

> At the petty sessions of Banbridge, from 11th October 1836 to 4th October 1838, there were 548 cases tried for the detention of webs beyond due time, and 32 cases for the embezzlement of yarn; one firm alone, employing only 1,500 weavers, had 115 cases tried within the time I have mentioned for detention of yarn, and three cases for embezzlement of the web.[46]

The motif of the underhand and fraudulent tradesman or merchant is, of course, known also in literature, and the image can be found at least as far back as medieval times in French *fabliaux* or among the popular social stereotypes satirized in *Estates Literature*, where tradesmen are often guilty of administering false measures and pass off substandard produce as worthy, merchantable goods. Folklore, a subject less

---

43 This information was communicated to me by the late Mairéad Dunlevy (pers. comm., June 2003), who in turn had received it from the late Dr Muriel Gahan, whose father, Townsend Gahan, worked as an inspector for the Congested Districts Board. **44** It should be borne in mind, however, that at the time Otway was preparing his report he was very much in favour of bringing the handloom weaving system to an end; this conviction may well have coloured some of his opinions and observations. **45** C. Otway, *Report of the royal commission on the hand loom weavers*, HC 1840 (43), xxiii, pt. 3, p. 613. W.H. Crawford, on the other hand, expresses the contrary view that 'quite a lot of fuss was made about weavers embezzling yarn but it was not so serious as it sounded, for comparatively small quantities could have been involved and inspection of the webs was a sufficiently effective deterrent', *Domestic industry in Ireland*, p. 54. **46** Ibid., p. 652.

removed from de Barra's realm of knowledge than the aforementioned examples, offers similar motifs. Here, for instance, the image of the unscrupulous merchant or tradesman is common: Stith Thompson in his *Motif-index of folk-literature* cites examples of stories concerning millers and tailors in which a closely related motif can be found.[47] Although the figure of the weaver in Irish folk tradition awaits proper treatment, certain tales and other narrative material (*seanchas*) occurring in published collections of folklore suggest that such a reputation for dishonesty is likewise echoed in native oral tradition.[48] A well known tale in Ireland, based on the motif of 'man admitted to neither heaven nor hell' (Q565)[49] and which recounts the fate of a dishonest tradesman after death, provides a good example. In this story, we encounter a weaver who, following a life of underhand dealing, reaches the gates of Heaven, only to be summarily dismissed by St Peter down to Hell and burdened on his journey with all the clews (*ceirtlíní*) he has embezzled while alive. To this fardel is added the embezzled skeins of a tailor whom he meets along the way and who slyly offloads them on to the unsuspecting weaver. On reaching Hell, the Devil refuses the weaver entry, believing mistakenly (owing to the latter's stuttering reply) that there are sixty weavers outside rather than one. He orders 'them' off, protesting a lack of space. Unwilling to give up, the weaver pokes his protuberant nose through the keyhole only to set it alight. He runs thence back to earth through rivers, streams and marshes in an effort to quench his burning nose and there he still remains in the guise of Jack-o'-lantern, presumably as punishment for the transgressions he committed during his lifetime.[50] Interestingly, the belief that Heaven was unattainable for weavers on account of their treacherous nature is actually mentioned by one of the artisans towards the end of the *Parliament* and the subject sets off a brief debate among the gathering.[51]

In the following oral account we learn how the weavers' distinctive brand of professional fraudulence came to acquire a particular name in Irish. The excerpt in question was collected in the 1940s by Donnchadh Ó Céileachair, the Irish-language short-story writer, from his father, Dónall Bán Ó Céileachair (1871–1950), a renowned tradition bearer from Cúil Aodha in west Co. Cork (who was also the source of the preceding tale). He has this to say about weavers generally:

47 S. Thompson, *Motif-index of folk literature: a classification of narrative elements in folktales, ballads, myths, fables, mediaeval romances, exempla, fabliaux, jest-books and local legends* (Bloomington, IN, 1955–8), pp 507–8. 48 See, for instance, P. Ó Crualaoi, *Seanachas Phádraig Uí Chrualaoi* (Dublin, 1982), pp 201–2. This is a collection of traditional lore (much of it in verse form) from west Co. Cork, which includes a typical story about weavers' fraudulent behaviour. See Irish Folklore Commission MS 822:481 for a further version of the story. 49 S. Thompson, *Motif-index of folk literature*, p. 261. Reference is made by Seán Ó Súilleabháin to this motif in his *Handbook of Irish folklore* (Detroit, MI, 1970), pp 68–9. 50 This version of the tale is given in D. Ó Céileachair, 'Conus a deintí éadach sa tseana-shaoghal', *Béaloideas*, 14 (1944), 285–6. 51 NLI MS G 656:165. The artisan in question was one Uilliam Ó Céileachair of Baile an Bhriotaigh. This was a widely held folk belief, see Ó Súilleabháin, *Handbook of Irish folklore*, pp 68–9.

Bhí sé d'ainm ar mhórán de na figheadóirí ná rabhadar ana-mhacánta. Bhídís a' coimeád cuid de ga'haon tsnáth a gheobhaidís chun abhrais a dhéanamh dóibh féin. Ní goid ná fuadach a thugaithí air sin – cribeáil a ghlaoidhtí air.[52]

(Many weavers had the name of not being very honest. They used to keep back some of the thread they received in order to make yarn for themselves. The practice was known not as theft or robbery but as 'cribeáil').

The latter term is most likely based on the English verb 'crib', which means to steal and is itself derived from thieves' slang.[53] It is telling that a specific term to describe the practice came into use in the Irish of the region, a fact which suggests that such fraudulence was all too common among weavers in that part of the county.

The physical appearance of the weavers in the *Parliament* is remarked on both directly and indirectly. Some of the mocking epithets given to characters in de Barra's work refer, for instance, to less attractive physical attributes or even deformity: *garbh-chliabhach* ('rough-bodied'); *cos-dhreoite* ('having a withered foot'); and *caol-scrogach* ('thin-necked') are just some examples. Although these epithets are suggestive of *The parliament of Clan Thomas*, there is no doubting also their association with the trade and with received ideas about its members' appearance, particularly when taken together with other internal evidence in de Barra's satire. At the beginning of the second book, for example, the new leader of the weavers, their 'bishop designate' (*easpag-d[h]amhna*), Tomás Firéast, is visited, while sleeping, by a spectral figure (*sighebhrogha*) whom Tomás recognizes from a cursory observation of the phantom's appearance to have once been a weaver:

> Bíogas Tomás as a shuan go bhfeacaidh ag colbha a leapa fuirm fir thrua, dhroch-dhealbhach agus naprúinín beag, smeartha óna imleacán go leath a cheathrún air agus drannadh beag gáire ina bhéal, ionnas go mba léir do as a fhionnachruth créad ba cheard dho, gurab ann ró rádh Tomás ris [. . .].[54]

(Tomás starts from his sleep and sees at the [outer] edge of his bed the outline of a man pitiful to behold and badly formed, who had on a small greasy apron (running) from his navel halfway down his thighs and was wearing a small grin on his mouth, so that it was obvious to Tomás from the phantom's old worn appearance what his occupation was, and so Tomás spoke to him thus [. . .]).

Furthermore, during the quarrel that ensues at the very end of the *Parliament* when weavers fight among themselves, some of the barbs they exchange centre on each other's ugly and slovenly appearance.[55] The notion that one could tell a weaver from his grubby and unhealthy look was common and is remarked upon by Otway in the

---

52 Ibid., pp 284–5.   **53** See *Oxford English Dictionary*, vol. iv *Creel-Dusepere* (Oxford, 1989, first ed. 1927), s.v. crib[1].   **54** NLI MS G 656:147.   **55** Ibid., pp 163–4.

aforementioned report. He describes as follows the weavers' working conditions and diet before alluding to the concomitant effects these usually had on their health and appearance:

> The physical condition of the weavers appears to me to be worse than that of any class of Irishmen. The length of time they continue at work, and the damp, unwholesome cabins they work in [a disgrace to any country that would permit such a state of things], appears one great cause of their inferiority. To this we must add their low diet [...] I could not pass a weaver by without knowing him to be one; and I never saw a weaver that had not dyspepsia written in his countenance.[56]

The tendency among weavers to fritter away their earnings on gambling and alcohol also comes in for censure by Otway[57] although he is careful not to suggest that such behaviour was confined only to members of the fraternity. This improvidence is hinted at in *The parliament of weavers* on a number of occasions. At the beginning of the first book, we are told that the leader of the trade, Séamas Ó Achiarainn, is virtually penniless despite his years of weaving, having no savings to boast of for his time and effort. Subsequently, it is implied that penury is the lot of the trade generally and their financial position is compared unfavourably to that of other professions (farmers, smiths, shoemakers and publicans) who have been prospering lately. Moreover, during the second assembly we learn that, in the weeks leading up to the parliament, weavers make a point of restricting themselves to one meal a day in order to save a shilling for beer on the occasion of their meeting. Such is the demand for alcohol at the gathering that two female weavers are obliged to leave their place in the parliament in order to offer assistance to the attending womenfolk in administering the ale. References to weavers' fondness for alcohol survive elsewhere in Gaelic literature: for instance, Co. Mayo poet, Antaine Raiftearaí (1779–1835), himself reputedly the son of a weaver, in a song of praise of the trade mentions how '[gur] maith é i dteach óil fear chaite an spóil' and in a poetic dialogue between Donncha Ó Céirín (a poet and journeyman weaver) and An Tiarna Barrach (a schoolmaster in Listowel), Ó Céirín is accused by the latter of having been reduced in circumstances through gambling and drinking ('imirt is ól ar bord is crosaibh an

---

56 *Report of the royal commission on the hand loom weavers*, HC 1840, p. 600. John Dickey, poet and journeyman weaver, describes himself as a 'a lazy-greasy weaver' in a composition he penned in 1818, see John Hewitt, *Rhyming weavers and other country poets of Antrim and Down* (Belfast, 1974), p. 21. A similar description, i.e. 'fiodóir smeartha' ('a greasy weaver'), is found in a Gaelic composition, 'Barántas an bhata', which one Séamas Ó Catháin composed, see P. Ó Fiannachta, *An Barántas 1. Réamhrá téacs malairtí* (Maynooth, 1978), p. 45 [B4 l. 241]. **57** *Report of the royal commission on the hand loom weavers*, HC 1840, p. 663. Crawford makes the point that because of the monotony of working at a loom for long hours 'many a weaver was glad of the excuse to leave his loom for a spree if the work was not too pressing', *Domestic industry in Ireland*, p. 34.

tsaoil do lagaigh do stóir is ní ceolta bladair mo scéal').[58] Clearly, such a store of stereotyped descriptions, which emphasizes the reputed greed and improvidence of weavers as well as their supposedly unhealthy appearance and unfailing dishonesty, influenced de Barra's portrayal of the fraternity and, to judge from oral sources, was not only current in his day but persisted well into the twentieth century.

CONCLUDING REMARKS

The terms in Irish employed by the author to describe different weaves and textiles, some forms of which are not known elsewhere, make the *Parliament* a rich source of Irish-language terminology on the subject. The great majority of these terms suggest manufacture from either wool or linen. Although the types of cloth (and weaves) mentioned in the enactments alter somewhat from the first book to the second, these changes are predominantly in line with the prevailing trends of regional production in the relevant branches of the industry in the final quarter of the eighteenth century and first quarter of the nineteenth. To cite an illustrative example, the only mention of mixed/union goods in the text, *slait lín et cotúin* ('a yard of mixed cotton', that is, one in which cotton weft was woven with a linen warp), occurs in the first part (1790) of the *Parliament*;[59] unsurprisingly no reference is made to such fabrics in the following book (1826) as 'mixed' cottons were already being replaced by the manufacture of pure cotton as early as the 1780s and were no longer common in the first quarter of the nineteenth century.[60] Despite the fact that de Barra was obviously

58 The lines quoted here are drawn from Ciarán Ó Coigligh (ed.), *Raiftearaí – amhráin agus dánta* (Dublin, 1987), p. 48 and Pádraig de Brún, 'Filí agus filíocht Chiarraí Thuaidh (1700–1850)' (MA, UCC, 1963), p. 428 respectively. Raiftearaí's description may be rendered literally as 'the caster of the spool is good in (= excels in) the public house' while the second quotation may be translated as: 'gambling and drinking as well as the crosses of this world have weakened your resources, and not an insincere "strain" is there in my account.' On a related note, Jane Gray makes some interesting observations on the social meaning of drinking in the poetry of the Ulster 'rhyming (weaver) poets' and on the perceived need for moral improvement among them found in their work, see Gray, 'Gender and uneven working-class formation in the Irish linen industry' in Laura L. Frader and Sonya O. Rose (eds), *Gender and class in modern Europe* (Ithaca, NY, 1996), pp 37–56 at p. 50. **59** NLI MS G 656:138 and 139. **60** For references to the rise in use of mixed cottons from the mid-eighteenth century and to their subsequent decline after the turn of the following century, see Bielenberg, *Cork's industrial revolution, 1780–1880: development or decline?*, pp 12–13 and 21ff as well as Rynne, *The industrial archaeology of Cork*, p. 114. The production of cotton was stimulated by a government bounty on mixed goods which came into place in the 1750s, see C. Ó Gráda, *Ireland: a new economic history, 1780–1939* (Oxford, 1994), p. 274ff. By 1790, machine-spun cotton had become stronger and it was used to replace the linen warp. Further, Brenda Collins (Irish Linen Centre and Lisburn Museum) informs me that by the mid 1820s mixed cottons 'were being power woven successfully and cheaply and so there would have been no market for handwoven ones, certainly not as far away from the English market as Cork' (e-mail communication, Apr. 2010).

quite familiar with the various processes involved in the production of cloth as well as with changing trends in fashion, and may himself have been the victim of dishonest weavers, it should be emphasized that the author offers no explanation anywhere in his work as to the specific nature of his grievances with the trade and its practitioners, that is, of course, presuming he had ever been so aggrieved. Needless to say, the question of auctorial motive or intention is problematic and the dangers of adopting an overly deterministic approach in the case of a work such as this need to be borne in mind. Although efforts have been made in the essay to delineate the relevant literary and socio-economic milieux as well as to describe some of the stock images of weavers that abounded in tradition and contemporary discourse, the parodic nature of *The parliament of weavers* along with its inter-textual relationship with *The parliament of Clan Thomas* complicate matters to a significant degree.[61] Ultimately, the meshing of literary strands and contemporary events remains the salient feature of the text and unquestionably lends colour, humour and depth to the work. The *Parliament* is of importance too as an unofficial (partly insider)[62] source, revealing as it does some of the ways in which weavers were apparently willing to exploit their knowledge of the technology they used on a daily basis for their own self-serving purposes; it also uncovers the resentment which this must have aroused in, at least, some of those who were accordingly duped by them.

What, then, of the reception of *The parliament of weavers*? De Barra's satire survived only in manuscript form until the early years of the twentieth century, when it first appeared in print.[63] The majority of extant Gaelic manuscripts date to the post-classical period and the bulk of these are paper manuscripts written prior to the 1830s. By the time Dáibhí de Barra finished his work, the scribal tradition had been in sharp decline for some years. In view of this, it is interesting to note that *The parliament of weavers* circulated to a certain extent in manuscript: in total seven copies of the work (or parts thereof) have come down to us and at least one other copy is now lost. The reception the text enjoyed is evidenced not only by surviving copies but, perhaps, more so by the knowledge that a contemporary of de Barra's, one Uileag Ó Céirín (or Ulick Kerins), from Castleisland in Kerry, who was by turns a poet, scribe,

61 For a comprehensive survey of parody and its various forms as well a discussion of intertexuality as it relates to parody, see S. Dentith, *Parody* (London, 2000).   **62** While I do not wish to suggest that the author was himself a weaver, I have chosen to employ the label 'partly insider' in this context to allow for the very strong possibility that de Barra (or those close to him) had frequent dealings with weavers, which, if true, would lend his work the (insider) perspective of those at the receiving end of the weavers' fraudulent practices.   **63** Such was also the fate of most Irish-language works of this kind during the eighteenth and first half of the nineteenth century: they were written, and circulated, predominately in manuscript form. The earliest edition of the text appeared during the years 1902–3, see É. Ó Foghladha, 'Parlaimint na bhFíodóirí', *Banba* Bealtaine (1902), 69–72; Nollaig (1902), 112–13; Féil Bhrighde (1903), p. 127. A second edition appeared some years later, see (author not given) 'Parlaiméid na bhFigheadóirighe: re Dathi de Barra ó Charrig Thuathaill', *Irish Rosary*, 17 (1913), 586–7, 667–8, 754–5, 842–3, 969–70. These editions comprise only one of the two books of the satire. The *Parliament* has yet to be translated into English.

bible teacher and weaver, took it upon himself – so angered was he by de Barra's satire – to write in prosimetric form a spirited response to the *Parliament*. In his work, which dates to 1845, Ó Céirín counters what he regards as an unwarranted attack on the weaving fraternity, who have suffered greatly in the preceding decades. Framed in the *barántas* tradition, his work not only attacks de Barra's motives but also casts aspersions on the latter's origins as well as calling into question his abilities as a writer. In the textual tradition, the *Parliament* and Ó Céirín's response are found together in the majority of surviving copies, clearly on account of the direct connection between the two works. Of greater interest is the fact that some of those who copied the work were themselves weavers or connected to the profession; this suggests that members of the trade showed more than a passing interest in the two works, and may indeed indicate that the *Parliament* and Ó Céirín's rejoinder excited a certain amount of debate on the subject among concerned tradesmen.[64]

---

64 The copyist of the portion of the *Parliament* that occurs in RIA MS 24 P 45:78–80 was one Daith Ó Lurcáine (David Larkin), a weaver resident in Fieries, Co. Kerry. Seán Ó Catháin, the scribe of the exemplar (and oldest known, but now lost, copy) of Ó Céirín's response (two copies of this exemplar survive, Cork Archives MS IE 0627 G. 8:151–61 and UCC MS T 11:239–56), was son of the famous Kerry weaver, Séamas Neamhurchóideach Ó Catháin (James 'Harmless' O'Keane), a resident of Brosna, see P. de Brún, 'Lámhscríbhinn Ghaeilge ó thuaisceart Chiarraí', *Stud. Hib.*, 4 (1964), 197–9.

Dominick McCausland and Adam's ancestors: an Irish evangelical responds to the scientific challenge to biblical inerrancy[1]

PATRICK MAUME

Dominick McCausland (1806–73), a Conservative lawyer from a Church of Ireland landed family, moved from writing on biblical prophecy to trying to reconcile a literal reading of Genesis with geology and archaeology. Among other things, he argued that Genesis described only the creation of Adamite man, allegedly the only form of humanity capable of generating civilization, while pre-Adamite races were condemned to stasis and disappearance before the expanding descendants of Japhet.[2] This essay discusses how McCausland's denunciations of evolutionary theory selectively impose material from contemporary popular science over a framework supplied by the pre-millennialist school of biblical interpretation.

Dominick McCausland was the third son of the landowner Marcus Langford McCausland of Roe Park, near Limavady. McCausland's father died when he was young; as a result, his upbringing was dominated by his mother, who recognized his intelligence and expected great things from him.[3] Initially, he was educated in England and the Royal School, Dungannon (1820–2), progressing to Trinity College Dublin, from where he graduated in 1827, winning the college gold medal for science. McCausland studied Hebrew,[4] a fact that indicated he was intended for the Church of Ireland ministry. Shortly after graduation he unsuccessfully sat the Trinity College fellowship examination (Fellows had to be clergymen); then, he broke down from overwork. After two years' convalescence, his mother urged him to try again, but McCausland chose to study for the bar. His decision was influenced by the fact that Trinity fellows were expected to be celibate, and perhaps his exposure to the anti-ecclesial views of John Nelson Darby, with whom his biblical commentaries suggest some affinity, also had an impact. Furthermore, although McCausland was a member of the Church of Ireland and one of his sons became an

1 Thanks to Paul Bew, Derval Fitzgerald, Greta Jones, David Livingstone and James McGuire. 2 For a history of pre-Adamite theory, see D.N. Livingstone, *Adam's ancestors: race, religion and the politics of human origins* (Baltimore, MD, 2008). 3 An elder brother, John Kennedy McCausland, distinguished himself as an officer in India in the 1840s and 1850s, becoming a lieutenant-general. 4 W.D. Ferguson in D. McCausland, *Sermons in stones; or, scripture confirmed by geology* (London, 1873), p. xxxi.

Anglican clergyman, he displays a noticeably 'low' ecclesiology; at one point he claimed that any genuine post-apostolic church of Jesus must be obscured and humbled. One of his criticisms of the Roman church was that it replicated the superseded Jewish temple priesthood; this was a standard Protestant accusation of judaizing against Rome, to which the equivalent Catholic accusation was that Protestantism displayed pharisaic text-based legalism.[5]

From 1837, although he lived in Dublin, McCausland practised on the North-West Circuit, which included his native Co. Londonderry. In 1859, he was appointed crown prosecutor by Conservative attorney-general James Whiteside.[6] Shortly after taking up this position, McCausland was elected father of the circuit (that is, senior barrister presiding at circuit dinners) by his colleagues, who liked his shyly courteous and conciliatory manner; he retained this position until his death (28 June 1873).

McCausland devoted his leisure to compiling and revising theological works. In 1841, he published *The latter days of the Jewish Church and nation, as revealed in the Apocalypse*; this was followed by *The times of the Gentiles as revealed in the Apocalypse* (1852). Both were revised and combined as *The latter days of Jerusalem and Rome as revealed in the Apocalypse* (1859).[7] In 1856, he published *Sermons in stones; or scripture confirmed by geology*, which had eleven editions in McCausland's lifetime and was translated into Italian, German, French and modern Greek.

The first edition of *Sermons in stones* advocated monogenism (the belief that all human beings descended from Adam and Eve, whose creation McCausland placed within the traditional biblical chronology);[8] but by 1864, when he published *Adam and the Adamite*, McCausland had adopted pre-Adamism, which was the belief that Adam was the ancestor of certain races only and other human races derive from separate earlier creations.[9] In this respect, McCausland was influenced by Edward William Lane, as is evident from several references to *The genesis of the earth and of man* (2nd ed. 1860).[10] Lane's arguments include ideas about the supposed superiority of inflectional Caucasian and Semitic languages over the agglutinative languages of other peoples, which McCausland replicates.[11]

McCausland's views of human history are expanded in his published YMCA lecture *Shinar* (1867), and receive final expression in *The builders of Babel* (1871), which traces the descendants of Ham, Shem and Japheth after their separation at the Tower of Babel; along with his previous major books, this can be seen as an universal history of mankind within a rethought biblical frame of reference, a genre familiar in earlier

5 D. McCausland, *Builders of Babel* (London, 1867), pp 198–9. **6** In 1867, McCausland lectured the Dublin Church of Ireland Young Men's Society on the Tower of Babel and how archaeology and ethnography allegedly upheld the inerrancy of scripture; Whiteside and his ally Joseph Napier used the YMCA to identify and encourage bright young Conservative recruits in the defence of church and constitution. **7** Throughout this article, *Latter days* will refer to this revised and combined volume. **8** McCaulsand, *Adam and the Adamite* (London, 1868), pp 163–4n. **9** *Adam and the Adamite* went through five editions, the last in 1882. **10** For example, *Adamite*, pp 171–3, 298. **11** Livingstone, *Adam's ancestors*, pp 100–3.

centuries but falling into disrepute even as McCausland wrote. Nonetheless, McCausland devoted great effort to revising his works to keep up with new research and rethink his ideas. According to the memoir by his friend William Dwyer Ferguson, which was affixed to the twelfth edition of *Sermons in stones* published shortly after McCausland's death, he revised the third edition of *Adam and the Adamite* by dictating revisions even when he could no longer hold a pen. But, for all McCausland's efforts, the Ferguson memoir conveys a strong sense of unfulfilled promise. McCausland's work is marked by pessimistic undercurrents that reflect both his pre-millennial belief that the Christian millennium would be preceded by a time of trial and apostasy, and the increasing embattlement of Church of Ireland Toryism in the era of disestablishment.

McCausland's first major work was a commentary on the Book of Revelation. Its prophecy schema resembles that of John Nelson Darby – futurist, dispensation-alist and pre-millenarian.[12] As such, McCausland believed that instead of the post-millennialist view that the spread of Christianity would continually improve the world, culminating in a thousand years' happiness before the return of Jesus,[13] the world would sink further into turmoil and apostasy until Jesus returned to defeat Antichrist and begin the millennium. And, as a futurist, McCausland held that although enough of the prophecies of the Apocalypse had been fulfilled to confirm their divine inspiration, most remain unfulfilled; these would be realized not throughout history past and present (historicism), but in a future age or dispensation (dispensationalism), beginning with the return of the Jews to Palestine, which McCausland thought was imminent. While McCausland regretfully noted the re-imposition of Ottoman rule over Syria (1840) after its temporary conquest by Mehmet Ali of Egypt (which some evangelicals predicted would lead to the return of the Jews), he predicted the region would remain chaotic until stability was achieved by restoring the Jews to their ancestral home.[14] Such futurism is based on a Protestant concern that the Bible should be self-interpreting, whereas historicism implies it can only be understood through extra-textual knowledge of obscure and perhaps fictitious events of medieval history.[15]

Like Darby, McCausland believed that the Bible's primary concern was with the Jews, and the era of the Gentile Church was a mere parenthesis.[16] However, whereas Darby expected true believers to be caught up into Heaven before the Tribulation presided over by Antichrist, McCausland predicted that rationalism would produce universal Gentile apostasy with true faith preserved only among the Jews during the Tribulation. Like many Protestant commentators, he saw Rome as the city of Antichrist, the Church of Rome as the mystery of iniquity described in scripture, and the rise of Tractarianism within the Church of England as a sign of reviving papal

12 For the Darbyite schema, see G. Marsden, *Fundamentalism and American culture* (Oxford, 1980). 13 McCausland repeatedly attacks this view; see, for example, D. McCausland, *Latter days of Jerusalem and Rome* (London, 1859), pp 369–70. 14 *Latter days*, pp 299–300. 15 Ibid., p. 295. 16 Ibid., pp 138, 308.

power.[17] He admitted that the Italian crisis of 1858–9, which coincided with the final version of his book, was destroying the temporal power of the papacy; but he believed its spiritual power, stronger and more deadly, would thereby increase. The conservative McCausland supposed that the then current tendency towards democracy would lead by inevitable reaction to despotism, and that the papacy, the most effective despotism, would triumph as a result. However, he differs from similar commentators in his insistence that the biblical Antichrist was not the papal institution but an individual future pope installed as temporal ruler in Jerusalem; his defeat by the risen Christ would lead to the millennium and the saints would rule the earth from the New Jerusalem (brought down from heaven) until a Satanically inspired revolt of subject peoples heralded the Last Judgment.

Certainly, other versions of millennialism predicted a world inhabited entirely by saints; but, this image of a race of saints ruling less regenerate humanity from an earthly New Jerusalem may also be an expression of colonial siege mentality. McCausland dourly predicts that the ability of Antichrist to disguise himself as an angel of light means that he will be a rationalist social reformer. He also suggests that the mark of the Beast would be offered as a compromise to those refusing to accept Antichrist as a religious leader but willing to acknowledge his political supremacy; this concept echoes contemporary Tory-evangelical condemnations of Whig compromise with political Catholicism.[18]

Further contemporary references can be found in McCausland's use of ethnographic research in seeking the lost ten tribes of Israel, whom he believed to have lapsed into idolatry and lost awareness of their identity. In *Latter days*, McCausland investigates the Karens of Burma[19] and the Hazara of Afghanistan and wonders whether the Afghans may be the lost tribes who will revert to Judaism and march eastward to rescue their brethren of Judah from Antichrist. He suggests that the recent opening up of the Chinese Empire (by the Opium War) was providential, since the lost tribes might be within its borders.[20] Of particular relevance to this essay, he argues that geological discoveries show that the earth was initially covered by sea without any dry land; hence it is apt that in its latter days there should be no sea, as is stated in the Apocalypse:

> May not this be fulfilled, without involving in its fulfilment physical impossibilities, by the conversion of the surface of our globe, by volcanic disturbances, into a world of islands, without any of those extensive continents or oceans which now exist?[21]

McCausland's thought is strongly binary; here Jew and Gentile, elsewhere scientist and religionist, or Semite and Japhetite. In each, McCausland presents himself as

---

17 Ibid., pp 441–2. **18** Ibid., p. 203. For an earlier pre-millennialist interpretation of nineteenth-century British and Irish history, with particular reference to Catholic Emancipation, see Patrick Maume (ed.), *Irish recollections*, by Charlotte Elizabeth Tonna (Dublin, 2004). **19** *Latter days*, p. 48. **20** Ibid., p. 300. **21** Ibid., p. 483.

expounder of the divine plan by which these divisions are to be healed. His reasoning is lawyer-like in combining insistence on strict respect for the text with the wildest creative interpretation, which is presented as unquestionably correct. For example, when discussing whether the apocalyptic prophecies of the Olivet Discourse refer to the destruction of Jerusalem in AD70 by Titus or its future beleaguerment by Antichrist, he suggests that Jesus predicted both events but Matthew and Mark omitted the first siege while Luke omitted the second. Everything is to be measured by Baconian inductive reasoning, which McCausland saw as the benchmark of truth.[22] In this way, Divine language must possess absolute precision[23] and sceptical Bible criticism heralds impending apostasy and persecution.[24] Though McCausland frequently uses typology, he insists the Bible narrative must be literal, not merely symbolic:[25]

> All this we have found to be consistent with the prophetic symbols, with the other scriptures, and with historic facts; while every other system of interpretation imposes the necessity of spiritualizing the language of the prophecy to an extent that is dangerous in principle, and which renders all reasoning unsatisfactory and inconclusive.
>
> That such a principle is most dangerous is manifest, when we consider that to construe the casting of Satan out of heaven as a figurative incident, entails as a consequence that the presence of Satan in heaven is also figurative; and then the record in the books of Job and Zechariah, of Satan appearing in the presence of God in Heaven, as the accuser, must be taken to be figurative likewise. Admitting that, how can the Christian resist the conclusion of the free-thinker, that the temptation or fall, or any other supernatural incident among the inspired records, is but an allegory or a myth?[26]

McCausland also suggests at various points that the original Greek of the Gospels supports his readings better than the English translation. And in *Sermons in stones*, McCausland similarly draws on his knowledge of Hebrew to modify standard translations of Genesis.

Sermons in stones argues that there is no conflict between scripture and geology; indeed, they actually confirm each other. Thus, McCausland rejects the claim by the Scottish Presbyterian leader Thomas Chalmers that Genesis describes a re-creation after the Earth's previous fauna were destroyed by catastrophe[27] because there is no positive proof for it. Many ancient species found in the geological record, he argues, still exist or existed in conjunction with man, and it is inconsistent with the principle

---

22 D. McCausland, *Sermons in stones; or scripture confirmed by geology* (London, 1873), p. xli.
23 *Latter days*, p. 135. 24 Ibid., pp 498–9. 25 Ibid., p. 134. 26 Ibid., pp 501–2.
27 *Sermons*, pp 117–18, 133–5, 138–9. For a discussion of Chalmers and variants of this theory envisaging pre-Adamite humans in the pre-catastrophic fauna, see Livingstone, *Adam's ancestors*, pp 83–91.

of divine economy to postulate the creation and destruction of a pre-catastrophic world for no apparent purpose:

> God is a God of Order. Consistency and regularity are stamped on every portion of His work, and proclaim that such are the distinguishing attributes of the great Architect of the heavens and the earth, and all that therein is. But this interpretation of His word represents Him as one who pursues different plans, at different times, for the production of similar effects; which, being a departure from the previously declared laws of nature, must be ascribed to a miraculous interference of the Deity, without any warrant, object, or necessity for it.[28]

McCausland deploys a variant of the 'day-age' theory associated with the Scottish Calvinist geologist Hugh Miller (1802–56)[29] to claim the geological epochs correspond to the days of creation; this confirms the Mosaic account providing 'evidence of the inspiration of Holy Writ … manifestly of a higher order than any which has been supplied by fulfilled prophecy'.[30]

Amid vivid visual descriptions of the different eras and their life-forms in a style drawn from contemporary popular science, McCausland offers emendations to the biblical narrative. For example, he suggests that the phrase normally translated 'the first day' should be '*a* first day'[31] (so the world could have existed previously); and 'without form and void' means only that the world was invisible and unfurnished.[32] He also posits that when God's spirit brooded on the face of the waters, this meant that from the second day the Spirit seeded the oceans with life and created submarine creatures, adding others on the third and fourth days. Thus, McCausland suggests, the earliest aquatic animals lack eyes because they were created before the light. The statement that 'all creatures that move' were created on the fifth day, which was taken to mean that no animals existed previously, actually means only 'all reptiles that creep'.[33] Furthermore, McCausland suggests that Moses did not specifically mention aquatic fauna (leading to Genesis being misread as saying that there were no living creatures before the fourth day), because in his divinely inspired vision he could not see under water! So, where Hugh Miller maintained that only the third, fifth and sixth days were discernable in the rocks, McCausland claims the first, second and fourth days are visible also.[34]

McCausland deploys John Tyndall's discovery that in the Carboniferous Epoch the atmosphere was dominated by carbonic clouds (now called the greenhouse effect)[35] as further evidence for his theories; he argues that the biblical reference to light being created on the second day and the sun, moon and stars on the fourth does not mean the heavenly bodies were created then, but that they became visible as the

---

28 *Sermons*, p. 137.   **29** M.A. Taylor, *Hugh Miller: stonemason, geologist, writer* (Edinburgh, 2007); *Sermons*, pp 82, 127–31, 139–41.   **30** *Sermons*, p. 243.   **31** Ibid., p. 170.   **32** Ibid., p. 154.   **33** Ibid., pp 206–7.   **34** Ibid., pp 146–7, 156–70.   **35** Ibid., pp 76–7, 196.

carbonic clouds dispersed.[36] McCausland identifies these clouds with the firmament of Genesis and is indignant with writers who point out (correctly) that the Hebrews thought the firmament a solid vault.[37]

McCausland adamantly maintains a hierarchical Great Chain of Being whereby God created each class of fauna separately in order of complexity, that he 'imposed a law of progress on himself',[38] that 'Each of the leading associate classes of the creation were in succession the monarchs of the world [before Man appeared]'. We are complacently told that insects were created in the Oolite period 'to feed on and enjoy the increasing bounties of Providence; while, on the other hand, new families of insectivorous creatures ... are introduced with them, to check their increase, and maintain the due proportion which a wise Creator has willed should at all times exist among the various races of animals on the earth'. This process continues when

> Man appears on the scene; advancing outwards from the uncivilized savage races of mankind to the civilized and civilizing sons of Adam. But the Creator is never absent; for the Power that infused life into the Eozoon of the Laurentian in the infancy of the world, is the same Power that breathed the breath of life into the nostrils of our forefather Adam.[39]

The last step in this process will be the millennium – the final age or Sabbath, when Man as he now exists will be supplanted by the glorified inhabitants of the New Jerusalem.[40] This brings McCausland into conflict with all forms of evolutionism:

> Very different is the development or transmutation theory, which was first proposed by Lamarck and De Maillet ... that organic life commenced in the lowest and most simple forms; and being endued with an inherent property of progressive improvement, it has advanced, by the operation of pre-ordained natural laws, from the inferior to the superior orders of beings without any interference on the part of the deity, or any exercise of his immediately super-intending power in the mundane economy ... This theory, so dishonouring to God and degrading to Man, was soon rejected as an absurdity by the common sense of mankind. It was however revived, with a little variation, by the author of the *Vestiges of the Natural History of Creation*.[41]

In particular, McCausland ridicules the consequent dispute about whether the monkey or the frog was the progenitor of humanity, mocking *Vestiges'* claim that it

---

36 Ibid., p. 172. **37** Ibid., p. 261; S.L. Jaki, *Genesis 1 through the ages* (London, 1992). **38** *Sermons*, pp 37, 92, 122. 'In [the fossils] we are permitted to study some of those links, of antique type and pattern, in the chain of being that unites the highest with the lowest species of organic life, and both with the omnipresent author of their existence'. *Sermons*, p. 92. **39** *Sermons*, p. 122. **40** Ibid., appendix A, pp 259–64; appendix B, pp 265–78. **41** Ibid., pp 220–3.

must have been the frog because it, like mankind, has a calf to its leg.[42] In relation to this question, McCausland writes:

> [It] has been recently revived with the publication of Dr Darwin's *Origin of Species*, in which an attempt has been made to solve the mystery of the creation of life, by seeking to establish the proposition, that every existing species has been produced by generation from previously existing species … It must be conceded that by the principle of natural selection we can account for the origin of many varieties of the same species; but that is far short of the proposition, that an accumulation of inherited varieties may constitute a species difference.[43]

McCausland then seizes on Darwin's diplomatic remark that all animals might descend from 'some one primordial form, into which life was first breathed':

> This admits that life has been produced upon our planet by one, if not more, divine creative fiats; and such being the case it is more reasonable, as well as more natural, to account for the appearance of distinct orders of living creatures, from time to time, by the exercise of similar acts of Divine power, than by a vain endeavour to link together animals in relationship by descent that are wholly dissimilar in organization, and in all the habits, propensities, and instincts of their lives.[44]

McCausland says the fossil record is less imperfect than Darwin maintains; hence if intermediate forms existed they would have been discovered.[45] Finally, he proclaims the origin of species is beyond human reason, only communicable by divine revelation: 'leaning on God's Word, and reading the written and the stony records together, we are preserved from all such whimsical reveries and dangerous speculations'.[46]

McCausland attacks Lamarck, Chalmers and Darwin throughout his later works. His central objection to evolutionary theory is that it implies a non-interventionist watchmaker God who set the earth in motion and, by extension, might be assumed not to intervene in human history as does the biblical deity, particularly in pre-millennialist interpretations:[47]

> Such is the theory of progressive development, which, admitting the existence of God, excludes Him from all immediate superintendence over the affairs of the world which he has created and furnished; and, by degrading man to the level of the brutes that perish, deprives his soul of all claim to immortality. But for these consequences, so strangely welcome to many a human heart living in a state of resistance to God, this fanciful dogma must have been long since

---

42 Ibid., p. 222n.   43 Ibid., pp 238–9.   44 Ibid., p. 230.   45 Ibid., p. 231.   46 Ibid., pp 231, 233.   47 Ibid., pp 224–7 (need for continuous divine intervention).

discarded by all reasoning minds as one of those amusing conceits which are frequently the offspring of perverted learning and misapplied research.[48]

Accordingly, McCausland is convinced that the biblical narrative indicates the fixity of species. Thus, when an ingenious apologist tried to explain how the world's animal species fitted in the Ark by suggesting that Noah brought a few species from which the later multiplicity developed through natural selection, his use of the Darwinian concept was seen by McCausland as sufficient to discredit him.[49] He expresses sheer disgust that 'The man of science, on alleged scientific grounds, derives Caucasian man, not merely from the lowest species of humanity, but descends to a lower depth to seek his parentage in the monkey, the ape, or the gorilla',[50] and that 'The reasoning of Darwin, Huxley, Lubbock and others of the same school of thought, relegate the existence of man to an endless series of natural procreation without any defined beginnings'.[51] He was confident, however, that the missing link between humanity and earlier species 'never has, and never will be, discovered'.[52]

Two appendices to the revised edition of *Sermons* polemicize against Baden Powell's essay in *Essays and reviews* (1860), which argued that the Mosaic cosmology contradicted the discoveries of science and hence could not be divinely inspired. McCausland disagreed with at least two of Powell's critics, the apologists Birks and McCaul. Birks reacted to Powell's criticisms by reviving Chalmers' claim that a cataclysm involving the extinction of all previous life preceded the six-day creation (or rather re-creation) of Genesis, while McCaul tried to combine the Genesis narrative with the nebular hypothesis of *Vestiges*.[53]

In *Adam and the Adamite* McCausland tries to harmonize scripture with geology, archaeology, history, language and ethnology: 'The physical sciences have been brought to bear on God's word and it must be defended and vindicated with the same weapons'.[54] If the Bible does not strictly establish the date of Adam's birth and genealogy, he proclaims, 'the whole fabric of the revelation must collapse'.[55] Thus, he supplies not only allegedly scientific arguments for his theory that all humanity except Caucasians and Semites are of pre-Adamite origin, but a discourse (with map) on the precise location of Paradise. In this way, McCausland habitually situates himself between the 'excesses' of scientist and 'religionist'. In *Sermons in stones*, Chalmers plays the latter role; whereas, *Adam and the Adamite* balances criticism of evolutionism with attacks on the degenerationist form of creationism associated with Archbishop Richard Whately, who argued that present-day primitive peoples descended from more advanced ancestors.[56] The degenerationist theory that the 'Negro and Mongol' developed from the Caucasian after Noah's Flood, and the rival view that Adam was black and the Caucasian a later development was dismissed by

---

48 Ibid., p. 227.   **49** *Builders*, p. 11.   **50** Ibid., p. 304.   **51** Ibid., p. 330.   **52** *Adamite*, p. 191.   **53** *Sermons*, appendix A, pp 259–64; appendix B, pp 265–78.   **54** *Adamite*, p. 4.
55 Ibid., p. 8.   **56** Ibid., pp 33, 73–5; *Builders*, p. 303. For a brief discussion of Whateleyan degenerationism, see P. Maume, 'The Orientalism of William Cooke Taylor' in R. Blyth & K. Jeffrey (eds), *The British Empire and its contested pasts* (Dublin, 2009), pp 77–94.

McCausland; he argued that that this idea possessed 'all the vices of the Lamarckian and Darwinian theories of the production of the species without any of their plausibilities'.[57]

In support of his pre-Adamite theory, McCausland offers a revised translation of the first chapters of Genesis, where 'Adam' ['Man'] and 'ha-Adam' are translated as 'the Adamite' with 'ish' (also conventionally translated 'man') meaning mankind as a whole.[58] McCausland proclaims that the divine commission to multiply and replenish the earth is addressed specifically to Europeans. Pre-Adamite peoples are stationary; they have no literature, their languages are like those of infants or deaf and dumb people.[59] Furthermore, he argues that without the Adamite there would be no worship of God as McCausland did not believe in the concept of natural religion preceding revelation.[60] The Chinese, according to McCausland, are descendants of Cain; originally nomads in Central Asia, they poured into China displacing the aboriginal peoples, and after the dilution to insignificance of Cain's Adamite blood, remained static and Godless.[61] The representative Semite, for McCausland, is the prophet contemptuous of institutions; the representative Japhetite is the scientific philosopher.

Proto-Indo European, according to McCausland, appeared at the Tower of Babel as the language of the descendants of Japheth; as proof he provides an elaborate narrative (drawing on various sciences, including recent archaeological discoveries) of their expansion into India and Europe. McCausland claims the earliest Hindu scriptures, the Vedas, are essentially monotheistic and reflect memories of the original revelations to Adam and Noah; he eagerly adopted Gladstone's suggestion that the Homeric poems display similar inspiration.[62] Gladstone's diaries show that he read both *Adam and the Adamite* and *The builders of Babel*.[63]

McCausland shows awareness of the difference between Neanderthal and Cro-Magnon man (he does not use these names), seeing the former as Stone Age aborigines and the latter as conquering Bronze Age Adamites.[64] He argues that the betaghs, or slave-class of Celtic society were aborigines subjected by the incoming Celts; and his view that the betaghs were eventually freed when Teutonic liberty

57 *Adamite*, p. 304. Livingstone is mistaken in stating McCausland's reference to the derivation of 'Adam' from 'red' implies he thought Adam might have been black (*Adam's ancestors*, p. 151), see *Adamite*, pp 185–8. **58** *Adamite*, pp 166–70. **59** Ibid., pp 110–11. **60** *Builders*, pp 20–2; *Sermons*, p. 124. **61** *Adamite*, pp 196–7, 254–63. **62** *Builders*, pp 29–232. **63** H.C.G. Matthew (ed.), *The Gladstone diaries*, VI (1861–8) (Oxford, 1978), p. 332, and *The Gladstone diaries*, VII (July 1871–Dec. 1874), pp 23–4. Gladstone certainly entertained pre-Adamite theories in the 1880s, but these do not appear to have derived from McCausland, since he emphasized the idea that Atlantis – in which McCausland took no interest – was the home of the pre-Adamites (letter to Sir Richard Owen, 23 Oct. 1885 in D. Lathbury (ed.), *Correspondence on church and religion of William Ewart Gladstone*, II (London, 1910), pp 107–9). This view implies that the pre-Adamites were mighty civilization-builders equal or superior in natural endowments to Adamic man – unlike McCausland's racially inferior pre-Adamites, but somewhat resembling the (Adamic) Hamites, whom McCausland postulates in *The Builders of Babel*. **64** *Adamite*, p. 54.

abolished such distinctions conveys how the English conquests of Ireland fitted into McCausland's overall schema.[65]

The builders of Babel purports to fill the gap in salvation history by explaining what the descendants of Ham and Japheth did between the Tower of Babel and the emergence of Greek civilization. Here, a larger role is played by the Hamites,[66] who in *Adam and the Adamite* are obscure and inconspicuous.[67] Here, they appear as city-dwellers, world-conquerors and explorers living by trade and 'combining military and mercantile power with the lowest religion and morality' in a manner that suggests misgivings about the commercial and social development of British and European civilization in McCausland's own epoch. However, there may be an Anglo–Protestant subtext, with the Hamites as the defeated Jacobites and the absolutist Catholic European monarchies – particularly the French – of the recent past. The highly speculative (not to say imaginative) nature of the whole construct is emphasized by McCausland's treatment of the Phoenicians. In *Shinar* (1867), he saw them as Semites,[68] but apparently realized that by making them racial Hamites (albeit Semitic in language) he could heighten the supposedly non-political nature of the Semites. Making the Phoenicians into Hamites could also strengthen his claim that civilizations not attributable to Japhetites were founded by Hamites. The pagodas of Burma and the step pyramids of Mesoamerica become evidence of Hamite/Phoenician settlement, and the erotically decorated temples of India are attributed to Hamite influence, compounded by the phallic worship of 'Thamulian' (that is, Tamil) aborigines. The biblical curse on Ham is fulfilled by cultural absorption and loss of separate identity, and McCausland predicts that the non-Persian cuneiform tablets of Mesopotamia (which he believed contained the literature of the Hamites) would, by divine decree, never be deciphered.

McCausland maintains Semites have no skill for government, but are always patriarchal and are naturally and instinctively religious. He argues that Old Testament Israelites showed little aptitude for kingship, except when copying their neighbours, and that the Arab conquests from the seventh century onwards were driven by proselytism rather than desire for territory. McCausland conveniently maintains that the sedentary populations of the Middle East are of Hamitic descent; the only 'true' Semites are desert Arabs and wandering Jews.[69] His discussion is strongly influenced by Ernest Renan, except that where Renan suggests this racial tendency led Semites to invent monotheism without any supernatural input, McCausland argues this tendency was divinely created and fostered to make the Semites fit bearers of the revelations received through the prophets. He even suggests Mohammed, though an impostor, might have been divinely raised up to spread knowledge of the God of Abraham. McCausland's division between Semites and Japhetites recalls Matthew Arnold's distinction between Celt and Saxon, except that where Arnold abandons

---

65 *Adamite*, p. 265.   **66** McCausland's pre-Adamite scenario excludes the traditional Christian racist belief that the Hamites were black.   **67** *Adamite*, pp 223–7.   **68** *Shinar*, p. 17.   **69** *Builders*, p. 25.

the biblical framework for nineteenth-century 'racial science', McCausland grafts contemporary ethnography onto the older framework. As Arnold advocates synthesis of Saxon and Celt, McCausland tries to reconcile Semitic religion and Japhetite science.

McCausland's account of Japhetite achievements, especially after the freeing of the mind from 'sacerdotalism' by the Reformation, rises to a near-ecstatic account of modern science and technology and the global dissemination of the Gospel – reminiscent of the post-millennialists he criticized. Isaac Newton opened the sanctuary of divine law; electricity and magnetism bring us closer to divine providence.[70]

> The vast material and intellectual wealth of Europe and America has accumulated from a very small capital in a comparatively short period of time; and if progress is to continue with the same multiplication of speed and volume that marks the progress of the last few years, the work of the Japhetite will soon be completed, and his destiny accomplished. Everything has assumed colossal dimensions. Monster exhibitions and monster armies – monster guns and monster ships – monster hotels and monster shops – are the order of the day. Luxuries and literature, formerly confined to the few, are now provided for the million; and the simple offspring of fire and water [i.e. the steam engine] is the source from which this mighty flood of innovations has issued on the earth.[71] ... Hurrying from place to place, bringing the ends of the earth and its inhabitants together by the rushing railway and the lightning speed of the electric telegraph, accumulating and extending knowledge that increases power, and concentrates force for production, and thereby multiplying and extending population throughout the earth, are the characteristics of our own times, and realize the prophetic decree of the enlargement of Japhet.[72]

His portrayal of a predestined conquest and resettlement of the world by Adamites (with the Celts driven to seek out the New World by onrolling waves of Teutonic settlement, the Teutons in turn being driven after them by the Slavs, who will follow suit across the Atlantic)[73] and the disappearance of all other races display the same sense that history is speeding up, while incidentally revealing horrifically racist attitudes:[74]

> Our Livingstones and Bakers, Grants and Burtons, sons of Japhet, are now exploring and seeking an entrance for our overflowing populations into the vast and hitherto unknown and misapprehended continent of Africa; and unless climate and soil forbid, the abode of the Negro will, in a few generations, be the emporium of commerce and the home of the Japhetite, in the

70 Ibid., pp 236–7. **71** Ibid., p. 269. **72** Ibid., pp 333–4. **73** Ibid., pp 220–1. **74** Ibid., pp 278ff.

same manner as the hills and valleys, the plains and prairies of the United States and British North America are now, and have been, the abode of the same people.[75]

A similar displacement by Japhetite settlers is predicted for China, Japan and South Asia.[76]

McCausland's last major refinement of his theories, however, displays pre-millennialist pessimism haunted by images of vanished civilizations displaced by divine judgment; his catalogues of technological accomplishment suggest a certain weariness and bewilderment at the pace of technological development since his youth:

> Here is a period in the world's history, styled by a prophet [Daniel 12:4] who wrote six hundred years before the Christian era, 'the time of the end', adding, 'many shall run to and fro, and knowledge shall be increased'. Whether this restlessness and enlargement of knowledge is intended to characterize 'the time of the end', or the period that is immediately to precede it, all must admit that it is remarkably descriptive of the present state of the civilized world.[77]

McCausland displays discernable unease at the process of massacre and bloodshed accompanying 'Japhetite' expansion, arguing both that it fulfils a divine decree and reflects the curse of Eden.[78] In the millennium, God will supplant the flawed Japhetite with a higher race and a better way of evangelization. Furthermore, he defends himself by pointing out that belief in monogenism has not prevented hideous mistreatment of primitive races.[79] McCausland insists that the redemption of mankind by the Adamite Jesus raises up the lesser human races also and that non-Adamites such as the Ethiopian eunuch baptized in the Acts of the Apostles are fully capable of salvation.

McCausland argues that where the Semite's failing is neglect of intermediate causes and attribution of everything to direct divine intervention, the Japhetites' besetting fault is rationalism, leading them to discover intermediate causes while ignoring Divine Providence.[80]

> The rapid advance of material civilization has never been accompanied by a corresponding advance in the moral culture of the community; on the contrary, it is found, that the higher the intellectual attainments, and the greater the prosperity, the more prevalent is the contempt or the perversion of God's word. The Babylon of the Revelation, which typifies the climax of

---

75 Ibid., p. 296. **76** Ibid., p. 183. **77** Ibid., pp 333–4. **78** *Adamite*, pp 266–7. **79** Ibid., p. 304. **80** McCausland originally stated this in *Shinar*, published as Irish disestablishment returned to the political agenda. *Shinar*, pp 44–5.

progressing civilization, presents to view a community which combines the highest commercial prosperity and the most refined luxury with a low moral condition and gross apostasy; and all are buried together on the confines of a better dispensation, typified by the New Jerusalem, which is to be the scene of a future reign of righteousness and peace on the earth.[81]

Thus McCausland brings his readers full circle, back into his earlier prophecy writings.

McCausland had a fairly significant contemporary readership and in 1911 was noteworthy enough for mention in the *Catholic Encyclopedia* ('Preadamites').[82] Now, he is only cited by racist exponents of Identity Theology, and to visit his works is to discover a buried intellectual landscape, its extinct fauna unable to adapt to changed conditions.

81 *Builders*, p. 283.   82 www.newadvent.org/cathen/12370a.htm (accessed 30 June 2009). For McCausland's critical reception, see Livingstone, *Adam's ancestors*, pp 104–5, 164; for his later use by white supremacists, see pp 198, 208, 218.

The Irish-Catholics-in-science debate: John Tyndall, Cardinal Cullen and the uses of science at Castleknock College in the nineteenth century

JAMES H. MURPHY

Over the last decade there has been something of a debate concerning the participation of Catholics in science in nineteenth-century Ireland. The empirical starting point for this debate is generally that of the conclusion of several surveys that Catholics constituted 10 to 15 per cent of scientists in Ireland at the time.[1] Because of the apparent lack so far of information on other measures of participation, this one piece of data has assumed an unusually central importance in the debate.

On the one hand, there are those who explain the putative lack of Catholic participation in science as being the result of the deliberate policy and actions of the Catholic Church:

> the Catholic Church in Ireland has not on the whole encouraged science or explicitly entertained scientific explanations of cosmic mechanisms and the evolution of life on earth. The church has been a counter-Enlightenment force and has generally obstructed the introduction and development of Enlightenment values in Ireland long after they had become part of the common intellectual currency of Protestant Europe and America.[2]

On the other hand, there are those who deny that there is any evidence that the Catholic Church ever discouraged science. Further, they explain the lack of apparent participation in a number ways: the lower socio-economic position of Catholics in society; and, more importantly, the dominance of Irish science by Ascendancy-controlled institutions of learning and by the British government, which employed an unusually large number of scientists in Ireland. Indeed, it has been argued that not only were Catholics institutionally excluded from science but that there was a hostility to Catholics in the very socially constructed nature of science itself as a form

---

1 J. Bennett, 'Science and social policy in Ireland in the mid-nineteenth century' in P.J. Bowler and N. Whyte (eds), *Science and society in Ireland: the social context of science and technology, 1800–1950* (Belfast, 1997), pp 37–47 at p. 38; N. Whyte, *Science, colonialism and Ireland* (Cork, 1999), p. 151. **2** J.W. Foster, 'Natural history in modern Irish culture' in Bowler and Whyte, *Science and society*, pp 119–33 at p. 126.

of knowledge.[3] Finally, some have argued that those claiming to detect a hostility in the Catholic Church towards science in Ireland may also subscribe to a deeper and more general critique of Catholicism as hostile to and of Protestantism as receptive towards scientific inquiry. This is a critique with antecedents in the nineteenth-century, but one which was influentially articulated by Robert Merton in 1938.[4] Whether the perceivers of Irish Catholic hostility to science would agree with this is uncertain. If it is the case, it would not only link this current debate with past international controversies, such as that over Max Weber's Protestant-work-ethic theory, but relate it to previous Irish debates such as that between Horace Plunkett and Michael O'Riordan at the beginning of the twentieth century over Catholicism's supposed role in the retardation of economic progress in Ireland.[5]

The debate over Catholics and science in nineteenth-century Ireland has also taken on a more specific focus, around the issue of the reception of Darwinism in Ireland. Some of those who perceive a Catholic hostility to science have attempted to show that the Catholic Church in Ireland was strongly hostile to Darwinism and that this revelation constitutes evidence of hostility to science in general. Even more particularly, the focus has been on the Catholic reception of the famous presidential address of the Irish man of science and supporter of evolution, John Tyndall, to the British Association for the Advancement of Science at its Belfast conference in 1874, an address that certainly caused concatenations of alarm in Belfast Presbyterian circles.[6] For the purposes of our present discussion, the important questions are: was the Catholic reaction as strong as has been claimed and, whatever its strength, what was its significance?

Tyndall's address was certainly polemical. It was an occasion on which 'the aggression of evolutionists towards Christianity reached its height.'[7] His preface to the published form of the address deliberately baited the Irish Catholic hierarchy:

> Cardinal Cullen [archbishop of Dublin], I am told, is also actively engaged in erecting spiritual barriers against the intrusion of 'Infidelity' into Ireland. His Eminence, I believe, has reason to suspect that the Catholic youth around him are not proof to the seduction of science. Strong as he is, I believe him to be impotent here. The youth of Ireland will imbibe science, however slowly; they will be leavened by it, however gradually.[8]

---

3 J. Bennett, 'Why the history of science matters in Ireland' in D. Attis (ed.), *Science and Irish culture* (Dublin, 2004), pp 1–14 at pp 5–6; J. Bennett, 'Science and social policy in Ireland in the mid-nineteenth century' in Bowler and Whyte, *Science and society*, pp 37–47 at p. 44; Whyte, *Science, colonialism and Ireland*, pp 6–7, 12, 15.   **4** E. Leaney, 'Vested interests: science and medicine in nineteenth-century Ireland', *FDR*, 2 (2006), 285–94 at p. 286.   **5** H. Plunkett, *Ireland in the new century* (London, 1904); M. O'Riordan, *Catholicity and progress in Ireland* (London, 1906).   **6** D.N. Livingstone, *Adam's ancestors: race, religion and the politics of human origins* (Baltimore, MD, 2008); A. Holmes, 'Presbyterians and science in the north of Ireland before 1874', *British Journal for the History of Science*, 41 (2008), 541–65.   **7** Foster, 'Natural history in modern Irish culture', p. 125.   **8** J. Tyndall, *Address delivered before the*

The Catholic reaction to Tyndall culminated in a public lecture given at the Rotunda in Dublin by the famous preacher, Tom Burke. 'The Catholic Church is not the enemy', Burke declared, 'but the friend and patron, and encourager of all true science, and all true scientific men'.[9] The Irish Catholic bishops responded with a pastoral letter, dated 14 October 1874 and published before the end of that month (and not in November 1874 as is usually stated).[10] Given Tyndall's provocation, it would have been odd had they not done so. In their letter, they did not criticize science per se, but what they saw as a polemical discourse around science by the proponents of materialism. For good measure, they adduced the Belfast address as providing evidence for the sagacity of their insistence on denominational university education in Ireland: 'The open profession of materialism, by men holding high rank in the schools of science, is an additional proof of the necessity of continuing with renewed ardour our exertions to secure for the Catholics of Ireland an education based on religion'.[11] Far from being outraged, indeed, they may privately have been pleased by Tyndall's attack. A sardonic editorial in the London *Times*, in grim congratulations of the Irish bishops, put the matter thus:

> They have discerned the opportunity of exhibiting to their followers in a concrete and visible form the spectre against which they have long been fighting a battle under the disguises of Queen's colleges [Ireland's secular university institutions] and Secular Education. Behold, they exclaim, the real tendency and ultimate result of these insidious inventions of Liberalism! ... A tribute of admiration is due to the promptitude which has so vigorously turned a rare opportunity to account. A confession of Materialism, however modified, in the president of the British Association, and delivered at Belfast, was, no doubt, a singular piece of good fortune to the opponents of a 'godless education', but the vigilance which takes instant advantage of it is none the less to be applauded.[12]

Tyndall emerges from this as a naïve blunderer who was playing into the bishops' hands. It is likely that Cullen and his fellow bishops were not greatly exercised by Tyndall or his address. For them, he was probably just another exponent of a hostile philosophical system from an alien culture. As Greta Jones remarks about articles on Darwinism in the *Irish Ecclesiastical Record* in the 1870s and 1880s, Catholic writers attacked '"modern thought" and Darwinism, the two seen as much the same thing'.[13]

There were several reasons why Darwinism may not have been the problem for Catholics that it was for some Protestants. For a start, Catholics did not rely solely on the Bible for guidance. Further, their tradition of interpreting scripture was multiple.

British Association assembled at Belfast, with additions (London, 1874), p. vii.   **9** T. Burke, *The Catholic Church and science* (Dublin, 1874), p. 11.   **10** *Freeman's Journal*, 31 Oct. 1874.   **11** *FJ*, 5 Nov. 1874.   **12** *The Times*, 31 Oct. 1874.   **13** G. Jones, 'Darwinism in Ireland' in Attis, *Science and Irish culture*, pp 115–37 at p. 129.

Medieval approaches, for example, had included literal, typological, tropological and anagogical methodologies. Finally, Catholics had generally not attempted to read the Bible as offering a source of information compatible with Enlightenment science. It was the attempt to do the latter that had really caused difficulties for so many British Protestants when faced with the findings of Darwin. This is generally and unhelpfully what is meant by 'reading the Bible literally' in popular accounts of the topic.

Tyndall, however, claimed to have had an even more specific occasion for his attack on the Irish bishops, as some have noted.[14] This was the supposed protest of students of the Catholic University of Ireland at the deficiency of their education in science. Indeed, his reference to Catholic youth in his attack on Cullen seems to be an allusion to this. However, whatever Tyndall may have believed about it, and, in this instance, his naïve misreading may have been to his own subjective advantage, there is certainly less substance in this supposed controversy than appears at first sight.

The Catholic University was an unendowed institution, without state recognition, under the direction of the bishops. Ironically, for this present discussion, its most successful division was the Catholic University Medical School, an enterprise not unconnected with science, whose students, through a circuitous route, were able to obtain recognized medical qualifications. The possible recognition and endowment of the Catholic University was such a contentious political issue at the time that it had brought about the resignation of the Liberal government in 1873, although they resumed office almost immediately afterwards. Tyndall's allusion to the university may have been his attempt to garner political advantage with British opinion, just as his attack on Catholicism in general certainly represented an embrace of the widespread international hostility to Catholicism of the time, which was specifically focused on Bismarck's *Kulturkampf* in Germany. *Kulturkampf* had its British supporters, not the least of whom was the former prime minister Earl Russell, of Ecclesiastical-Titles-Act fame, whose broad historical survey, *Essays on the rise and progress of the Christian religion in the west of Europe, from the reign of Tiberius to the end of the Council of Trent* (1873) had culminated in a treatment of the case of the truculent parish priest of Callan, Co. Tipperary; the latter had cannily presented his own very personal dispute with Cardinal Cullen in terms of the extension of an aggressive papal power.

The episcopal board at the Catholic university had indeed received a document or memorial representative of the views not so much of the students of the Catholic University as of a group of Dublin middle-class professionals. Little came of it, but its contents were leaked to the newspapers, leading its authors, led by the future lord mayor, Charles Dawson, to protest that it was far from the aggressive document that was presented. The *Freeman's Journal* lamented that it had been misrepresented as 'an

14 Leaney, 'Vested interests', p. 286; Whyte, *Science, colonialism*, p. 25; J.W. Foster, 'Nature and nation' in J.W. Foster (ed.), *Nature in Ireland: a scientific and cultural history* (Dublin, 1997), pp 409–39 at p. 430; J.W. Foster, *Recoveries: neglected episodes in Irish cultural history, 1860–1912* (Dublin, 2001), pp 37, 39.

uprising of the Catholic youth against the views and policy of the ecclesiastical authorities'.[15] It was in fact thirty pages long and seems mostly to have dealt with the administrative deficiencies of the university, though the *Times* report on it focused almost entirely on its remarks about science, leading to the probably erroneous conclusion that that was its principal focus.[16] It certainly did contain criticisms of the university's deficiencies in science, wonderfully reversing its episcopal recipients' own rhetoric by urging them, with a droll earnestness, to arm the university's students against modern error through a proper understanding of science, lest they abandon the Catholic University for Trinity College or the Queen's colleges, or, worse, start reading Darwin, Tyndall et al. for themselves.

Nonetheless, there was some discontent in certain quarters about science in the Catholic University. However, the cause of any deficiency was more likely to have been in the lack of finance than in any principled hostility to science. The university was chronically underfunded and the early 1870s were crisis years for it financially, as it slackened off on its fund-raising in erroneous anticipation of impending government funding. Its income shrank by 40 per cent during this period.[17] Indeed, when, shortly after receiving the document and most likely in response to it, the bishops appointed Dr Gerald Molloy as professor of Natural Philosophy, it was announced that he was going to spend £750 of his own money 'to procure for the university the newest and most costly apparatus necessary to illustrate his lecture'.[18] His equipment, when it arrived, was in fact to elicit widespread admiration.

If the Catholic University's science deficiencies had more to do with money than antagonism to science, the motives of the authors of the memorial had probably less to do with a liberating love of pure science than with the social and economic needs of an *arriviste* Catholic middle class. 'No one can deny that the Irish Catholics are miserably deficient in science education', they were reported to have written. 'That deficiency is extremely galling to us. In a commercial sense it involves a loss to us, while in a social and intellectual sense it is a positive degradation'.[19] Beneath the parody of theological anxiety, it seems, there was after all a serious *bourgeois* agenda at work to do with money and social status.

This brings us at last to the case of Castleknock College. Founded in 1835 by the Vincentian congregation, with aspirations to be a partial seminary, it had become by mid-century one of the three leading Irish Catholic boarding schools for middle-class boys. Gerald Molloy had been at school there, as had the future Admiral Sir Henry Kane, son of Sir Robert Kane, one of Ireland's leading scientists.

Before the 1878 Intermediate Education Act, it was a widespread custom for secondary schools to showcase their academic standards at public events, to which distinguished guests would be invited as assessors. These events, called the

---

15 *FJ*, 3 Dec. 1873. **16** *The Times*, 2 Dec. 1873. **17** E. Larkin, *The Roman Catholic Church and the Home Rule movement in Ireland, 1870–74* (Chapel Hill, NC, 1990), p. xx. **18** *FJ*, 12 Dec. 1873. **19** *The Times*, 2 Dec. 1873.

Academical Exercises or the Publics at Castleknock, took place in the college at the end of the school year on 19 July. In theory, this was a form of external moderation of academic standards. In practice, it was a type of promotional advertising for the school: invited guests, who included lawyers, doctors, clergymen, professors and sometimes the lord mayor of Dublin, were treated to an entertaining display of learning, some speechifying and prize-giving, and then to a good lunch. In the early years, the emphasis was on reciting the odes of Horace in Latin, with a little light algebra, recitations from Racine and Molière in French, a debate between pupils, the acting out of scenes from a play and, finally, the exertions of the college band.[20]

As the years wore on, however, a certain tedium began to creep into the proceedings. Novelty was required and novelty was supplied. The report on the Publics in July 1869 in the *Freeman's Journal* thrilled as follows:

> The experimental philosophy at Castleknock has been always a treat; yesterday assuredly was not an exception. The subject chosen was chemistry. 'Tis very difficult to popularize scientific matter. The difficulty can be realized by those only who have made the attempt. Master Fowler, however, in the judgment of all, succeeded wonderfully. He was clearness and precision itself, yet his language was plain and familiar, scarcely a technical term from beginning to end. His manner was the theme of universal admiration. I must say Master Downes gave great assistance by the dexterity with which he illustrated by experiment the laws laid down by his companion. Master Fowler developed, enforced and illustrated the laws of chemistry till the smallest child in the hall had them pictured on his imagination. When the properties of oxygen and hydrogen came to be illustrated, the experiments were really brilliant. Master Fowler concluded, amidst applause, by exhibiting a beautiful fountain, which was illuminated by a pillar of lime heated to whiteness by the oxy-hydrogen flame.[21]

As Master Fowler and Master Downes looked in justifiable pride at their audience at the end of their demonstration, perhaps their gazes met that of Paul Cardinal Cullen, who was presiding over the event and who had come, along with four other bishops, apparently to applaud this display of science, though at least the cardinal was sitting on a throne for the occasion. But it must also be recorded that among the wonders demonstrated on these occasions were experiments that had been developed by none other than John Tyndall himself, such as Tyndall's Tuning Forks, which illustrated sound as a wave effect and the Sensitive Naked Flames, which measured pitch and tone quality: 'The extreme sensitiveness of the Sensitive Flames as they responded to every hissing sound caused great wonder!'[22] Master Downes was on

---

20 J.H. Murphy, 'A history of Castleknock College' in J.H. Murphy (ed.), *Nos autem: Castleknock College and its contribution* (Dublin, 1996), pp 1–154 at p. 16.   **21** *FJ*, 21 July 1869.
22 *Castleknock centenary record* (Dublin, 1935), p. 110.

hand again the following year, in 1870. This time the topic was physics and his experiment was on spectrum analysis. However, the demonstration obviously did not reach the triumphant heights of the previous year, as the *Freeman's Journal* correspondent noted that '[t]o preserve the auditors from the possible effect of even a lucid explanation of an abstruse question, the spectrum analysis – they were now invited to listen to a French dialogue'.[23]

Scientific display was the central attraction for the golden jubilee celebrations of the college in 1885. Once more, they did Tyndall proud:

> In halls specially darkened for the purpose might be seen the spectrum analysis with the electric light; microscopic objects; living specimens thrown on the screen by lime light; arrangements for Tyndall's experiments with the dark-heat rays, as also for fluorescences; screen experiments for crystallization; electric breast-pin and hair-pin. So much for the darkened rooms. There was besides the photograph, a working model electric railway; working model steam railway; freezing mercury in a red-hot crucible; numbers of microscopes and polariscopes attached, for inspection; large sectional models of the eye and ear; sensitive and vowel flame apparatus; electroplating. One of the really remarkable instruments was a loud-speaking telephone, recently acquired by the college.[24]

Electricity was installed as well as the telephone. Shortly thereafter, an indoor heated swimming pool was built, the largest at the time in the United Kingdom.[25] By the end of the 1880s, Castleknock College was bubbling with chemical reactions, humming with electricity and electric light, and steaming with hot water, and, in the early years of the twentieth century, would soon be buzzing with radio signals and flickering with the early use of cinema.[26] It had become a veritable tomorrows-world of science and technology.

But there was scientific substance behind the technological display. Science education, physics, chemistry and natural philosophy had been a priority in the curriculum since the early 1850s and the college claimed to have equipped its physical hall 'with the most elaborate and up-to-date apparatus, so that it was one of the outstanding physics laboratories in the country'.[27] Pupils were taught by experiment and themselves took part in experiments. Edward Gaynor was an outstanding chemistry teacher and wrote a textbook on the subject. Physics was in the hands of the polymath R.C. Bodkin, whose pupil Joseph Slattery was the pioneer of X-rays in Australia, the Australian government issuing a postage stamp in his honour in the late twentieth century. Bodkin presumed scientific literacy and could write with insouciance in the college *Chronicle* in 1896, 'Everyone knows what an Induction Coil is and how the spark is produced in the outer coil and is of very high tension'. In the

23 *FJ*, 21 July 1870. **24** *Centenary record*, p. 128. **25** Murphy, *Nos autem*, pp 65–6. **26** *Centenary record*, pp 174, 176. **27** Ibid., p. 193.

late 1880s, the college acquired extensive astronomical equipment. Grants for science were available to schools whose pupils took part in the examinations of the Science and Art Department of the Council of the Committee on Education, South Kensington, London. Castleknock was notable for its participation in these exams, particularly in the 1890s. Science remained a priority at Castleknock, even though the effect of the Intermediate curriculum was to reduce the number of Irish pupils taking science towards the end of the nineteenth century.[28]

David Newsome's classic study of English public schools, *Godliness and good learning*, traces the crisis brought about not only by Darwinism but by the German biblical higher criticism that had preceded it.[29] This led to a shift between an alliance of religion and the intellect, the godliness and good learning of his title, into a more defensive connection between religion and physical prowess, as in the muscular Christianity of Charles Kingsley. The preacher of one of the sermons delivered in 1935 to mark the centenary of Castleknock College was keen to assert that the college, whose religion he was careful to portray as 'masculine', had maintained that synthesis between godliness and good learning that had broken down in England:

> When Castleknock College was founded one hundred years ago by the Vincentian Fathers, Modernistic Liberalism, which has since devastated English thinking, was capturing Oxford and its spirit was spreading to Ireland. That spirit stood for the divorce of science from religion. It is said the virtue could not be intellectual, goodness could not be great, conscientiousness could not be heroic, that religious men must be dull and tiresome. Castleknock and its traditions always stood for the antithesis of that false spirit. Its teachers were, at the same time, men of learning and piety, of faith and good fellowship ... Here was no conversing with science by day and lodging with religion in the evening.[30]

Complacency and self-congratulation tend no doubt to be the hallmarks of centenaries. Yet if we place this passage alongside a passage quoted earlier from one of the recent proponents of the Catholic-hostility-to-science theory, we may observe that this sermon is making a rather remarkable claim. The earlier passage, perhaps somewhat loosely, took the supposed Catholic hostility to science as a symptom of a wider Catholic rejection of the Enlightenment. The passage we have just heard, however, is claiming that it is precisely because Catholicism had immunized itself against Modernistic Liberalism, no doubt a close cousin of the Enlightenment, that it had had no hesitation in embracing science with confidence and enthusiasm.

No doubt this overstates the matter, and presents an unrealistic picture of an Irish Catholicism sealed off from Anglo-Saxon influences. But there may be something

---

28 Murphy, *Nos autem*, pp 72–3.   **29** D. Newsome, *Godliness and good learning* (London, 1961).   **30** *Castleknock College Chronicle* (1936), pp 8–9.

worth thinking about it in it. In general, my own view is that the debate over Catholics in science has tended a little towards the recondite. The issues involved are not only those of science, philosophy and theology, but also of rhetoric, politics, popular culture and, yes, money and social status.

'A pure school of science': the Royal College of Science for Ireland and scientific education in Victorian Ireland[1]

CLARA CULLEN

INTRODUCTION

In 1864, a government committee, appointed to inquire into the scientific institutions in Dublin that received government funding, reported that

> [They could not] see why such of the youth of Ireland as wish to devote themselves to the establishment or management of such manufactures as depend on the application of any science, or such as wish to prepare themselves for the business of life, either in Ireland or elsewhere, should not have the same facilities afforded them in Dublin as those of England have in London.[2]

Its subsequent recommendation was that the existing Government School of Science at the Museum of Irish Industry (MII) in Dublin should be expanded to become 'a public scientific institution as in London [the School of Mines at Jermyn Street], under a proper system of responsibility, with examinations and prizes or certificates of competency'.[3] Three years later, the Royal College of Science for Ireland (RCScI) was established. This new college offered courses in scientific education at a number of levels and was the first comprehensive attempt made in the United Kingdom by the British government to give state-aided higher scientific and technical education. Its establishment pre-dated the Royal College of Science in London by twenty years. The college continued into the twentieth century and it reflected the continuum of the efforts in Victorian Ireland to make scientific education more accessible to those interested in science but who could not, or did not wish to, pursue an academic degree in any of Ireland's universities.

However, the history of the RCScI has never been addressed in any detail. In the

1 I would like to acknowledge the help and support I received from the UCD Humanities Institute of Ireland in making the resources of the Institute available to me for my research.
2 *Report from the Select Committee on Scientific Institutions, Dublin; together with the proceedings of the committee, minutes of evidence, appendix and index*, p. xxxiii, HC 1864 (495), xiii, 1 (hereafter *Select Committee ... 1864*). 3 *Copy of minute of Committee of Council on Education relative to scientific institutions and instruction in Dublin*, p. 2, HC 1866 (42), lv, 239.

most recent history of University College Dublin (UCD), the author acknowledged that the contribution of the RCScI and of its predecessor, the MII, to the university has yet to be written.[4] The two main publications on the college are William F. Barrett's *Historical sketch of the Royal College of Science* (1907) and a pamphlet published by the College's Association in 1923.[5] These, together with a few articles and some unpublished theses on the history of science and of technical education in Ireland, principally those by John F. Kerr (1957), Brian Kelham (1957), Kieran Byrne (1982) and, most recently, by Enda Leaney in 2003,[6] are the full written record of an institution established in 1867 and which continued as an educational institution for almost sixty years, until it became part of UCD's faculty of science in 1926.

THE ROYAL COLLEGE OF SCIENCE FOR IRELAND: THE VICTORIAN YEARS

The RCScI was established following the recommendations of a number of government commissions. The first was the Select Committee of Scientific Institutions of 1864, which had recommended that the functions of the Government School of Science at the Museum of Irish Industry (MII) might be extended, its title possibly changed and that it 'might be made an independent institution of great utility to Ireland'.[7] This recommendation resolved a very public battle begun in 1862 as to which Dublin institution, the MII or the Royal Dublin Society (RDS), should be responsible for the provision of scientific education in Ireland, outside the universities. The final structure of the proposed college was based on the recommendations of yet another government commission two years later, headed by the Irish scientist, the earl of Rosse, which provided very detailed recommendations 'on the scope of the instruction to be given, the examinations for testing it, and the certificates etc. to be awarded to successful students'.[8]

A treasury minute of January 1867 constituted the college, appointing the erstwhile director of the MII, Sir Robert Kane, as dean (after an internal struggle with

---

4 D. McCartney, *UCD, a national idea: the history of University College Dublin* (Dublin, 1999), p. xix. **5** W.F. Barrett, *An historical sketch of the Royal College of Science from its foundation to the year 1900* (Dublin, 1907); *The College of Science for Ireland: its origin and development, with notes on similar institutions in other countries, and a bibliography of the work published by the staff and students (1900–1923)* (Dublin, 1923). **6** K.R. Byrne, 'The origin and growth of technical education in Ireland, 1731–1922' (PhD, UCC, 1982); B.B. Kelham, 'Science education in Scotland and Ireland, 1750–1900' (PhD, Victoria U of Manchester, 1968); J.F. Kerr, 'The development of the teaching of science in Ireland since 1800'(PhD, QUB, 1957); E. Leaney, '"The property of all": public access to scientific education in nineteenth-century Ireland' (PhD, U Oxford, 2002); B.B. Kelham, 'The Royal College of Science for Ireland (1867–1926)', *Studies*, 46 (autumn 1967), 297–309. **7** *Select Committee ... 1864*, pp xxii–xxiv. **8** *Report of Commission on College of Science, Dublin; minutes of committee of council for education directing abolition of office of director of Museum of Irish Industry; and of all correspondence that has taken place*, p. 2, HC 1867 (219), lv, 777 (hereafter *Report ... College of science ... 1867*).

the Department of Science and Art (DSA) in London),[9] with a staff consisting of professors of physics, chemistry, applied chemistry, geology, applied mathematics, botany, zoology, agriculture, engineering, and mining and metallurgy.[10] The following November, the new institution opened its doors to students and in 1868 yet another government commission concluded that

> In the College of Science, Ireland possesses an institution which, in the number of its professorships and general course of study, is more complete as a pure school of science than anything of the kind existing in Scotland or England.[11]

Such a glowing description obscured a very different reality. The circumstances in which the new college began might be described, at best, as inauspicious and, more accurately, as chaotic. Having been established after a series of confrontations between the RDS, the British Treasury, the DSA in London and public opinion in Ireland, it was against a background of bureaucratic policy-making, personal agendas and antagonisms, administrative confusion, disruption and departmental negotiations that the RCScI came into being. The new college was housed in the converted Georgian house in St Stephen's Green that had been the Museum of Irish Industry and that had been condemned by the 1864 committee as inadequate for its purpose. However, it was in this inadequate and converted building that the RCScI remained until 1911. In the months between ending science classes at the MII in May 1867 and opening the new college in November, the building had to be remodelled for its new purpose. The first academic session was described by the dean, Sir Robert Kane (who may have been showing some bias), as follows:

> Nothing was ready; not more than one-half of the professors were actually appointed; the museum was all broken up; the professors that were appointed had no place to lecture, and altogether the institution was in a complete state of collapse, I might say; and consequently no persons presented themselves for the lectures, practically, but the persons who had obtained exhibitions, and who consequently were paid to attend there.[12]

The ongoing reconstruction work in the museum building was not the only factor that caused problems and delayed the opening of the new College of Science until

9 *Report from the Commission on the Science and Art Department in Ireland; vol. 2, Minutes of evidence, appendix and index*, pp 113–69 at pp 122, 152–3, HC 1868–9 [4103–1], xxiv, 43 (hereafter *Report ... on the Science and Art Department in Ireland, vol. 2*). **10** *The College of Science for Ireland: its origin and development, with notes on similar institutions in other countries, and a bibliography of the work published by the staff and students* (1900–1923) (Dublin, 1923), pp 9–10. **11** *Report from the Commission on the Science and Art Department in Ireland; Report, vol. 1*, p. xxxiii, HC 1868–9 [4103], xxiv, 1 (hereafter *Report ... on the Science and Art Department in Ireland, vol. 1*). **12** *Report ... on the Science and Art Department in Ireland, vol. 2*, p. 403.

the middle of November. The new college council met for the first time on 10 September 1867, to discuss how the academic objectives recommended by the 1866 Rosse Commission should be implemented and to draft a programme for the next session, which commenced on 4 November 1867.[13]

THE COURSES

As defined by the 1866 commission, the object of the new college was to supply, as far as practicable, a 'complete course of instruction in science applicable to the Industrial Arts, especially those which may be classed broadly under mining, engineering and manufactures, and to aid in the instruction of teachers for the local schools of science'.[14] Four faculties – mining, engineering, manufactures and agriculture – were established, although the faculty of agriculture was a last-minute addition to the list of subjects and was abolished in 1877.[15] Later, in 1885, a faculty of chemistry was planned and in 1896 a new faculty of applied physics and physical science was established, followed shortly afterwards by a faculty of natural science and the re-instatement of the chair of agriculture (and rural science) in 1899. By the end of the century, practical courses in many subjects – including zoology, physics, spectrography, engineering and electro-technology – had been expanded or added to the original curriculum. In all of these subjects, the principles of scientific education established in the MII continued – practical instruction in the college's laboratories supplemented the theoretical teaching in the classrooms of the RCScI.

The full-time course was to be a three-year one, with students specializing in one particular subject area in their final years. Successful students were awarded the diploma of Associateship of the Royal College of Science for Ireland (ARCScI). To encourage prospective students, the DSA offered a number of scholarships, or Exhibitions, which were tenable for three years study at the college and which were awarded on the results of the department's public science examinations each May. To the value of £50 per annum, these scholarships brought a number of students from Britain to Ireland and, until the end of the century a significant proportion of the Associate students were not Irish,[16] giving the impression that the college was more a British than an Irish institution: 'There is a feeling among young men here, that, by going to these classes and attending such institutions, they are going some way to make Englishmen of themselves, or to make Protestants of themselves'.[17]

13 Minutes of Council, 10 and 11 Sept. 1867 (University College Dublin Archives (hereafter UCDA), RCSI/1); *IT*, 30 Sept. 1867. 14 *Report ... College of science ... 1867*, p. 2. 15 This professorial post was given to E.P. Davy, erstwhile professor of agricultural science at the RDS, who occupied the post until 1877. 16 Kelham, 'The Royal College of Science', p. 304; *Royal Commission on University Education (Ireland)*, appendix to the third report, p. 544, HC 1902 [1229] xxxii, 1(hereafter *Robertson Commission ... 3rd report*, appendix). 17 *Report from the Royal Commission on Technical Instruction. 2nd report with appendix*, vol. iv: evidence ... relating to Ireland, p. 16, HC 1884 [c.3981–III], xxxi (1), 1 (hereafter *Commission on Technical*

Nevertheless, significant numbers of Irish students did avail of the scientific education offered at the RCScI and although the college was non-denominational and kept no records of religious affiliations, at least half of the students were Catholic.[18] The majority of these were the non-associate (or occasional) students who could register for single subjects in the college's academic and laboratory courses for a fee of £1 or £2 for each course. Certificates were awarded to those who were successful in various subjects of the college's sessional examinations. As had been the case with the certificates awarded to successful students at the MII, the RCScI certificates were recognized as qualifications for some branches of the civil service, and for entry to military colleges and a number of universities.[19] After the establishment of the Royal University of Ireland (RUI) in 1880, science courses at the RCScI were recognized by the new university and the college directory for 1882–3 included information that 'the classes of chemistry, botany and zoology qualify for graduation in medicine in the Royal University of Ireland, and are especially adapted to the requirements of that university'.[20] Apart from university students, the opportunity to take individual courses in the college's curriculum was availed of by teachers who wished to acquire a DSA qualification as science teachers. Other students included:

> [E]ngineers of established reputation and professional experience wishing to extend their knowledge of chemistry, chemical analysis, metallurgy and assaying ... but by far the greater proportion of the occasional students are those whose friends and relations have a substantial stake in the country, either as owners of landed estates, or property in industrial enterprise, established manufacture or commercial undertaking.[21]

Although the 1864 Select Committee had recommended that the evening courses of lectures on various scientific topics, which had been one of the most popular features of the MII educational programme, should be continued, no funding was made available for them in the government grants to the new college. Kane had voiced his concerns regarding the 'abolition of what was its most popular element in its old form; that is to say, the system of scientific instruction to which pupils were admissible for small nominal fees';[22] and, together with some of his colleagues, attempted to continue to provide some evening courses, but they were 'voluntary on the part of the lecturers, and entirely distinct from the regular systematic course of instruction

Instruction, 2nd report, vol. 4). **18** *Royal Commission on University Education (Ireland)*, final report, p. 122, HC 1903 [1483], xxxii,1 (hereafter *Robertson Commission ... final report*). **19** Minutes of Council, 28 Nov. 1867 (UCDA, RCSI/1); *Robertson Commission ... 3rd report*, appendix, pp 551, 554. **20** Minutes of Council, 1 Mar., 17 May and 14 June 1882 (UCDA, RCSI/2). **21** *Robertson Commission ... 3rd report*, appendix, p. 548. **22** *Report from the Select Committee on Scientific Instruction; together with the proceedings of the committee, minutes of evidence and appendix ... 1868*, p. 154, HC 1867–8 (432), xv, 1 (hereafter *Select Committee on Scientific Instruction ... 1868*).

in the college'.[23] In 1879, formal courses of evening lectures were re-introduced, 'to place the college on a better footing ... [and] make it more widely known'.[24]

THE PROFESSORS

Not all the new teaching posts had been filled by the time the first term opened and it would appear that the process of selecting the new professors was, to some extent, informal. Edward Hull, who succeeded Joseph Beete Jukes as local director of the Geological Survey in Ireland on the recommendation of Roderick Murchison in 1869, was also given 'the additional appointment of Professor of Geology in the Royal College of Science'.[25] Similarly, in 1867, Robert Stawell Ball, tutor to the earl of Rosse's children, recalled:

> I received a letter from my valued friend, Dr Haughton, in which he told me that ... if I offered myself as a candidate for the post [of professor of applied mathematics], and if Lord Rosse would support my application, I should probably be appointed ... The post of a professor presented itself to me as a considerable advance on my position ... and my application was successful.[26]

Serious questions were raised about some of the new appointments. There were allegations that the new appointments were made to exclude Catholics from teaching posts at the college; this view supported by the fact that the only three Catholics appointed in 1867 were Sir Robert Kane (the dean), William Kirby Sullivan (the professor of chemistry) and William Plunkett (the assistant chemist), all of whom had been on the staff of the MII. It was also alleged that the appointments were made in London for anti-Irish reasons.[27] Given the loyalty of the majority of the MII professors to Robert Kane, it is probable that some new professors were selected by the DSA because their loyalty would be to the department rather than to the old regime of the MII. What is certain is that from 1867 until 1900, all of the appointments to the college were made in London by the DSA and professors were appointed to their

---

23 In 1867–8, 'Thirteen evening lectures on science of a more popular character are being delivered during the session by the dean of faculty and several of the professors, at a fee of 6d. for each course. These lectures have been well attended, principally by artisans'; *Sixteenth report of the Science and Art Department ... [1868–69]*, p. x, 1868–9 [4136], xxiii, 131. **24** Minutes of Council, 5 June 1879 (UCDA, RCSI/2). **25** E. Hull, *Reminiscences of a strenuous life* (London, 1910), pp 30–1. **26** R. Ball [W.V. Ball, ed.], *Reminiscences and letters of Sir Robert Ball* (Dublin, 1915), pp 80–1. **27** G. Sigerson, 'The Royal College of Science for Ireland' in G. Sigerson, *Modern Ireland: its vital questions, secret societies and government; by an Ulsterman* (London, 1868), p. 201; Sullivan to Monsell (National Library of Ireland, Monsell papers, MS 8318 (5)); G.B. Bradshaw, *Condemned for their country; or, 'No Irish need apply': an authentic, but startling, expose of the delinquencies of the South Kensington Museum; and a plea for the projected 'Royal Irish Institute'* (Dublin, 1868).

posts with no reference or consultation with the council of the college,[28] which for one writer confirmed his belief that 'The Royal College of Science for Ireland has an imposing name, but in reality it is to be in abject dependence on South Kensington'.[29]

Nevertheless, the majority of the new appointments were eminent men in their respective scientific fields. Although a few moved on to other posts within the first few years, the majority of the professors appointed to the RCScI remained with the college for much of their careers. Among these were the physicist William Fletcher Barrett, the geologists Edward Hull and Grenville Cole, and Alfred Cort Haddon, who was described by Greta Jones as 'the Darwinian evolutionist par excellence',[30] and who was professor of zoology from 1880 until 1901.[31] There was also the entomologist George Herbert Carpenter (an Englishman who had studied science at the RCScI) and William McFadden Orr, professor of mathematics from 1890 and who transferred to UCD when the college became part of that university. Almost all of the professors were experienced teachers, were active in professional associations and in the societies in Dublin relating to their particular disciplines, wrote for the scientific journals and published both learned monographs and text books.[32] They also contributed to scientific initiatives in Ireland and many of them travelled widely in pursuit of scientific knowledge. Haddon, for example, organized his anthropological expedition to the Torres Straits while a professor in the RCScI and, prior to that, he had conducted scientific expeditions around the Irish coast funded by the Royal Irish Academy (RIA) and the RDS. They collaborated with colleagues in the other scientific institutions in Ireland, were members of the RDS and the RIA and many were Fellows of the Royal Society (FRS) – an honour which R.L. Praeger considered 'a scientific honour more prized than those which any university can confer'.[33] They represented a wide spectrum of the sciences of their day and brought their professional experience and commitment to their teaching.

CHALLENGES AND PROBLEMS

Whatever the reasons behind their appointments, all of the teaching staff faced a serious challenge in implementing the objectives and achieving the aims of the new

28 Minute books of the Council of the RCScI (UCDA, RCSI/1–6, 1867–1901). **29** *The Chronicle*, 16 Nov. 1867 (UCDA, MII/7). **30** G. Jones, 'Contested territories: Alfred Cort Haddon, progressive evolutionism and Ireland', *History of European Ideas*, 24 (1998), 195–211 at p. 195. **31** He resigned as 'the Department [DATI] can give me no assurance that the Chair of Zoology … will be placed on a satisfactory basis'; Minutes of council, 1 Oct. 1901 (UCDA, RCSI/7). **32** For a bibliography of the publications of the students and staff of the RCScI from 1900 to 1923, see 'Contributions to pure and applied science published by the staff (past and present), Fellows and associates of the College of Science for Ireland during the period 1900–1923', *The College of Science for Ireland*, pp 25–53. **33** R.L. Praeger, *A populous solitude* (London, 1941), p. 200; quoted by G. Jones, 'Catholicism, nationalism and science', *Irish Review*, 20 (1997), p. 56.

institution. Initially, the professors had no security of tenure, being on temporary contracts for the first seven years, and until the end of the century their salaries continued to be at a lower level than their colleagues in Britain.[34] The institution to which the new professors were appointed was riven by internal disputes, divided loyalties and personal antagonisms in the early years;[35] furthermore, there was the dual administration of academic dean (Sir Robert Kane) and college secretary (Frederick Sidney) who had been appointed as 'the agent and representative of the department in all business, whether immediately connected with instruction or not'.[36] This dual administration continued until the end of the century and imposed severe constraints on the executive role of the council of professors at the RCScI, as all decisions regarding staffing, expenditure and changes in the college's curriculum had to be sanctioned by the DSA in London.

One serious problem in the college was the poor standard of scientific education in Ireland. This had been a problem for the teachers at the MII that Kane had attributed to 'our secondary schools, [which] owing to the peculiar character of the older universities for which they educate, their training is almost exclusively classical' although he paid tribute to the Christian Brothers, who 'have some schools of a very superior description'.[37] Certainly, in the early years of the RCScI, the education standard in mathematics and the sciences of some of the first-year students was so poor that the numbers who failed to make the grade into second year was high, often as high as 50 per cent Therefore, the professor of applied mathematics had to provide classes in mathematics for the associate students. A result of this was that there was no selective entry to the courses at the college until 1887, when an entry examination in mathematics was established.

The college did not have the popular appeal of its predecessor, and the higher fees of £1 to £2 for each course of occasional lectures at the college, rather than two or three shillings charged by the MII, must have made the new college economically inaccessible for many. Also, when the college was established in 1867, practical teaching in science was not commonplace even in England. In Ireland, where (except for the urban areas and the industrial areas in the north-east of the country) the principal industry was agriculture, the potential benefits of the detailed practical instruction it offered were barely appreciated and, as Robert S. Ball recalled, the educational programmes were 'greatly in advance of their times'.[38] This lack of a public visibility and presence is reflected in Sullivan's comments in 1884 that 'The

---

34 These professors were on temporary contracts for the first seven years and 'not entitled to claim compensation in the event of their offices being abolished'; *Report ... College of Science ... 1867*, p. 7; *Royal Commission on University Education (Ireland)*, appendix to the third report, p. 550, HC 1902 [1229], xxxii, 1. **35** For details of the negotiations and disputes prior to and immediately after the establishment of the RCScI, see *Select Committee ... 1864; Report ... College of science ... 1867*, p. 2; *Report ... on the Science and Art Department in Ireland, Vols 1–2*; Copy of letter from Sullivan, Jukes and Barker to the Duke of Marlborough, 13 Mar. 1867 (NLI, Mayo papers, MS 11,200 (1)). **36** *Report ... College of Science ... 1867*, p. 6. **37** *Select Committee on Scientific Instruction ... 1868*, pp 37, 157. **38** Ball, *Reminiscences*, p. 87.

people of Dublin, who have been crying out for technical education lately, do not seem to know that they have had in their midst for the last twenty years one of the most complete polytechnic schools in Europe'.[39] A contributing factor was that the RCScI qualification of 'associate' was regarded by many as inferior to a university degree. Joseph O'Reilly, professor of mining and mineralogy at the college from 1869 until 1890, held this view:

> Any establishment which does not pretend to train its students to what is called a liberal profession has much to contend with in this country, there being for a long time an extremely marked prejudice against any vocation which seems to be even connected with trade.[40]

However, the biggest challenge facing the professors and lecturers in the RCScI was their physical environment. The old building in St Stephen's Green was never suitable for its new purpose and as courses expanded it became critically overcrowded. The annual reports of the college council to London were constant in their request for better accommodation, in 1899 describing the old building at Stephen's Green:

> [It is] very unsuitable for a college ... several of the lecture rooms are attics, low roofed, ill ventilated, badly lighted and, in winter, insufficiently heated. None of the laboratories is of sufficient size; some, like the lecture rooms, are attics; some are underground basements, into which daylight seldom penetrates. There is no engineering or mechanical laboratory whatever. In not one department of the college is there a place where professors or students can uninterruptedly pursue delicate experiments ... The professor [of geology] ... regrets that there is no room to introduce a stove into the [geological] laboratory, and that it still has to be heated by lighting the gas in winter ... The students have repeatedly complained of the want of facilities.[41]

Despite the poor conditions, the professors at the RCScI continued to develop and expand the courses they taught. Practical physics was taught there when it was taught nowhere else in Ireland and a physics laboratory was established to support its practical instruction. Although no facilities or funding was provided in the college and despite the poor accommodation in the old building in St Stephen's Green, the college's professors did make significant contributions to research in their areas of scientific expertise, their research quite often funded by outside institutions.[42] On

39 W.K. Sullivan, 'Technical instruction in Ireland', appendix to *Second report of the Royal Commissioners on Technical Instruction*, vol. III, pp cvii–cxix, HC 1884 [3981–II].   **40** *Commission on Technical Instruction, 2nd report*, vol. 4, p. 69.   **41** *Forty-sixth report of Department of Science and Art*, pp 261–2, HC 1899 [C. 9191], xxvii, 245.   **42** See *Fourteenth report of the Department of Science and Art*, HC 1867 [3853], xxiii, 1 to *Forty-sixth report of the Department of Science and Art*, HC 1899 [C.9191], xxvii, 245; *Robertson Commission ... 3rd report*, appendix, p. 552.

occasion, this led to conflict with other interests in Ireland, especially towards the end of the century. Haddon, for example, who had conducted ethnographical surveys of the communities of the Aran Islands as part of his research on progressive evolutionism, came into conflict with advocates of Ireland's Gaelic and cultural revival, Yeats in particular. In Greta Jones' words, 'Haddon saw Irish folklore as evidence of the evolutionary history of European peoples from primitive to complex societies. Yeats saw it as a mark of Irish uniqueness'.[43]

Overall, the professors taught and conducted their research in a political environment that changed rapidly in the second half of the nineteenth century. The development of a new style of Irish nationalism, linking the Irish cultural identity with education and Catholicism, caused concern regarding the continuing independence of scientific research.[44] The professor of physics, Barrett, reflected this concern in 1902, arguing that 'For thirty-three years the College of Science has preserved an unbroken record of freedom from religious and sectarian dispute, and it would, I think, be an unfortunate thing if it were handed over to a denominational university'.[45]

THE STUDENTS

The number of students who registered in the early years of the college was small. In the first session there were only seven students who registered for the full diploma course and most of these were Exhibition scholars who were government-funded. The numbers gradually increased: by 1896, 181 students had graduated from the College. The associate students could be divided into three classes: those who intended to be engineers, those who intended to become manufacturers and a number who hoped to become science teachers. The majority of the graduates left Ireland and found employment abroad. They obtained appointments as inspectors of national schools, as consulting chemists to manufacturers, and in the Indian Civil Service, as research chemists in factories, engineers in Ireland, England, South Africa, Australia and in the army, in the Patent Office, in the geological surveys of Ireland and Scotland, and as teachers and lecturers in schools and colleges in Britain and Ireland.[46] Among those students were Joseph Reilly (later professor of chemistry at

---

43 Jones, 'Catholicism, nationalism and science', 59 n. 22.   44 For studies of the various strands of nationalism as they affected the scientific environment in Ireland, see Jones, 'Contested territories'; G. Jones, 'Catholicism, nationalism and science', *Irish Review*, 20 (1997), 47–61; G. Jones, 'Scientists against Home Rule' in D.G. Boyce and A. O'Day (eds), *Defenders of the union: a survey of British and Irish unionism since 1801* (London, 2001), pp 188–208; G. Jones, 'Darwinism in Ireland' in D. Attis and C. Mollan (eds), *Science and Irish culture: why the history of science matters in Ireland* (Dublin, 2004), pp 115–37.   45 *Robertson Commission ... 3rd report*, appendix, p. 228.   46 *Directory of the Royal College of Science for Ireland. Session 1902–1903* (Dublin, [1903]), pp 18–31; *Robertson Commission ... 3rd report*,

University College Cork), Thomas Wheeler (later professor of chemistry at University College Dublin) and Thomas Dillon (professor of chemistry at University College Galway).

A significant number of the occasional students took the classes in science and attended laboratory sessions at the RCScI but completed their university degrees elsewhere, in TCD, the Catholic University or the RUI. Some were engineering students, some medical students, and others students who intended to take an arts degree, but who wished to take honours in science.[47] Of the rest, a substantial number were local manufacturers and business men or their sons. Robert Galloway, who had been the first professor of chemistry, described the wide range of backgrounds of his students in 1885:

> They used to come for miles round Dublin, some of them were engaged in smelting works, others in gas works, others in soap works, in pharmaceutical establishments, in chemical works (owners as well as managers), in manure works, in photographic establishments, in mineral water factories; some were teachers, others were practicing physicians, others students in TCD, and some who were in non-manufacturing business have since become, from the knowledge they acquired, chemical manufacturers, and some have become inventors'.[48]

Galloway's view was supported by a Dublin city councillor, John Mulligan, formerly a student and a strong advocate of technical education in Dublin, who believed that 'the classes were of great advantage to pupils who were engaged in manufactories in Dublin'.[49]

In the 1880s, all the courses and examinations were opened to women, although they were excluded from competing for scholarships until the end of the century. In fact, women students had attended the occasional courses at the RCScI since 1867, when after the representations of one of the women who had attended the MII,[50] it was decided that 'Female students should be admitted to enter for the separate Courses of the Professors as heretofore to the Classes of the Irish Industrial Museum'.[51] By the mid-1880s, about one sixth of the students were women. Many were students at Alexandra College Dublin or at the other women's colleges, such as the Dominican College of St Marys' and Victoria College Belfast, and later took up a career in teaching. Others had academic ambitions, and of the nine women who

appendix, pp 545–7. **47** *Select Committee on Industries (Ireland)*, p. 452. **48** *Select Committee on Industries (Ireland)*, p. 465. **49** *Commission on Technical Instruction, 2nd report, vol. 4*, p. 10. **50** For the history of women students at the MII see Clara Cullen, '"Laurels for fair as well as manly brows": women at Dublin's Museum of Irish Industry, 1854–1867' in M. Mulvihill (ed.), *Lab coats and lace: the lives and legacies of inspiring Irish women scientists and pioneers* (Dublin, 2009), pp 1–13. **51** Minutes of meeting, 28 Nov. 1867 (UCDA RCSI/1). All the professors present voted in support of the proposal 'with the exception of Professor Dickson, who confined his objection however to his own subject'.

were the first graduates of the RUI in 1884, the majority had been students at the RCScI.[52] Some of these women students continued in the sciences, like the chemists Mary Robertson and Genevieve Morrow and botanist Matilda Knowles who, with her sisters, studied at the college between 1895 and 1896. From the 1880s, when the barriers to the admittance of women to the medical professions were lifted, there were numbers of women students who attended courses in the RCScI as part of their medical studies. These included the first woman to register at the Royal College of Surgeons in Ireland, Agnes Shannon, and Emily Dickson, the first woman to become a fellow there in 1893. Eva Jellett, one of the first women admitted to courses at the Catholic University medical school, and who was followed by Kathleen Lynn (1899), Everina Massy (1900), Isabella Ovenden (1904) and Ada English (1904) all studied at the RCScI.[53]

NEW BUILDING, NEW CENTURY

By the last decade of the century, the old building in St Stephen's Green was severely overcrowded. The demands of scientific education had increased enormously since the foundation of the college in 1867. There were new courses and additional subjects contributed to the pressure on the existing faculties. The college council's repeated pleas for a new building and proper facilities for teaching and research were finally heard and in 1899 a committee, established to consider what new buildings were required, recommended 'the erection of a new and extended college, contiguous with the Science and Art Museum in Kildare Street, and that the curriculum of the college should be enlarged by adding more practical work without interfering with the pure science at present taught'.[54] The same year, the new Department of Agriculture and Technical Instruction (DATI) took responsibility for the college 'with the object of its forming part ... of the system of technical instruction as related to Agriculture and Industries, which the Department have been commissioned to establish in Ireland';[55] and the subjects offered by the college were revised. Mining was abolished as a faculty and new courses in agriculture and rural science were introduced. Fellowships were established, research studentships set up and a new building was finally approved. In 1904, the foundation stone was laid by Edward VII and in July 1911 his son George V opened the new buildings.

In the new college, the student numbers increased but not to the extent anticipated, possibly due to the establishment of the National University of Ireland (NUI) and the opening of UCD in 1909. Two years later, the British treasury, concerned

52 Occasional students register, 1867//8–1905/6 (UCDA, RCSI/165). **53** I. Finn, 'Women in the medical profession in Ireland, 1876–1919' in B. Whelan (ed.), *Women and paid work in Ireland, 1500–1830* (Dublin, 2000), pp 102–19; Occasional students register, 1867//8–1905/6 (UCDA, RCSI/165). **54** *Report of the committee appointed to inquire into the buildings and site of the Royal College of Science for Ireland*, HC 1899 [9159]; *College of Science for Ireland*, p. 11. **55** Minutes of council, 4 June 1901 (UCDA RCSI/7).

about 'the somewhat excessive proportion of the teaching staff to the number of students at the college' threatened to review the situation.[56] World events overtook this threatened review. The business of the RCScI council for late 1914 was principally to discuss and support applications of students to temporary commissions. In subsequent years, as well as academic arrangements, the college minutes record correspondence asking for deferral of examinations as the erstwhile students were on active service 'somewhere in France'.[57] Some of the college's rooms were given over to the packaging of sphagnum moss as surgical dressings for the hospitals on the western front and in 1917, the Department of Agriculture requisitioned some rooms (including the professors reading room), 'for two or three weeks ... for food production work'.[58]

1918 and the end of the First World War saw a flurry of letters from former students about the completion of their qualifications.[59] Political events in Ireland were reflected in changes in the college; a number of staff retired in 1922, taking up the offer of retirement in consequence of the change of government.[60] Numbers in some of the classes were decimated – including eighteen final year associates who transferred to engineering courses in universities in England because of the uncertain political situation in Ireland.[61] In August 1922, just as the college council was planning the next academic year, the provisional government ordered the closing of the college to the students 'in consequence of the disturbed state of the country'.[62] This was deferred when UCD

> offered the use of 85 and 86 St Stephen's Green for classrooms and such laboratory accommodation as might be required pending the re-opening of the College ... [and] it was explicitly stated that the co-operate [sic] entity of the college should be maintained.[63]

However, on 4 May 1926, the last meeting of the College of Science council was held in the council chambers of UCD.[64] Subsequently, the college buildings became home to UCD's faculties of science and engineering until these faculties moved to Belfield. The government again moved in and in 1991 the College of Science in Merrion Street became Government Buildings.[65]

56 Minutes of council, 11 Nov. 1913 (UCDA, RCSI/9). 57 Minutes of council, 21 Feb. 1918 (UCDA, RCSI/10). 58 Minutes of council, 23 May 1917 (UCDA, RCSI/9). 59 Minutes of council, 21 Feb. 1918 (UCDA, RCSI/10). 60 UCDA RCSI/62 (1). 61 UCDA, RCSI/62 (5). 62 Report of the arrangements for the work of the college, session 1922–3 (UCDA, RCSI/62 (14–15)). 63 Ibid. 64 Minutes of Council, 4 May 1926 (UCDA, RCSI/11). 65 *IT*, 2 Jan. 2010.

CONCLUSION

Despite the eminence of the professors and the comprehensive courses on science, the Royal College of Science for Ireland never captured the popular imagination in Ireland. It may have been ahead of its time in Ireland in the technical and scientific education it offered; however, the qualification of associate was not a university degree and the accommodation in which it functioned until 1911 was totally inadequate. At the same time, the RCScI was, as its professor of experimental physics W.F. Barrett believed,[66] in 'a unique position among the educational institutions' of Ireland.[67] Its emphasis on the practical application of scientific theory and the research interests of its professors ensured that the educational programmes of the college were at the forefront of scientific development and research, in Ireland and internationally.

Following the policy of its predecessor, the MII, that its courses should be open to all without 'distinction of class, creed or opinion ... [and] there is no monopoly of sex',[68] the college's determined non-sectarian policies meant that for Catholics in Dublin, whose options regarding higher education were limited to TCD or the CU, the RCScI offered the opportunities for scientific education in a non-denominational environment acceptable to all. With inadequate funds and very limited and unsuitable facilities, it did provide access to scientific education for many before the establishment of the technical schools in Dublin. The college's policies of access for all was particularly important for the 50 per cent of the population who were female and who, until the twentieth century, had little access otherwise to advanced courses in scientific subjects.

These courses were provided in the most challenging of circumstances – poor facilities, an unsuitable building and, in the early days, a very ambivalent attitude on the part of its managers in London. The institution and the efforts of those who taught and who studied there deserve to be better remembered.

66 Barrett was also a governor of the Technical School of the City of Dublin, a member of the Technical Education Committee and a founder of the Royal Irish Association for the Technical Training of Women. 67 *Robertson Commission ... 3rd report*, appendix, p. 225. 68 *FJ*, 21 Oct. 1859.

Practical science and religious politics: the Glasnevin botanic gardens' Sunday opening controversy, 1861

VANDRA COSTELLO

The opening of the Glasnevin botanical gardens on Sunday, 18 August 1861 marked the end of a hard-fought battle between advocates of public education and sabbatarians. This conflict between the aims of practical science and religious practice in Ireland echoed similar developments in England and Scotland and was part of a much wider controversy which preoccupied much of the political discourse relating to scientific and educational institutions during the latter part of the nineteenth century. The behaviour and education of the working classes would, it was said, be greatly improved by the opening of public gardens, museums and picture galleries.[1] The nineteenth-century city was dirty, over-populated and disease-ridden. The fashionable city squares were closed to the Dublin public and there was little for workers to do apart from visiting public houses, which moved one writer to note: 'In the continental cities where public institutions are far more freely thrown open than with us, no traveller has his feelings outraged by the scenes of filthy brutal drunkenness on a Sunday, so common in those regions of stricter and bitter observance'. In contrast to the 'educated man', who could spend the day at home in quiet contemplation with his books, 'the uneducated cannot remain at home; he must go somewhere to recreate and enjoy himself. He finds the public house alone open'.[2]

The Victorians believed that clean air and open spaces were health giving. In Dublin, houses close to open spaces could be sold or let at a premium.[3] There was a moral imperative to keeping the working classes busy at all times and the provision of places of recreation was seen as a way to improve both their mental and physical health and moral conduct. As George Woods Maunsell put it, 'Places reserved for the amusement of the humbler classes would assist in weaning them off the low and debasing pleasures such as drinking houses, dog fights and boxing matches they enjoyed theretofore'.[4] Following a report in 1826 on the state of London's royal parks, George IV instructed that 'the whole range and extent of the parks should be thrown

---

1 *Daily News*, 8 Feb. 1856.   2 *Irish Builder*, 4:7 (Nov 15 1862), p. 295.   3 72 St Stephen's Green was described as 'a most convenient and healthful habitation for a respectable family', *FJ*, 3 May 1820. Mountjoy Square and Gardens were a draw for houses on Gardiner Street, *FJ*, 26 Apr. 1816.   4 G.W. Maunsell, *Reasons for opening St Stephen's Green and converting it into a public park* (Dublin, 1859), p. 5.

open for the gratification and enjoyment of the public'.[5] From the mid-nineteenth century onwards, Sunday access was became a more pressing issue.

Developments in Dublin sparked the English movement for Sunday access to scientific and educational institutions. In 1841, the Dublin Zoological Gardens in the Phoenix Park was the first of the scientific institutions in Ireland or Britain to open its doors to the public on Sundays.[6] Sir Dominic Corrigan, giving evidence to the Royal Commission on Art and Science said

> I can hardly give you an idea of the obloquy and opposition we incurred from that; and for that I think we deserve very much credit, for we were the first public body in the United Kingdom that opened the institution under its control to the public on Sundays.[7]

Corrigan stated that opening on Sundays had the welcome effect of 'withdrawing the people from public-houses, and bringing them into the open air . . . making them well-tempered and civil'.[8]

When the Crystal Palace opened in London for the Great Exhibition of 1851 it was planned that it would always be open to the public after one o'clock on Sundays.[9] When attempts were made to renege on this promise, the problem was overcome by the issue of shares to the public which granted an automatic right of entry, as a member of the company, to the gardens on a Sunday. The *Belfast Newsletter* was of the opinion that the Crystal Palace's Sunday opening policy was a 'blow struck at the sanctity of the English Sabbath', in which 'mammon worship carried the day'.[10] Following Dublin's example set at the Zoological Garden, Kew Gardens opened to the public on Sundays in 1853. The *Gardener's Magazine* reported that 'the experiment of opening the gardens at Kew to the public had been an unqualified success' – in 1858 the number of visits was 404,090 and in 1859–60 was 384,698[11] – while *The Times* noted the 'vast benefits to the people of the artisan class resulting from the opening of Kew Gardens'.[12] Hampton Court Palace gardens followed suit shortly afterwards. In 1855, the Manchester Botanical Gardens voted to open their gardens to the public on Sundays by a vote of 265 to 234, but as the requisite two-thirds majority was not reached, the motion was not carried.[13] Undeterred, the pro-Sunday opening movement gathered support.

5 S. Lasdun, *The English park, royal, private & public* (London, 1991), p. 130.   **6** *Pall Mall Gazette*, 10 Apr. 1869.   **7** Ibid.   **8** Ibid.   **9** *Leeds Mercury*, 28 Aug. 1852.   **10** *Belfast Newsletter*, 21 Dec. 1857.   **11** *Gardener's Weekly Magazine*, Jan.–June 1860, p. 229.   **12** *The Times*, 6 Apr. 1869.   **13** *Manchester Times*, 7 Mar. 1855.

THE BOTANIC GARDENS AT GLASNEVIN

The Royal Dublin Society opened the botanic gardens at Glasnevin in 1795. The Gardens' functions were primarily practical and educational and included agricultural trial plots and a large herb garden for medicinal purposes. The gardens were initially open to the public on weekdays and remained so until 1801, when the RDS decided to admit only those with cards.[14] After Ninian Niven's appointment as curator in 1834, the agricultural purpose of the gardens had been overtaken by the pursuit of botanical knowledge. This was facilitated by the arrival of plants from around the world and by continuing contact and dialogue with the botanical gardens of Kew and Edinburgh. Since their establishment in Glasnevin, the gardens had been a boon to the area; adverts for houses for sale boasted that 'the goodness of the air, and its vicinity to the botanic garden make it a desirable residence'.[15]

Glasnevin was part of a wider recreational interest in practical botany in mid-Victorian Dublin. Summer schools on botany were held by Dr Wright at Dr Steven's Hospital.[16] Royal Horticultural Society shows were regarded as highlights of the social calendar, attracting huge crowds to view exotics such as orchids and azaleas. The viceregal lodge sent peaches and hyacinths grown for the lord lieutenant, while nurseries sent their best flowers for display in large marquees set out on the lawns of the Rotunda. The spring show of April 1861 was reported to have had such a great and illustrious turnout that 'Cavendish Row and its neighbours were filled with carriages waiting to get in'.[17]

THE PRO-SUNDAY-OPENING MOVEMENT IN DUBLIN

In the 1850s, a pressure group campaigning for Sunday opening of public facilities was established in England. The object of the National Sunday League, founded in the 1850s, was 'to obtain the opening of the public museums, libraries and gardens on Sunday, in London and in the towns of England, Ireland and Scotland for the instruction, recreation and innocent amusement of the working classes'.[18] Sir Joshua Walmsley MP, an advocate of non-sectarian education, was the first president of the league.[19] In 1856, Walmsley laid a motion for the relaxation of the law to allow the British Museum and the National Gallery and other institutions to open on Sundays. The motion was defeated by 376 votes to 48.[20] The English group may have prompted the establishment of a similar movement in Dublin. Following the establishment of the National Sunday League, a campaigning organization to re-open St Stephen's Green as a people's park was founded. This it was said would be 'of great

14 *IT*, 6 Apr. 1861. 15 *FJ*, 16 May 1816. 16 *IT*, 22 Apr. 1861. 17 Ibid., 26 Apr. 1861.
18 *Manchester Times*, 23 Feb. 1856. 19 C.W. Sutton, rev. M. Lee, 'Sir Joshua Walmsley (1794–1871)', *Oxford Dictionary of National Biography* (Oxford, 2004), online ed., accessed 29 Oct. 2010. 20 *Manchester Times*, 23 Feb. 1856.

public advantage and conducive to the health and enjoyment of the inhabitants' of the city.[21]

The idea of opening the botanical gardens in Glasnevin to the public on Sundays was tied into debates about public opening in general. Sunday opening had first been mooted in 1854. The RDS committee of botany opposed this on the grounds 'that without greatly increasing the staff of assistants, for which there are no adequate funds, or depriving those now employed of their only day of rest' the garden could not be opened on Sundays.[22] However, it was the society's council rather than the botany committee that objected to opening the garden to the public. In 1858, Dr Frazer suggested that the gardens be opened for public promenade once a month during the summer but was forced to withdraw the motion after opposition from the council.[23] In June of that year, the botany committee recommended that the gardens be opened to the public, free of charge on Saturdays from 2 to 6 o'clock during the summer months.[24] This measure automatically excluded members of the working classes who worked in trade or in service whose only day of rest was on Sundays.[25]

THE IRISH PRO-SUNDAY OPENING COMMITTEE

In January 1861, the Committee for Science and Education of the English privy council received a letter from Sir Thomas Larcom enclosing a pamphlet by the pro-opening committee. The privy council in England declared that it had 'no hesitation in expressing [the] opinion that these gardens should be freely opened to the public as the Kew Gardens are', but before issuing instructions to the Royal Dublin Society, it canvassed the opinion of the lord lieutenant, who was clearly in favour of Sunday opening.[26] In January 1861, a 'Conference of Friends' of the movement to open the botanical garden was held in the Prince of Wales Hotel in Dublin. It was proposed that the garden be opened after divine service at 2pm. The chairman of the group, James Houghton, and other members of the RDS noted that Sunday opening had been proposed at council three times already and at each time had been outvoted.[27] The main argument of the pro-opening movement was that the garden was publicly maintained and that as such should be available to all. Sunday opening had been successfully tried in London and on the continent and should be extended to all classes of the people in Dublin.[28] As it stood, the garden was 'practically inaccessible to the mass of the population of Dublin under the present system of admission'.[29]

Prominent among the group lobbying to open the gardens were members of the Roman Catholic and Jewish faiths. The editor of the *Catholic Telegraph* said 'religious objection was an insult to the people of this country as it asserted that the people of

21 Maunsell, *Reasons for opening*, p. 7.   **22** RDS Committee of Botany Fair Minutes, 1857–77, 27 Mar. 1861. All RDS manuscripts referred to are found in the Royal Dublin Society's library, Ballsbridge, Dublin.   **23** Ibid., 3 May 1858, 7 June 1858.   **24** Ibid., 7 June 1858.   **25** Ibid., 31 Oct. 1859.   **26** TNA; PRO ED 28/12/153, 22 Jan. 1861.   **27** *IT*, 31 Jan. 1861. **28** Ibid.   **29** Ibid.

Ireland were unfit for what was freely granted elsewhere on the continent and in England'. The Jewish representative, Maurice Solomons, said the Irish people wanted equality with England and 'to have no brand placed on them of inequality of race, or creed or class'.[30]

Leading members of the RDS attached themselves to the campaign and accusations of sectarianism soon emerged.[31] An influential minority was convinced that religious bigotry was behind the society's determination to keep the botanic garden closed on Sundays. Lord Talbot de Malahide said he would and could not believe that the Society's governing council's refusal to open the garden was not based on religious considerations.[32] Testimony in support of the Sunday opening movement was also provided by some larger landlords who had traditionally allowed their estates on Sundays. At the January 1861 meeting, J.R. Barry stated the 'beneficial effects of affording the peasantry the opportunities for healthful, innocent recreation on a Sunday evening' on his own estate.[33] Lord Cloncurry, a strong supporter of Sunday opening, who opened his gardens on Sundays to his 'humble neighbours' said that no injury had been caused to his plants.[34]

Trades unions and guilds in Dublin took an interest in the developing debate and many allied themselves to the Sunday opening movement. Trades associations were active in organizing petitions and it was hoped to canvas every house in the city, which one trade unionist said was 'a labour of love and goodwill'.[35] For example, the secretary of the Operative Painter's Society had, with the help of a brother operative, obtained signatures of 132 householders in favour of Sunday opening.[36] However, some unions took a more submissive view. For example, a meeting of the Society of Plasterers advocated the opening of places of exercise and amusement for the working classes, but felt that Sunday opening of the Botanical Gardens was a matter for the RDS, 'the proper guardians of the place'.[37]

Support for the pro-opening committee had increased when it met again the following month. This time, the meeting was composed of members of the RDS, including 'several MPs and professors, men of the first eminence, merchants, traders and representatives from several trades'.[38] The pro-opening committee argued that its manifesto was 'greatly benevolent in character', seeking merely to provide a fit recreational outlet for the working class:

> it is in accordance with the good spirit of our times, which would freely open up to our toiling classes such innocent and civilizing enjoyments of a visit to our beautiful garden ... on their only day of leisure.[39]

Despite the pleas of the pro-opening committee, the RDS council claimed that it had 'no power to comply with their suggestions'.[40]

30 Ibid.; RDS Minute Books, 19 Mar. 1861. **31** *IT*, 31 Jan. 1861. **32** RDS Minute Books, 27 May 1861. **33** *IT*, 31 Jan. 1861. **34** RDS Minute Books, 27 May 1861. **35** *IT*, 22 Feb. 1861; *IT*, 15 Feb. 1861. **36** Ibid., 31 Jan. 1861. **37** Ibid., 22 Feb. 1861. **38** Ibid. **39** Ibid. **40** RDS Committee of Botany Fair Minutes, 1857–77, 28 Feb. 1861.

A formidable counter-movement opposed the Sunday opening movement throughout the United Kingdom. When a partial opening of the Leeds Botanical Gardens was proposed for Sundays,[41] the *Leeds Mercury* in 1851 editorialized vehemently that

> Mr Hume and his associates have long been urging on the legislature to open the British Museum and National Gallery on Sundays, which would mean that 'the popish festival will at once supersede [the Sabbath] – a mass in the forenoon; – then the park, the picture gallery, or the ballroom for the rest of the day ... it is ten times more alarming than was that papal aggression of 1850'.[42]

This fear of a continental-style Sunday was foremost in the minds of the anti-Sunday movement in Leeds, who were of the view that if the council were to sanction the opening of the gardens that it would give a sense of 'authority' to the 'continental idea of the Sabbath day', which 'may be expected to lead to a similar practice ... in the conduct of various establishments'.[43]

Sentiments in Scotland ran high: not only did Scottish sabbatarians want to keep all gardens and scientific or educational establishments closed, but petitions were sent to Queen Victoria pleading with her 'to put a stop to the assemblage of the higher classes in their equipages in the parks on Sunday'.[44] The Sabbath Observance Committee of the Established Church Assembly of Scotland protested that opening the Edinburgh gardens on a Sunday would lead to Sabbath desecration elsewhere and that, if this was sanctioned by the legislature, it would 'convert a local violation of the Sabbath law into a national sin'.[45] In addition to this national sin, opening on Sundays 'would have the effect of violating the consciences of most of the men employed in the garden, and either depriving them of their Sabbath's rest, or removing them from their situations on behalf of others less trustworthy'.[46]

As pressure from the Committee for Sunday Opening of the Dublin garden mounted, those determined to keep the gates firmly closed to the public rallied and in April 1861 the opponents of Sunday opening met in the Metropolitan Hall to discuss tactics.[47] Support for the opposition came mostly from the Protestant and non-conformist churches, with the synod of the Presbyterian Church in Ireland and the Sabbath Alliance in Edinburgh sending letters of approbation to the opposition committee.[48] Although non-conformist support was strong, the anti-opening committee was composed overwhelmingly of prominent members of the Church of Ireland. Clerics including the dean of St Patrick's Cathedral were heavily involved. The movement's argument was framed in sabbatarian terms. The stated aim of the

---

41 *Leeds Mercury*, 14 Aug. 1841. **42** Ibid., 22 Jan. 1853. **43** Ibid., 28 Aug. 1852. **44** *Glasgow Herald*, 1 Oct. 1856. **45** *The Times*, 8 June 1863. **46** H.R. Fields and W.H. Brown (eds), *The Royal Botanic Garden Edinburgh, 1670–1970* (London, 1970). **47** *IT*, 30 Apr. 1861. **48** RDS Committee of Botany Fair Minutes, 1857–77, 23 May 1861.

group was to fight against the proposed 'desecration of the Lord's Day'. It was horrified at the attempts to 'Parisiennize' the city. Sunday opening of gardens was merely the first point in a process that would ultimately end in the scandalous opening of theatres and ballrooms on the Sabbath. It concluded with a dire warning that 'all things go by slow degrees – if the botanical gardens opened, then the college gardens and Portobello etc. would follow!'[49]

Aided by the *Irish Times*, the anti-opening committee began a 'dirty tricks' campaign; an editorial in the paper alleged that the pro-opening committee's meetings were unruly and that the atmosphere 'was aggressive and [that there was] threatening conduct and that nobody could talk'. Other slurs included accusations that the leaders of the pro-opening committee were guilty of 'agitation' and 'luring little boys into signing the petition'.[50]

THE PRIVY COUNCIL AND THE RDS

The sabbatarian movement had failed to attract governmental or political support. In fact, both the privy council and the treasury were in favour of Sunday opening. In January 1861, the privy council Committee for Science and Education received a letter from the under secretary, Sir Thomas Larcom, enclosing a pamphlet by the pro-opening committee. The privy council declared that it had 'no hesitation in expressing its opinion that these gardens should be freely opened to the public as the Kew gardens are'.[51] The treasury increased the pressure on the RDS open the garden on Sundays by threatening to withdraw grants. The secretary of the treasury wrote of the difficulties involved 'with respect to the grants of public money … in the case of an institution, which, though mainly supported by parliamentary grants, claim the privileges of a private society' and informed the privy council of his intention to bring the matter to the notice of the House of Commons prior to the next vote on financial allocations to the RDS.[52]

From this point on, the argument escalated and there was a flurry of correspondence between Dublin and London and a number of council meetings were convened to urgently put an end to the matter. The privy council recommended that the RDS open the gardens to the public on Sundays forthwith as, in its opinion, 'the people of Ireland seem to be well entitled to this boon from the RDS'.[53] The privy council reminded the society that in 1836 the government had suspended the vote of the society until it was fully and unequivocally admitted that the property of the society was held 'for the public use of the institution only so that the public shall be entitled to the full and entire use thereof'.[54] The council further argued that it

49 *IT*, 30 Apr. 1861. **50** RDS Minute Books, 27 May 1861. **51** TNA:PRO ED 28/12/153, 22 Jan. 1861. **52** TNA:PRO ED 28/13/12/121, 2 May 1861. **53** TNA:PRO ED 28/13/41, 15 Mar. 1861. **54** TNA:PRO ED 28/13/12/83, 30 Mar. 1861. To underline that this was the case, they reminded the society that over a period of six years from 1854 to 1860 subscriptions from individual members averaged on £1,336, while the annual grant

was its duty to 'render public grants as conducive as possible to the improvement of the habits and tastes of the people and to affording them the means of healthful recreation' and said that the RDS should deal with this subject not from the view of a private society, but as a public institution who would 'afford to the working classes of Dublin all the facilities for visiting the Glasnevin gardens they can'.[55] It is clear from committee minutes and correspondence that the privy council felt that the reluctance of the RDS to open the gardens on Sundays was motivated by a combination of sectarianism and elitism.

The RDS decided to defy the threats being issued by the privy council, arguing that the council had no right to interfere in the workings of a private society whose majority consistently voted against Sunday opening.[56] The RDS convened a special meeting to discuss their predicament on 27 March 1861.[57] At the meeting, a reply was drafted to the privy council, referring the council 'to their former report on this subject presented at the meeting of the society held on December 7th 1854; and to state that the committee see no reason now to depart from the opinion expressed therein'. They also stressed that 'composed as this society is of all denominations and classes, may be considered a fair representation of the opinion of the educated portion of the citizens on this question'.[58] In a further response two months later, the RDS denied that it rested its objection to Sunday opening, on the basis of its being a private organization unaccountable for the support it received. Instead, it protested vaguely that there were myriad other reasons, mainly that they represented public opinion, for which

> there [were] reasons of <u>local</u> and special application in connexion with the <u>peculiar situation</u> of the botanical gardens of Glasnevin, which present cogent reasons why the society should view the opening on Sundays with grave apprehension.[59]

In subsequent a letter, it argued that opening the gardens on Sundays would prove prohibitively expensive.

London, however, was not convinced by the society's arguments. The privy council dispensed with the society's financial claim and argued that the public opening of Hampton Court and Kew gardens cost just £150 extra a year.[60] On 1 June 1861, a final and firm communication was made to the RDS by the English

---

besides special grants from the state averaged upwards of £6,000, excluding extra grants for the erection of conservatories and general maintenance and an average of £1,180 per annum raised by cattle shows. **55** TNA:PRO ED 28/13/12/83, 30 Mar. 1861. **56** RDS Minute Books, 27 May 1861. **57** RDS Committee of Botany Fair Minutes 1857–77, 21 Mar. 1861. **58** Ibid., 27 Mar. 1861. **59** Letter from the RDS dated 18 May 1861 to Norman MacLeod; TNA:PRO ED 28/13/12/121, 2 May 1861. **60** RDS Minute Books, 27 May 1861. The elitist motives of the RDS are underlined by the fact that the honorary secretary George Woods Maunsell who was anti-Sunday opening was a leading proponent of the campaign to re-open St Stephen's Green to the public.

privy council stating that 'Parliamentary motions will be made to oppose votes submitted on behalf of the RDS for funds and the question will be raised how far a society largely assisted by public funds is at liberty to claim independence of the control of the government'.[61]

THE GLASNEVIN SUNDAY-OPENING DEBATE IN PARLIAMENT

When the RDS' council learned that the issue of Sunday opening was to be raised in parliament, they sought representation at the debate. The council resolved to send the secretary and assistant secretary to London forthwith, authorizing them to

> take such steps as may appear to them to be necessary, as will explain fully to the members of parliament and the government, the true state of the circumstances bearing on the question now at issue between this society and the Science and Art Department.[62]

Steele appears to have had little influence on the direction of the debate. The liberal politician Lord Granville wrote to Lord Carlisle, the lord lieutenant, outlining the events:

> You will read in today's papers an abridged report of an interesting discussion in the House of Lords on the subject of the opening of the Glasnevin Gardens on a Sunday. Lord Clancarty introduced the question in a moderate speech, and was supported by the bishop of Carlisle, who spoke on the general principle of not opening any places of recreation to the public on a Sunday. Lords Eglington, Donoughmore, Monteagle, Talbot de Malahide, and the bishop of Down and Connor all regretted the decision to which the Royal Society of Dublin have come – the feeling appeared to be general (if not unanimous) in the house. At the same time, all the speakers deprecated 'a collision in the House of Commons, as the loss of the grant which might ensue, would be of great disadvantage to the Irish public'.[63]

The council of the Royal Dublin Society had begun to grasp the hopelessness of their position. Meeting after the parliamentary debate, the council stated that the society 'fully recognized the authority of parliament to impose any conditions they may think beneficial to the public' and expressed the readiness of the Royal Dublin Society to defer to such authority; however, as the question was now pending in the

---

61 TNA:PRO ED 28/13/12/, 1 June 1861; RDS Committee of Botany Fair Minutes, 1857–77, 11 June 1861.   **62** RDS Committee of Botany Fair Minutes, 1857–77, 11 June 1861, 13 June 1861.   **63** Letter dated 28 June 1861, RDS Committee of Botany Fair Minutes, 1857–77, 4 July 1861.

House of Commons, it was inappropriate to ask the society to reconsider a deliberate decision so recently arrived at by a very large majority of its members.[64] At a special meeting of the Royal Dublin Society convened on 11 July, Steele reported on his trip to London, where he had sent a circular to MPs he felt favourable to the society's view, soliciting their attendance in the house and support of the society's estimates.[65] He reported that the debates had gone badly, however. In the House of Commons, the view of MPs was unequivocal – all sides were in favour of Sunday opening. The secretary reported that it appeared to him that 'if a division had taken place on the matter, the number in its favour would not be less than 3 to 1'.[66] The house had voted the annual subsidy of £6,000 on the condition that it should not be distributed until the society had opened its botanic garden to the public on Sundays.[67]

On 14 July, the council of the society finally capitulated, but not without considerable resistance. It resolved with reluctance to recommend the opening of the garden on Sundays.[68] Before implementing the decision, however, it decided to convene a special general meeting to discuss the matter, which allowed opponents of the opening a final chance to make their arguments. The society's membership appears to have split according to party and ideological lines, with the Tories and militant Protestants urging that the RDS should refuse the treasury grant and continue with its course of Sabbath observance, while supporters of the Liberal party and Catholics applauded the privy council's decision. Lord Clancarty, a strict sabbatarian, declared that he 'approached the subject with very great distaste and reluctance, as it was a most unpleasant one to handle'. He underlined the society's view that it was the 'conscientious opinion of many members [that Sunday opening was] a needless desecration of the Lord's Day' and that he was not surprised to have seen in the public papers, and to have heard from individuals, strong expressions of astonishment, and feelings amounting almost to indignation, that the ground that the society had so long maintained should now be receded from.[69]

The Sunday opening was, in the minds of some, now linked to a loss of autonomy for the society. Lord Clancarty displayed a characteristic reluctance to submit the society to the wishes of parliament. He urged the society to spurn the parliamentary grant, clogged as it was 'with an unjustifiable condition', and found the requirement to continue correspondence with the privy council 'disagreeable' as he felt it had been 'so needlessly offensive'. He concluded with admission that subscriptions alone would be inadequate to maintain the society and that the interests of the public, as well as of the society, required some sacrifice of personal feeling.[70] One member, John Foley, said that the society would 'disgrace' itself in the eyes of the world if it capitulated for the sake of retaining the government grant; 'Whether it was upon the higher consideration of Sabbath observance, or the lesser ground of preserving the gardens for the purpose of science … the majority of the society voted before for

64 RDS Committee of Botany Fair Minutes, 1857–77, 4 July 1861.   **65** Ibid., 11 July 1861. **66** Ibid., 11 July 1861.   **67** Ibid., 13 July 1861.   **68** Ibid., 13 July 1861.   **69** *FJ*, 26 July 1861.   **70** Ibid.

keeping the gardens closed on Sunday'.[71] By contrast, advocates of Sunday opening saw no harm in taking public opinion into account. Matthew O'Reilly Dease, a liberal Catholic, thought the society 'was doing a wise act and one in accordance with the spirit of progress and enlightenment'. As to the religious question, and the quantity of extraneous matter introduced, he wished it to be noted that he entirely dissented with the views held by Lord Clancarty.[72]

On 1 August, the council agreed to make the necessary arrangement to open the gardens to the public on Sundays free of charge between the hours of 2.30 and 7pm.[73] The botanical gardens were finally thrown open to the public on Sundays on 18 August 1861 and the measure was a resounding success, from 700 visitors on the first day of opening, attendance ran to 15,700 on one Sunday alone in October of that year. A total of 78,132 people attended the gardens over twelve Sundays.[74] The Committee of Botany were pleased with the outcome and declared that it was 'very satisfactory'. The crowds now flooding into the gardens on Sunday were well-behaved:

> the police and other persons employed have no doubt been active in preserving order among such large multitudes as have congregated together, but independent of them, the people themselves have behaved in the most orderly and decorous manner – with the exception of boys occasionally running through the plants, and leaping over the beds, no further wanton mischief has been done so far as your directions go.

The committee noted that 'some pots [had been] knocked off stages in conservatories due to the narrowness of the passages, but that this was purely accidental and that the staging should be widened'.[75]

After the Glasnevin gardens opened, the MP for Galway, William Gregory, and the National Sunday League pressed for the opening of the Edinburgh botanical gardens, with Gregory noting that drunkenness in Dublin had decreased on Sundays since the gardens had opened.[76] However, opposition from sabbatarians remained stout. The Free Church of Scotland's Revd Dr James Begg remarked that it was 'very painful that the Scottish Sabbath should be interfered with by the representative of an Irish popish constituency – by the representative of one of the most degrading popish communities in the world'.[77] The Sunday opening campaign had more success in Ireland, however. Shortly after the botanic gardens were opened, a Committee for the Opening of St Stephen's Green began to gather momentum and the green was finally opened to the public in 1877.[78]

The debate surrounding the Sunday opening of the Glasnevin botanic gardens was not a scientific debate at all. Instead, it reminds us that the Royal Dublin Society

---

71 Ibid.   **72** Ibid.   **73** RDS Committee of Botany Fair Minutes, 1857–77, 1 Aug. 1861.
74 Ibid., 11 Nov. 1861.   **75** Ibid.   **76** *Caledonian Mercury*, 10 June 1863; *The Times*, 5 Nov. 1862.   **77** *Caledonian Mercury*, 10 June 1863.   **78** *FJ*, 4 Nov. 1863.

and its scientific mission were entangled with political and social conflicts of the day. The RDS was itself divided in many of the ways that Irish society was divided, and any controversy encouraged the cracks between factions to emerge. The Sunday opening controversy is reminiscent of a similar conflict over the black-beaning of the Catholic archbishop of Dublin, Daniel Murray, in 1835. Murray's refusal of membership in the society also resulted in public outcry, accusations of sectarianism and threats to withdraw the government grant.[79] The society's eventual capitulation in both cases demonstrates the fragility of its position as a privately run institution with significant government patronage.

---

79 K. Bright, *The Royal Dublin Society, 1815–1845* (Dublin, 2004), ch. 5.

The learned gentlemen are in town: the British Association meeting of 1857 in Dublin's popular press

SHERRA MURPHY

Judging from appearances up to the present, the meeting in Dublin promises to be one of the most successful and brilliant reunions of the association that has ever taken place. A very large number have already taken out members' and associates' tickets, and fresh arrivals from England, the Continent and the provinces are hourly expected.[1]

In late August 1857, the British Association for the Advancement of Science convened their peripatetic annual meeting in Dublin, bringing influential figures from the British scientific establishments and distinguished international guests to the city for a week of scientific and social exchange. The association's second conference in the city was widely covered in the daily press and in popular journals, with the *Freeman's Journal* in particular devoting copious, densely packed column inches to the minutiae of each day's activities. Careful reading of period accounts, however, reveals a subtext behind the reportage. As Elizabeth Tilley points out in her writing on the *Dublin University Magazine*, historians must seek to countenance the social and political undercurrents behind the recounting of events when utilizing the popular press as a factual source.[2] Periodical publications in nineteenth-century Ireland operated as a form of social discourse that must be understood as more than a collection of disinterested facts; then as now, facts were dependent upon a background and context for the fullness of their meaning. Press reports on the British Association meeting in Dublin reveal a number of circumstances and developments that illuminate the relationship between the scientific establishments of London and Dublin in the mid-nineteenth century.

Late nineteenth-century Irish newspapers and journals embodied forms of motivated representation, wherein the framing of events was habitually coloured by the political convictions of publishers, with each cohort of readers forming a general grouping of political and social positions. It is somewhat surprising, therefore, that the reports on the British Association meeting were broadly enthusiastic and

1 *FJ*, 27 Aug. 1857; also printed verbatim in the *Evening Freeman* and *The Nation*. 2 E. Tilley, 'Charting culture in the *Dublin University Magazine*' in L. Litvack and G. Hooper (eds), *Ireland in the nineteenth century: regional identity* (Dublin, 2000), pp 58–65.

supportive, when papers and magazines ranging from nationalist to unionist might be expected to differ around a large public event involving key figures from British scientific, government and mercantile bodies. When placed in context, the apparent agreement within the press may be read in terms of mid-century concerns around the precise nature of Ireland's nationhood, and its representation within British spheres of influence. The institutions that hosted the meeting, chiefly Trinity College, the Royal Dublin Society and the Royal Irish Academy, were especially occupied by the open questions around Ireland's status as a nation and its position within the structures of the empire. In his study on the same period, Joep Leerssen makes the point that:

> the quest for a national identity was twofold; it was national in its trans-partisan agenda, attempting to work out a shared sense of identity applicable to all Irishmen and transcending their internal sectarian and social differences; it was also national in that it attempted to distil such an invariant and universally shared awareness out of a contentious and conflict-ridden past, transcending thereby the violent vicissitudes of history and extracting from them an essential and unchanging principle of Irishness.[3]

Leerssen touches on the continuum between synchronic and diachronic nationhood, wherein immediate local conflicts are measured against the experience of a lengthy chronicled history, in an attempt to develop a collective identity. The nineteenth-century Irish scientific establishments sought to help shape such a 'shared sense of identity', through their ongoing efforts in fields of discovery such as geology and natural history. The scientific and cartographic studies that detailed the structures and populations of the island also established concrete signifiers of the nation, which could be understood and internalized by the entire population. Pioneering studies in geology, for instance, were ways of describing each region's physical particularity while establishing the shape, age and structure of the island as a whole, uniting its inhabitants through a common understanding of its most basic elements. Ongoing discoveries took their places within an unfolding context of geological time, framing each new discovery against a growing sense of the nation's antiquity as theories of geological time developed. The series of geological maps made from these studies provided a visual form through which local variations could be understood in the context of a unified whole. The development of geology in Ireland is inextricably linked to Richard Griffith, who was also deeply involved with the RDS throughout his life. He consistently presented his studies, maps and findings at British Association meetings, starting with the earliest form of his geological map at the 1835 Dublin meeting and continuing throughout his career. His progress was eagerly monitored by colleagues in Britain, who had ambitions toward creating a comprehensive map

3 J. Leerssen, *Remembrance and imagination: patterns in the historical and literary representation of Ireland in the nineteenth century* (Cork, 1996), p. 4.

of the geology of the British Isles, and looked to him for accurate material on Ireland.[4]

The scientific committees within the Irish learned societies perceived themselves as 'trans-partisan', asserting that the collection and dissemination of scientific information was outside the purview of political partisanship. However, their membership profiles, with a preponderance of landed, mercantile and military connections, largely drawn from Anglo-Irish backgrounds, problematize any assertions of neutrality in the period. As civic bodies, the hosting organizations and their memberships generally advocated a version of nationhood that was multifaceted, though narrowly focused; beneficial to their interests and social positions, uniquely Irish in character and committed to the union.

Unusually for the period, the transmission of the conference proceedings in the press was broadly uniform in approach, emphasizing the particularity of Ireland through the subject matter of conference papers and reports on social events. The press also underlined the economic and practical implications of local scientific activities as demonstrative of Ireland's increasing sense of self-reliance and progress. Both the press and the local organizers appear to have been prompted in this regard by what Michel Foucault would term 'normalizing judgment'. Local organizers worked to bridge the divide of an unequal power relationship, within which London largely controlled access to funding, networks of publication and parliamentary influence; it was imperative, therefore, that Ireland be demonstrated, as fully as possible, to be secure, resourceful and fully committed to the overall goals of union. Pro-union perspectives and support for the imperial project are predictable, given the overwhelmingly Anglo-Irish makeup of the Irish learned societies, but press accounts of the events also indicate a more general attempt to counter the relentlessly negative representations of Ireland and the Irish at large in the English press. The standardized caricatures of the *Punch* cartoon, depicting the Irish as demonic, lazy, filthy, duplicitous or violent, were repeated to varying degrees throughout large swathes of the British press.[5] The Dublin organizers of the British Association meeting appear have been at pains to form convincing counter-representations, foregrounding diligence, progress and stability, which were then adopted and disseminated by the popular press.

Whether through explicit agreement or through an unspoken sense of shared purpose, the learned societies and the local press presented a united front for the appraising eye of the British Association. Ireland was exposed for the week to the penetrating gaze of the English scientific establishment, and the Irish men of science responded as though they were being examined, responding to scrutiny from their influential peers as though sitting an unwritten test. As Foucault notes, examinations have particular functions in hierarchies of power:

4 For a full discussion of Griffith's maps, see G.L. Herries-Davies, *Sheets of many colours: the mapping of Ireland's rocks, 1750–1890* (Dublin, 1983).   5 These ideas have been fully and famously treated in L.P. Curtis, *Apes and angels: the Irishman in Victorian caricature*, 2nd ed. (Washington, DC, 1997).

> The examination combines the techniques of an observing hierarchy and those of a normalizing judgment. It is a normalizing gaze, a surveillance that makes it possible to qualify, to classify and to punish.[6]

Though strict Foucauldian readings of Anglo–Irish power relations are often unhelpfully reductive, his summation of the examination's purposes is germane here. The annual meeting, in its way, functioned as a form of examination with a prominent social dimension. The British Association understood itself as the arbiter of emergent studies in the fields it encompassed. Its closely interwoven structures of social and professional relationships formed a self-referential and self-regulating mechanism of orthodoxy. Jack Morrell and Arnold Thackray, in their work on the early history of the Association, identify twenty-three men as central to its formation in 1831, and their correspondences reveal an intricate fabric of debate, observation and scrutiny from which a series of conventions for the practice of British science emerged. Scottish chemist James F.W. Johnston suggested in a letter dated 11 July 1831 that 'The efficiency of the society will be destroyed if the terms of admission be too lax', and proposed that membership be open to 'all interested in science', but that to have a vote, a member must have published on his subject.[7] The association's core membership remained tightly connected, and conforming to its internal rationales was essential for access to networks of information and professional correspondence. Anne Secord observes that 'it was the elaborate etiquette of polite society that allowed the emergence of networks because it enabled one to know who to trust', and that strict hierarchies of social interaction governed the exchange of scientific correspondence in the nineteenth century.[8] Ireland's men of science seem to have been determined to use these interactions to strengthen their reputations, as both scientists and Irishmen, displaying the quality of the work taking place under the auspices of their respective organizations, thus widening pathways for productive future relations with the centres of English science.

The opening address of the meeting, delivered by its president, Revd Humphrey Lloyd of Trinity College Dublin, was fully covered in the *Freeman's Journal*. The article lists the dignitaries present for the inaugural proceedings: William Whewell, founding association member and master of Trinity College, Oxford was there, as was John Lord Wrottesley, president of the Royal Society and a frequent member of royal commissions on scientific topics.[9] The list continued with lords, earls, generals, professors, barristers and members of parliament represented in abundance. British Association meetings followed well-established protocols, wherein science was framed by the 'etiquette of polite society', annually cementing personal and professional bonds. Presentations of recent research in key disciplinary areas were delivered

6 M. Foucault, *Discipline and punish* (London, 1977), p. 184. **7** J. Morrell and A. Thackray, *Gentlemen of science: early correspondence of the British Association for the Advancement of Science* (London, 1984), p. 41. **8** A. Secord, 'Corresponding interests: artisans and gentlemen in nineteenth-century natural history', *British Journal for the History of Science*, 27:4 (1994), 383–408 at 389. **9** *FJ*, 27 Aug. 1857.

by members to their fellows, supplemented by public lectures and demonstrations, the whole augmented by public and private social events. Mounting a well-organized and stimulating event for these men and their peers would elevate the status of the Irish scientific establishment within London's administrative structures, such as the Department of Science and Art, bringing the benefits of increased attention and funding. The Irish learned societies carefully configured the event to demonstrate a resilient and buoyant Ireland, which, having banished the effects of the Famine, was eager to advance as a modern scientific, industrial and agricultural force alongside England. Exhibiting the island for the normalizing gaze meant representing Ireland as both partner and subject in the imperial context, a participant in empire-building but simultaneously a docile and loyal subject nation. The several papers on the trans-Atlantic cable then being laid between Valentia Island and Newfoundland placed Ireland at the centre of a vital advance in communications, with massive implications for the administration and security of the empire. Conference papers from members of Dublin's learned societies treating Irish subject matter, such as William Andrews' overview of the sea fisheries of Ireland, David Moore's botanical analysis of the plants forming turf bogs, or John O'Donovan's ethnological observations on the ancient Irish,[10] formed part of a growing body of material that represented a nation with abundant resources and significant economic potential, with a sense of the unique richness of its own past and a desire to demonstrate Ireland's attractive qualities to a central administration more accustomed to focusing on famine, rural unrest and the threat of rebellion.

Two papers differ from the general norm in their reportage; predictably, the *Dublin University Magazine* and *The Nation* adopted differing stances, though both in ways that underline the desire to represent Ireland favourably to the assembled association membership. As Charles Withers et al. observe:

> Newspaper reports are particularly valuable where they differ through editorial view or political affiliation or where they may be used in combination with other evidence, not least because they then highlight social and intellectual distinctions within such general terms as 'reception', 'audience' and 'science'.[11]

These two influential publications stand in for the opposing poles of nineteenth-century Irish politics and their concomitant conceptions of nationhood. Though diametrically opposed in their political goals for Ireland, they are here in concert with the overall aims of the learned societies in representing Ireland to the visiting

---

10 *Report of the twenty-seventh meeting of the British Association for the Advancement of Science, held at Dublin in August and September 1857* (London, 1858). 11 C. Withers, R. Higgitt and D. Finnegan, 'Historical geographies of provincial science: themes in the setting and reception of the British Association for the Advancement of Science in Britain and Ireland, 1831–c.1939', *BJHS*, 41:3 (2008), 385–415 at 410.

scholars. In introducing the British Association meeting, the conservative *Dublin University Magazine* proceeded with characteristic hyperbole:

> The British Association is now paying its second visit to Dublin. Of the twenty-seven sessions of this rotary parliament of science, one was held in our city in 1835, and another in this year. During the interval, Ireland has learned much; she has awakened from a dream of petty independence, to cast her lot heartily with the sister island; she has given up agitation for industrial rivalry.[12]

Clearly eliding the complexity of contemporary political conditions, this opening paragraph summarizes common themes in conference proceedings and many press accounts; a desire to discard the recent past, to depict Ireland as politically secure, and to represent Ireland's emergent scientific modernity as partner to union. The nationalist weekly, *The Nation*, took a contrasting point of view, delivering sharp commentary on the British administration, but lauding Irish contributions to science. In welcoming the Association in the 29 August edition, the editors attribute the decline of science in Ireland to British rule, asserting that the scholars would find 'relics of a glorious past, evidence of a miserable present' and that 'when Ireland ceased to be independent, the arts and sciences fled the land'.[13] On 5 September, *The Nation* synopsized the contents of conference papers that treated of Irish culture and economic independence, focusing heavily on John O'Donovan's researches into the antiquity of the Irish race as described in ancient texts, quoting Giraldus Cambrensis' twelfth-century manuscript stating that the ancient Irish 'grew up by nature into most beautiful, tall, symmetrical and well-formed persons, of well-formed and well-coloured faces'.[14] The paper chose to foreground the genealogy of Irish culture and learning to lobby for the concept of a historically independent Irish nation, supported by reference to ancient manuscript sources. *The Nation* was anomalous in that it used the occasion to take a critical stance, though it did so by effectively using the frameworks of British science to imply a nationalist perspective through reporting the proceedings of the conference; it also praised the association, while maintaining its nationalist stance. Whether intentional or not, these two diametrically opposed political organs effectively maintained a consonance of civilized discourse for the British Association membership through their representations of the nation. The representation of Ireland was a key theme throughout many of the week's activities, but focusing on a few examples will tease out indications of general tendencies.

The Royal Dublin Society availed of the British Association meeting to inaugurate its new Natural History Museum, offering the building as a venue for scientific lectures and social events. On 27 August, a warm, pleasant Thursday evening, the building and its newly installed collections were unveiled at a *conversazione* attended by over 2,000 people. Published accounts of the opening highlighted local contrib-

---

12 *Dublin University Magazine*, 1:217 (1857), 18.   **13** *The Nation*, 29 Aug. 1857.   **14** Ibid., 5 Sept. 1857.

utors, emphasizing Irish names of international repute such as Richard Griffith of the Geological and Valuation Surveys, and Thomas Oldham of the Indian Geological Survey. The depiction of Ireland as stable, socially advanced and fashionable are discernable in the report on the museum's opening night:[15]

> The number of guests received by the society on this occasion was upwards of two thousand, comprising the *elite* of every rank and fashion of our city – almost every class of society was represented – the nobility and the gentry, the dignitaries of both churches, the judicial bench, the learned profession, men eminent for their literary and scientific achievements, merchants, manufacturers &c. Indeed, we may say, without exaggeration, that there was scarcely a man of note in Dublin at this season who was absent.[16]

Large public events were signatures of the British Association's approach to popularizing science, with detailed exchanges of current scientific research enlivened by public and private social occasions. The Dublin meeting provided local organizers with opportunities to parade the city's civic attractions; they arranged an afternoon promenade at the zoo, a fete at the botanical gardens and an evening *conversazione* at the Royal Irish Academy. Trinity College launched a new museum, and the Royal Dublin Society's new museum hosted several important events. Press accounts of the social gatherings consistently reinforced the convivial atmosphere, stressed the large attendances, emphasized rank and fashion, and extolled the orderliness of the attendees. These reports must be understood through the lens of period representations; the British popular press was frequently peppered with references to conflict in Ireland. In the previous decade, a steady stream of press reports on O'Connell's Repeal movement and the Young Irelanders, as well as regular reports of land disputes and associated violent incidents, had reinforced a perception of Ireland as unruly and uncooperative in Britain's public imagination. Reports on the Famine had consistently portrayed Ireland as helpless and retrograde. The learned societies appear to have made a concerted, coordinated effort to counter these images by representing the island's first city as a smaller version of London, with civic amenities comparable for its size. The Dublin papers proffered the city, its civic spaces and its citizens as equal in sophistication to anything the British capital had to offer. The description of the Natural History Museum's opening night in the *Freeman's Journal* implied an orderly democracy within Dublin's leading scientific establishment, specifically suggesting an absence of sectarianism. Throughout its history, the RDS had consistently declared its organization free of religious and political bigotry despite its Anglo-Irish majority, and this particular report underscores that assertion, though the society had been criticized by the *Freeman's Journal* on numerous occasions on those very grounds.

15 Transcription is from the *Freeman's Journal*; the same account printed in the *Evening Freeman* and the *Dublin Evening Post*. The *Dublin Evening Mail* printed an abbreviated version, apparently adapted from the above.   16 *FJ*, 28 Aug. 1857.

As described in the *Freeman's Journal*, the displays of natural materials, books and images assembled for the opening night suggest the complexity of the ways in which the study of nature also described the relationships of science and the learned societies to the ongoing project of understanding the nation as an entity, both physically and conceptually. The displayed specimens represented their species or types, but simultaneously stood in for people, places, events and ideas. An extended extract describing the cases on the first floor indicates a sense of the logic behind the selections for the initial exhibition:

> One of them contained a series of edible crustacea, and among them were quaint specimens of lobsters, enormous crabs &c. Another contained a series of edible molluscs – such as oysters, cockles, periwinkles &c., both these cases being instances of what might be done in the way of economic zoology. The next case contained the splendid collection of fossils made by our countryman, Captain McClintock RN, from the Arctic regions. A large case, which extended nearly across the entire room, contained the collection of Arctic birds made by the same gallant officer; who, amid all the horrors of the inhospitable Antarctic [sic] regions, did not forget the cause of science, but brought home these unique collections, which will long bear ample witness of his preserving zeal and energy. The other half of this case contained a collection of birds from the Crimea, made during the Russian war by Assistant Surgeon Carte of the Light Dragoons. We could not but feel pleased and gratified of seeing thus prominently brought before the notice of foreigners and our English friends the results of Dr Carte's research in Crimean zoology, and we doubt if since the days of Pallus any such collection has been made; and this one too when engaged in the laborious duties of that war. The next case, in order of progression through the room contained a case of our own native Lepidoptera, which the Royal Dublin Society owe to the labours of the well-known entomologist the Revd Joseph Hunt. Part of this case was occupied with portions of the collections made in India by Professor Oldham and the honourable G.S. Gough.[17]

This extract is an example of the ways in which the Dublin organizers showcased Irish contributions to the progress of natural science, as well as to the overall goals of the empire. The displayed specimens from the Crimea, Australia, Africa, the Arctic and India were primarily collected by Irish officers and doctors serving in British regiments deployed in colonies and protectorates. In this context, the animals, plants and fossils carry a subtext of imperial service in specific regions that echoed current events. The text of the article emphasizes the service records of the collectors as well as the quality of the collections, situating them both within a definition of nationhood, which suggested that Ireland, while a unique entity, was also beneficial to the

17 Ibid.

stability of the Empire. The short descriptions of the indigenous materials reinforce this idea by stressing economic potential; the display of local crustacea and molluscs is cited as an example of the potential for 'economic zoology', implying that Ireland is re-imagining its use of resources through a scientific approach, applying the lessons of the Famine to explorations of alternate conceptions of nutrition, harvesting and capital.

The Arctic collections were the work of the Anglo-Irish explorer Francis Leopold McClintock, who had left six weeks previously on what would be his final trip to search for the remains of Sir John Franklin's lost expedition. A popular public figure, McClintock was also a keen natural history amateur and frequent contributor to the RDS collections. McClintock was a Victorian hero, lauded in the popular press for his ongoing devotion to Franklin's fate and to Lady Franklin's parliamentary efforts on his behalf, a man of action and purpose who persisted in the face of physical danger and governmental indifference. Walter Houghton identifies hero-worship as one of the defining tropes of the period, largely promulgated by Thomas Carlyle, who referred to it as 'the basis of all possible good, religious or social, for mankind'.[18] The materials associated with McClintock would have been legible as the remnants of heroic acts, standing in for the man himself in his absence. They also testified to his efforts in mapping and claiming unknown territory in the northwest regions, and in the collection of rare and previously undiscovered specimens, increasing the archive of human knowledge, at risk to himself. This description of McClintock in the moderately nationalist *Freeman's Journal* establishes him as an exemplar who transcends divisions, a representation of admirable and heroic Irishness. The items in the cases and their descriptions in the press act as reminders that influential sectors of Ireland's population shared the value systems of the British Association's overall membership.

One of the more celebrated attendants at the annual meeting gave a widely publicized talk at the new museum on 31 August. David Livingstone spoke about his travels in Central Africa, during what proved to be a brief return to Scotland. Most Dublin papers gave succinct notice of the talk, but the *Dublin Evening Mail* printed a full synopsis of it, as well as Lord Lieutenant Carlisle's remarks afterward. Again heavily attended, with a catalogue of the city's important personalities present, Livingstone's lecture was a compendium of period attitudes toward exploration, religion, race and ideology, which are fully treated elsewhere. More relevant in this context are the crown representative's comments to the assembled company:

> I will only say that the interesting region which has been the theatre of his journeying, that while the high behest of empire and of justice may now be calling upon some of our countrymen in that other great continent of the olden world to the discharge of stern and painful duties, I trust that in that Africa to which Europe owes such great attainment, our countrymen may

---

18 W.E. Houghton, *The Victorian frame of mind* (New Haven, CT, 1957), pp 305–10.

never be called upon to discharge any other mission than those which relate to extended commerce, increasing civilization and Christian philanthropy (loud applause).[19]

This single sentence does several things simultaneously: it foreshadows the scramble for Africa, references Ireland's role in the intensifying Sepoy Rebellion, and places Ireland firmly in the position of partner to, rather than opponent of, the empire. A large spread of images depicting events from India and the rebellion were published in the *Illustrated London News* that week,[20] and all the local papers covered the progression of the battles alongside their coverage of the British Association meeting, giving special attention to Irish regiments such as the Bengal Fusiliers (later the Munster Fusiliers). The comments delivered by the empire's seat of power on the island suggested a version of homogenous nationhood that presented itself as a foregone conclusion, ignoring domestic conflicts and ongoing calls for Irish independence in various forms, as well as strong Irish support for the Sepoy Rebellion in nationalist circles, consistently used by *The Nation* to signal that Ireland may soon follow suit.[21] Carlisle's response to Livingstone's talk provided an opportunity for making distinctions between classes of subjecthood in an overall taxonomy of power. Geography and intent merge here to form a series of telescoping representations; Africa as an opportunity for enlightened improvement at the furthest margins of civilization, India as an ancient but wayward civilization in need of guidance and discipline, and Ireland as helpmeet, sharing a sense of duty and purpose within Great Britain's unfolding global enterprise.

The published accounts of the events at the new museum touch upon complex Victorian discourses of science and exploration as viewed through period lenses of heroism, service, knowledge and utility, and they function as representations of admirable Irishness acceptable within an imperial context. Due to the complexities of national allegiance in the period, this is ticklish territory, which the organizers attempted to navigate by means of conference papers that treated the unique qualities of Irish nature and culture, and which simultaneously emphasized the island's modernity and its antiquity. Their representations, however, situated Ireland in a delicate subject position within the hierarchies of the period; they demonstrated a distinct Irish identity, though not an independent one; proposed Ireland as a nation, but not nationalist; described it as part of the empire, but not a colony. Leerssen observes:

> The difference between province and nation, crucially, involves a sense of historical individuality: the fact that Ireland looks back into a past that diverges from the English or British one, that traces its antecedents through a root system of its own.[22]

19 *Dublin Evening Mail*, 1 Sept. 1857. **20** *Illustrated London News*, 5 Sept. 1857. **21** M. Kelly, 'Irish nationalist opinion and the British Empire in the 1850s and 1860s', *Past & Present*, 24 (2009), 127–54. **22** Leerssen, *Remembrance and imagination*, p. 147.

The tricky business of navigating between a sense of 'historical individuality' and normalized imperial subject was further demonstrated in the events organized toward the end of the conference. Spectacle was an important aspect of the annual conference, and the Irish organizers fulfilled this in a distinctive way. Rather than laying on fireworks displays or public demonstrations of new electrical devices, they arranged a series of trips to iconic locations as part of the conference proceedings:

> Our readers are aware that, in addition to the meetings of the sections, the scientific lectures, the *conversaziones* and promenades which attend every meeting of this distinguished institution, several excursions of more than usual interest have been organized – namely, an excursion through some of the more picturesque localities in Wicklow, a visit to Lord Rosse's monster telescope, a geological examination of Lambay, and an ethnological excursion to the Arran Islands. Pleasure and instruction will thus be most agreeably and profitably combined.[23]

The country itself was displayed to visiting and local scholars as living evidence of topics covered in conference papers. Ireland, in essence, became a representation of itself through being presented as an active subject of study. The press reported the proceedings of these trips, the *Evening Freeman* and the *Freeman's Journal* providing detailed coverage by sending along a correspondent with each group. The trip to the Aran Islands, led by William Wilde of the Royal Irish Academy, concerned itself with the history, antiquities and monuments of the islands. With a particular focus on Inis Mór and Dún Aengus, the group of seventy strong was lodged by local families and in a small hotel, and walked the sites on the island. At Dún Aengus, they were treated to an alfresco banquet between the cliff and the ruins, after which a meeting of the geography and ethnology section of the association was conducted with all due ceremony *en plein aire*; following the meeting, a bagpiper played and a number of the party danced a jig.[24] In addition to Wilde, the trip's cadre of local luminaries included George Petrie, John O'Donovan and Eugene Curry, the reigning experts in antiquities and Gaelic language, culture and history. The three scholars were famous, in part, for their pioneering and influential work during the Ordnance Survey, which Leerssen argues was instrumental in creating a separate and distinct Irish identity:

> One particularly important result of the Ordnance Survey at the ideological level was, then, that the sense of place and the sense of past became mutually linked and almost interchangeable, and that Ireland itself, as a geographical space, became inescapably also a vessel laden with the place-names, monuments, memories and cultural cargo of a Gaelic past.[25]

---

23 *FJ*, 28 Aug. 1857. **24** *Evening Freeman*, 7 Sept. 1857. **25** Leerssen, *Remembrance and imagination*, p. 103.

It was the majesty of the Gaelic past that Wilde intended to bring to life for the visitors, using the Aran Islands as an unspoiled example of Irish antiquity and folk-ways. His display and framing of the ancient and ecclesiastical ruins on the islands, aided by Petrie, Curry and O'Donovan, were a means for representing the distinct particularity of Ireland, separate from England, though with related motifs. The size and remote location of the structure, framed by the dramatic backdrop of cliffs and sea, as well as the large group of locals who had gathered to observe the unusual event, were all presented by Wilde as concrete examples of myth, history and antiquity that could be found nowhere else. In his post-luncheon address to the group, arrayed on the grass in the sunshine at the base of the fort, he indicated the methods and ambitions of Irish antiquarian scholars:

> Now, why have I brought you here, and more particularly here, where I stand at this moment to address you? ... I now point to the stronghold prepared as the last standing place of the Firbolg aborigines of Ireland ... Of that race we have a written knowledge. We can but make such conjectures as the light of recorded history has afforded us, reading it, comparing and referring it to what they have left us in these litanies of stone. It has been one of my fondest hopes to render Aran an opposition shop to Iona. (hear).[26]

Wilde here conflates past and place as suggested by Leerssen, making them speak to a verifiable cultural history, while placing Ireland's ancient material remains on a footing with one of the most evocative sites in the British antiquarian tradition. Wilde then addressed an appeal for the preservation of the site to the locals gathered around the edge of the proceedings, which Curry repeated in Irish. Pre-eminent botanist and antiquarian Charles Babington said that:

> as an English member of the association, he felt bound to express the gratification he had enjoyed. He wished to call their attention to the fact that the antiquities of these Isles of Aran, with all their singular interest, were scarcely known beyond the Channel (hear, hear). He had heard of Aran, it is true, but the interesting character of its antiquities was utterly unknown to him. He begged to move the thanks of the meeting to Dr Wilde, without whose unparalleled exertions their trip would never have taken place.[27]

The spectacle of Inis Mór itself, its dramatic beauty, quaint locals and richness of archaeology, provided a living experience that mere fireworks could never match, presumably leaving a lasting impression on the visiting scholars and beginning the career of Dún Aengus as a tourist site. The effects of Wilde's efforts and the reactions of the assembled dignitaries are transmitted through the detailed recording of the excursion in the press, which also served as a set of representations for the local

26 *Evening Freeman,* 7 Sept. 1857.　**27** Ibid.

readership. Wilde's framing of the islands and their treasures as rare, ancient and unspoiled underlined the value of Irish heritage for the reader, who could then enjoy satisfaction at the positive reactions of the visiting dignitaries.

The meetings of the British Association were integral aspects of the Victorian imperial project of knowledge production and dissemination. The administrative structures and civic institutions of the period were engaged with their own versions of the theory of everything, attempting to collect, define and classify all known phenomena in a bid to understand the fundamental shape of life, and to marshal the globe's territory and resources. Thomas Richards describes these efforts as the creation of an archive, with knowledge production as its central purpose:

> Unquestionably, the British Empire was more productive of knowledge than any previous empire in history. The administrative core of the empire was built around knowledge-producing institutions like the British Museum, the Royal Geographical Society, the India Survey and the universities.[28]

The Dublin meeting was a way of demonstrating Ireland's significant contributions to that project, with its scientific institutions, museums, surveys and their related studies operating in agreement with their analogues in the rest of the British establishment. If knowledge was power, the Dublin men of science made a concerted bid to figure at the centre of that power through their production of useful information and knowledge. The Dublin organizers and the local press largely succeeded in getting the attention of the British scientific establishment, as the meeting was subsequently dubbed one of the most successful in years. The British press, however, was another matter; the Dublin correspondent for London's paper of record, *The Times*, complained:

> The morning papers groan under the weight of the reported proceedings of the British Association yesterday ... Twelve or thirteen columns of the minutest type are devoted to the reading of the papers, to the exclusion of almost every other topic of public interest. A *conversazione* in the evening at the Royal Dublin Society's house in Kildare Street wound up the second day's feast of reason.[29]

Followed by short reports on agrarian murders and cattle disease, this brief, dismissive account likely did little if anything to raise Dublin's profile in the public imagination of the capital. Subsequent reports in the same week were also brief, and conveyed nothing of the complexity and excitement of the event.

Reports of the meeting in the news and popular press must be understood against the background of wider conditions. *The Times* often reflected a vision of Ireland as

---

28 T. Richards, *The imperial archive* (London, 1993), pp 3–4.   **29** *The Times* [London], 29 Aug. 1857.

a semi-foreign backwater, unworthy of column inches unless it was causing trouble. Local reports, in contrast, illuminate the learned societies' 'trans-partisan agenda' of developing a national identity from an objective scientific framework, but these must be understood in terms of period tensions and conflicts. Questions around the fundamental nature of 'Irishness' remain open to this day, and the learned societies' observations around them centred on heady admixtures of class, breeding, education, locale, status and political loyalty, often wrapped in a cloak of scientific objectivity. To arrive at a nuanced understanding of the representations in the conference papers and in the press it is necessary to take period conditions fully into account. Leerssen makes cogent points regarding literary texts, which hold true for the press:

> Literary texts float like icebergs in a sea of discourse, are nine-tenths submerged in a larger discursive environment which is chemically (if not physically) identical to their own substance, out of which they have crystallized and into which they will melt back.[30]

The complex discourses around Ireland, England, nature, culture, power and identity are all deeply embedded within the papers presented to the conference and in press reports describing the events of the meeting. The appearance of a consonant set of sympathies between the organizers and the press are evident in the final stages of the meeting, where President Revd Lloyd underscored the importance of the daily press to the success of the endeavour:

> Before he closed, they would suffer him, on behalf of the association, to thank the gentlemen of the press who had been unremitting in their attention and labours to record the proceedings of the association since it assembled (loud applause), and he believed he might fairly say that those proceedings, and the results obtained in the several sections, as well as in their general meetings, had never been so fully or truly reported (renewed applause).[31]

---

30 Leerssen, *Remembrance and imagination*, p. 2. **31** *Evening Freeman*, 4 Sept. 1857.

Index